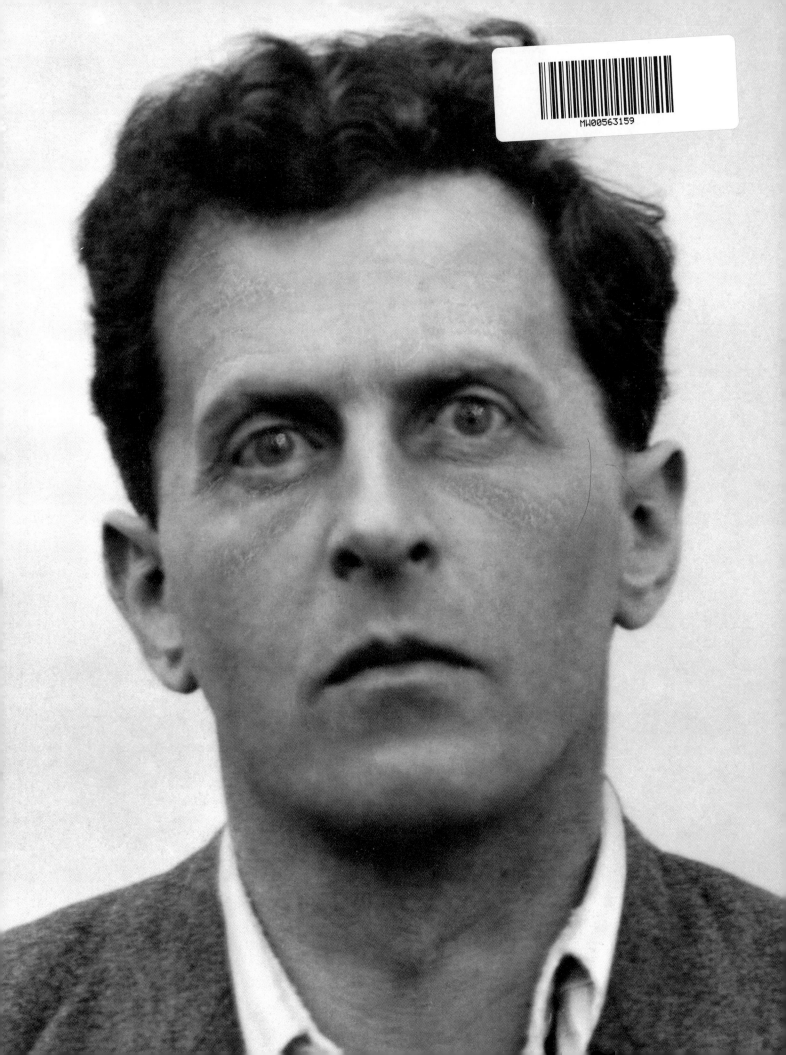

Paul Wijdeveld

Ludwig Wittgenstein

Architect

The Pepin Press

To the memory of my father, to my mother.

First published by The Pepin Press in 1993
Reprinted in 2000

ISBN 90 5496 048 5

A CIP record for this book is available from the
publisher and from the Royal Dutch Library,
The Hague

Produced by
The Pepin Press
PO Box 10349
1001 EH Amsterdam
The Netherlands
Fax (+) 31 20 4201152

Design: Mark van Wageningen, Amsterdam

Printed in Singapore

Note to the second edition

Compared to the first edition (The Pepin
Press/MIT Press/Thames and Hudson/Wiese
Verlag 1994) this paperback edition has been
slightly abridged as far as the introductory chapter and the chapters on Paul Engelmann and on
his sketchbook for the Kundmanngasse are concerned. However, no fact or argument of any relevance to the subject of the book has been
omitted. Furthermore, the appendix containing
the sketches that were not discussed in the text,
as well as the notes, which were almost all
source references, and the index have been left
out. Students of Ludwig Wittgenstein and Paul
Engelmann who should like to consult these are
kindly referred to the first edition. Finally, a few
factual mistakes (I am especially grateful to Otto
Kapfinger for drawing my attention to them) and
a number of printing errors have been corrected.

P.W.

Contents

Acknowledgements

I am greatly indebted to the relatives, friends and acquaintances of Ludwig Wittgenstein, Margaret Stonborough-Wittgenstein, Paul Engelmann and Jacques Groag who generously helped me in bringing to light the facts necessary for me to write this book and gave their permission to publish the many documents and photographs which illustrate them: Major John J. Stonborough, his wife Mrs Veronica Stonborough and their son Mr Jerome Stonborough, the late Mrs Marielies Stonborough, Mrs Marguerite Sjögren-Respinger, Mr Pierre H. Stonborough, Mr O.F. Karban, Mr and Mrs Paulus Auer, Mrs Katarina Eisenburger-Sjögren, Mrs Cecilia Sjögren, Mrs Milli Vogl, Mr Ben Richards, Mr Gilbert Pattison, Mrs Joan Bevan, Ing.Arch. Zdeněk Hynek and Mrs Jitka Hynková-Müller, Mr Vladimir Müller, Mr Werner Kraft, Dr Josef Schächter, Mr Willi Groag, Mr Jan Groag, the late Mr Yehuda Kurt Unger, Mr Otto Schiller, Dr Max Zweig, Dr Amos Handel, Mrs Hanna Blum, Mr Azaria Rapoport, and someone who in spite of her invaluable help wished to remain anonymous.

I would also like to thank those people who generously placed at my disposal results of their own research and who assisted me with many valuable suggestions: Michael Nedo, text editor and biographer of Ludwig Wittgenstein, whose private Wittgenstein archive provided many indispensable documents and pictures, who established some important contacts and with whom I had many fruitful discussions; Prof. Bernhard Leitner, who published the first documentation of the Kundmanngasse from which he has given me permission to reproduce some photographs here, and who allowed me access to his correspondence with the late Heinrich Postl; the architect Otto Kapfinger, who gave invaluable information and advice; Prof. Ottokar Uhl, through whose mediation it has been possible to publish important material here from the survey of the Kundmanngasse made during its renovation; Prof. Yehuda Safran, who paved my way to Israel; Prof. Vladimír Šlapeta, who made the first systematic enquiries into the lives and works of Paul Engelmann and Jacques Groag; the late Dr Willem Frederik Hermans, who published valuable contributions on the life and work of Ludwig Wittgenstein in Dutch, together with important photographic material; Mr Rudy Vrooman, who generously placed at my disposal his unique series of photographs of the Kundmanngasse before its renovation; Dr Burckhard Rukschcio, biographer of Adolf Loos; Ray Monk, biographer of Ludwig Wittgenstein, with whom I had a number of interesting exchanges of thought; and Dr Michael Levin, Curator of Architecture at the Tel Aviv Museum.

I have also had important assistance from the following institutions: the Bulgarian Cultural Institute which owns and occupies the Wittgenstein House, which generously opened all rooms and cupboards for my investigation and provided the photographers with all the time and assistance they needed; the Paul Engelmann Archive in the Jewish National and University Library, Jerusalem; the Brenner Archiv, Innsbruck; the Getty Center for the History of Art and the Humanities, Santa Monica, California; the *Adolf Loos Archiv* in the Albertina, Vienna; the *Bundesdenkmalamt,* Vienna; the *Magistrat der Stadt* Wien, the departments *Stadt- und Landesarchiv, Landesbildstelle* and *Baupolizei*; the *Österreichische Nationalbibliothek* and its *Bildarchiv*, Vienna; the *Wiener Werkstätte Archiv* in the *Österreichisches Museum für angewandte Kunst,* Vienna; The Bertrand Russell Archives in McMaster University, Hamilton, Ontario; the *Landesbildstelle Berlin*; the University Library of the Delft University of Technology; the University Library of the University of Amsterdam; the *Universitätsbibliothek Trier;* the Netherlands Organization for Scientific Research.

For permission to publish and quote material I am indebted to Wittgenstein's literary executors, Prof. G.E.M. Anscombe and Prof. G.H. von Wright.

I am especially grateful to Pepin van Roojen, who gave me the opportunity to write this book; to Jeroen Koolbergen, who acted as a go-between; to Prof. Manfred Bock, who tactfully guided me into the domain of the history of architecture; to Prof. Eduard Sekler and Prof. Stephen Toulmin for kindly agreeing to read the manuscript; to Cor van Schaik for a number of beautiful black and white photographs and for his outstanding reprographic work on most of the plans reproduced in this book. I offer special thanks for various reasons to Ireneus Spit, Erik van Loenen, Joris van den Worm, Ton Amir, Alexander Valeton, Martien Koning, Martin de Zoete and Peter Vos.

Amsterdam, autumn 1993/winter 1996
Paul Wijdeveld

Introduction

During 1926–28 the philosopher Ludwig Wittgenstein (1889–1951) acted as the architect of a city mansion in Vienna which was commissioned by his sister, the society lady Margaret Stonborough-Wittgenstein. Although one would not expect a philosopher to enter such a technical profession, Wittgenstein practised architecture with the same independence of purpose and the same relentless perfectionism as he had shown previously, and would demonstrate subsequently, in his philosophical pursuits.

At first sight the house looks like an example of early modern architecture that cannot be attributed with certainty to any particular school. A closer inspection, however, reveals that the design and the many peculiar details of its construction are so unique within the context of early twentieth century architecture that one is led to suspect that it must be the result of the deliberate application of 'the' principles of 'Wittgensteinian aesthetics' under the direct supervision of the philosopher himself. But unlike most philosophers Wittgenstein never developed a systematic theory of aesthetics and wrote only a little on the subject. Moreover, the house was not built on his own initiative and it was not meant to be a representation or illustration of his philosophical ideas, though its austere atmosphere inescapably reminds one of the rigour of his thinking. What made him an architect at that particular moment in his life was the situation in which he found himself, the possibilities which the project presented, and pressure from his sister. It is also true that in the initial stages of design and construction he worked closely with his friend Paul Engelmann, who originally received the commission and who was a pupil of Adolf Loos, the great Viennese modernist architect whom Wittgenstein knew well.

This book attempts to shed more light on the many questions raised by the design of the house, and to examine the possible connections between Wittgenstein's architectural exercise and his philosophical work. From this study it is hoped that it will emerge not only as an interesting architectural undertaking, but also as an significant landmark of early twentieth century Viennese culture.

A philosopher's exercise in architecture

Within the family circle the house is named the Kundmanngasse, according to Viennese tradition, after the street in which it stands. The history of public interest in it runs parallel to the history of public interest in Wittgenstein's life and philosophy. It was only after the posthumous publication of his second main work, the *Philosophical Investigations* (*Philosophische Untersuchungen*, 1953) that the wider scholarly and lay public became gradually aware of his thinking. Before that he had been known to only two groups of people. The first was the 'Vienna Circle' of logical positivist philosophers and scientists who, during the years of the building of the Kundmanngasse, had meetings with him following the publication of the *Tractatus logico-philosophicus* (*Logisch-philosophische Abhandlung*, 1922), his first main work. The second group was the small circle of pupils and friends in Cambridge, where, after completion of the Kundmanngasse, he became first a Fellow and later a Professor of Philosophy at Trinity College. In a historical sense, therefore, the Kundmanngasse characterizes the contrast between Wittgenstein's 'earlier' and 'later' philosophy which commentators on his work used to make an issue.

The *Philosophische Untersungen* became the starting point of the Anglo-Saxon school of the philosophy of language centred around Wittgenstein's pupils in England and the United States. The *Tractatus logico-philosophicus* remained a major point of reference of the logical positivist school which flourished in the United States where most of the members of the Vienna Circle found refuge from Nazi-Austria. Only in the last two decades has the connection between 'later' and 'earlier' work, as indicated by Wittgenstein himself, been recognized and the Kundmanngasse could be seen as the symbolic bridge between both. At the same time it has become apparent that Wittgenstein could be regarded as the most important thinker of our age. Also much material has been brought to light concerning his life, resulting in the publication of some serious biographies.

Until the end of the 1950s Ludwig Wittgenstein's architectural venture was known only to his family and friends. Wittgenstein's sister, Margaret Stonborough-Wittgenstein, lived in it until her death in 1958, with an interruption of seven years caused by the Second World War, during which the house was damaged. Notwithstanding its remarkable design the Kundmanngasse seems never to have been mentioned in any of the leading architectural journals or any other publication before the war. It is first mentioned in print in 1951, in the obituary notice written by Wittgenstein's friend Ludwig Hänsel:

It is characteristic of him that during the years between his teaching at public schools ... and his professorship [in Cambridge] he built the villa in the Kundmanngasse (in the IIIrd district of Vienna) for his sister Margaret Stonborough (He gradually took over from the original architect P. Engelmann). It is a house of great spiritual beauty, austere, noble, without any ornament. (We are close to Adolf Loos, by whom he was befriended, but, I believe, in a more rigorous reach.)

The Kundmanngasse, front elevation, present situation.

Although the neighbourhood is not sufficiently interesting to attract visitors, the house did draw the attention of passers-by with an eye for architecture, and evoked their predictable comment: 'It looks as if it was designed by Loos, but it cannot be by Loos.'

In 1958 G.H. von Wright, one of Wittgenstein's literary executors, published the first biographical sketch in which he described the house in similar terms to those of Ludwig Hänsel. Six years later it was mentioned for the first time in an architectural guide, *Wiener Bauten 1900 bis heute* ('Viennese buildings from 1900 till today'), and in 1965 the first eyewitness report and photograph of the house was printed in the Italian magazine *Aut*

The Kundmanngasse, spring 1929.

aut. In 1968 the Dutch writer Willem Frederik Hermans published some photographs of the Kundmanngasse, together with a first more elaborate account of Wittgenstein's life before he went to live in England in 1929. The reminiscences of Wittgenstein's friend and co-architect Paul Engelmann had appeared a year earlier, but for reasons that will be explained in a later chapter Engelmann hardly mentions their collaboration in designing the Kundmanngasse. In 1969 the Viennese architectural journal *Bau* reproduced official plans of the house for the first time. These bear the signatures of both Wittgenstein and Engelmann.

In summer 1971 investigations concerning the Kundmanngasse were accelerated because it was in imminent danger of being demolished. Margaret's son, Thomas Stonborough, who had lived in the house since her death in 1958, had offered the notoriously impractical house, horribly expensive to run, for sale to a real estate developer who intended to construct a high-rise hotel building on the site. Protests by architects, art historians and philosophers from around the world, organized by the architect Bernhard Leitner, whose article on the house in *Art Forum* in 1970 for the first time extensively showed the importance of its architecture, forestalled its destruction in the final hours before demolition, when it was declared a protected monument. However, almost all the century-old trees in the large garden, which formed a perfect counterpoint to the austerity of the house, had been cut down.

But the Kundmanngasse's rescue had not been completely successful; due to the lack of funds necessary to enable the building to be adapted for some new purpose, it fell into decay. In 1973, Leitner published the first major photographic documentation, *The Architecture of Ludwig Wittgenstein*, which aroused the interest of a wider public but it was not until 1975 that a purchaser was found who wanted to maintain the building: the Bulgarian Embassy in Vienna decided to house its Cultural Institution in it.

Between 1976 and 1977, the Kundmanngasse was extensively, but not very expertly, renovated under the direction of a Viennese firm of architects. At the same time the setting of the house was spoilt by the erection of a 140 foot (45 metres) high building in the former garden, as a result of which the original entrance gate was moved to the Parkgasse, so destroying the magnificent drive. However, during the renovation a group of students of architecture under the guidance of Thomas Sperling and Prof. Ottokar Uhl made an extensive survey of the house, thanks to which a number of important data on the original measurements and materials were recorded, though other specifications had already been lost.

At about the same time, interest was first shown in Viennese intellectual and artistic culture of the *fin de siècle* and the subsequent period of the *finis Austriae*. It arose from studies such as William Johnston's *The Austrian Mind* (1972) and *Wittgenstein's Vienna* by Allan Janik and Stephen Toulmin (1973). This gave rise to widespread interest in the philosopher's life and work within its cultural-historical context. From that time Wittgenstein's architectural achievement has been the subject of a number of publications, of which the more important are listed below.

In *La casa di Wittgenstein*, Francesco Amendolagine (1975) made a serious attempt to interpret Wittgenstein's work in architecture by seeing it as an important, even 'aphoristic', stage in the transition from his 'earlier' into his 'later' philosophy. Benedetto Gravagnuoli wrote a monograph on Adolf Loos in 1981, examining the former's cultural-historical context and later architectural work. This took Wittgenstein's ideas and 'architectural lesson' into account for the first time. The essays of Günther Gebauer, Rüdiger Ohme, and Lothar Rentschler which were published in 1982 with the survey of the Kundmanngasse mentioned above, tried to shed more light on the architecture of the Kundmanngasse by a morphological and semiotic analysis of stylistic similarities between Wittgenstein's philosophy and his architectural design, and by making an associative visual comparison of stylistic characteristics throughout the history of architecture. The impressive photobiography of Ludwig Wittgenstein by Michael Nedo and Michele Ranchetti (1983) printed for the first time some of Paul Engelmann's sketches for the house, hitherto unknown photographs of the exterior and interior of the Kundmanngasse before the Second World War, and some other important documents and texts. The brochure by Otto Kapfinger, produced in 1984, which is available to visitors to the present Wittgenstein House, and the catalogue to the exhibition which celebrated the centennial of Wittgenstein's birth in the Wiener Secession (1989), unearthed more information on the building's history. Finally, Jan Turnovský's extraordinary essay (1987), a metaphorical digression on an interesting detail of Wittgenstein's design that was not in fact realized, cannot be ignored.

However, none of these texts can be regarded as a comprehensive account of Ludwig Wittgenstein's architectural statement, either because their main subject matter is something different, or because they lack sufficient study of the source material. The latter is, indeed, quite complicated. Until

Margaret Stonborough-Wittgenstein.

halfway through the 1980s essential material concerning the building history of the Kundmanngasse and the lives of those who played a role in it was barely accessible or even traceable. Besides, the material is quite widely dispersed which impedes study. A second source of difficulty is the nature of the subject matter; on the one hand it requires sufficient understanding of Wittgenstein's philosophy and life, on the other it is necessary to have some knowledge of the history of architecture. Even so the publications mentioned above are indispensable, because they ask the right questions, many of which were first formulated by Allan Plattus in his review of Leitner's documentation, and by Jacques Bouveresse in his commentary on Gebauer's and Rentschler's essays – questions to which this book seeks to obtain answers.

'For doubt can only exist where there is a question'

The questions can be raised from three different viewpoints. The first considers the house as an architectural object: Which formal elements are to be found in its design? What are its roots in the history of architecture? What is its relationship to contemporary architecture and how should its 'modernism' be understood? How can we be sure about the extent of Wittgenstein's contribution to the design when we know that his friend Paul Engelmann originally received the commission and drew up the first plans? How does the candidness of Wittgenstein as the 'sincere dilettante-architect' express itself both in the materials and design of the finishing of the house, and in the solutions he chose for the design of the mechanical and electrical parts of the house, such as the door and window furniture and lighting? In what way do they form an integrated whole and do they add to the overall architecture of the house as such?

To be able to answer these questions it is first necessary to reconstruct the history of the construction of the house and the specifications of the design in its completed condition. It is also necessary to reconstruct the way it was furnished and decorated because, as will become clear, the interior had to tie in with the furniture and *objets d'art* which belonged to Margaret Stonborough. Leitner's photographic documentation is the main source for researching many details of construction that were lost during the incompetent renovation. Leitner's work is complemented by the photographs of Hermans (1967), by documentary photographs of the Bundesdenkmalamt (1969, 1971), by the important series of snapshots illegally taken by Rudy Vrooman in 1975, and by photographs made during the survey of 1976. However, when these records were made, the house first was inhabited by Margaret Stonborough's son and then, from 1971, it was empty, so they do not contain any information as to the original interior. The photographs by Moritz Nähr (a professional photographer who worked for the Wittgenstein family on many occasions) proved to be of extreme importance. Taken between 1926 and 1933, they not only show the house under construction, but also attest to the deliberate experiments with the furnishing of the rooms which were carried out in the first years after its completion. Equally important are the drawings and water colours made by Ludwig's sister Hermine, a fairly competent draughtswoman, which show the interior around the same time. For this book all these sources have been studied as a whole for the first time, together with previously unknown plans of the house that were still in the possession of the Wittgenstein family.

The existing literature contains many inaccuracies regarding the history of construction of the Kundmanngasse. Besides the absence of a reliable reconstruction of the house it does not contain the exact list of demands made by Margaret, nor does it establish the degree of her involvement, although we know that as patroness she wished to play an active role in the design. It does not give definite answers to the questions as to why Paul Engelmann was chosen as the initial architect, to what extent the architecture of the house was determined by his designs, and why he retreated into the background. For a long time Engelmann's sketches of the plan and elevations, which were the starting point of Wittgenstein's revisions, were hardly accessible and were not studied very seriously until the first tentative discussion in Kapfinger's brochure and in the catalogue of the Wittgenstein Exhibition of 1989. Moreover, Engelmann's architectural education — he was one of the first pupils of the great Viennese innovator of 20th century architecture, Adolf Loos — and the relationship of his earlier architectural work to the Kundmanngasse have not yet been assessed. As for the contents of contacts between Wittgenstein and Loos, who were friends and were aware of their mutual influence, these have never been studied in depth either. The nature and degree of the involvement of a third architect, Jacques Groag, whose presence has been suggested by some authors, has still to be examined. For example, Vladimír Šlapeta explored the architecture of both Engelmann and Groag as being Loos's pupils from Olomouc in Moravia, and pointed to some formal similarities between their respective works and the Kundmanngasse. Finally, until now there has been no discussion of the coherence between the architecture of the Kundmanngasse and Wittgenstein's earlier ideas on design and architecture.

Consequently, the existing interpretations of the relationship of the Kundmanngasse to both Loos's modernism and modernism in general must be regarded as provisional. For instance, almost all authors recognize the influence of classicism in the design of its elevations, its interior finishing, and its spatial setting. However, the similarities and differences regarding Loos's classicist inspiration and tendencies have only been hinted at, while the role of Engelmann's design in this respect has never been discussed. Rentschler explores the classicist aspects of the Kundmanngasse in great detail, contrasting them with late baroque architecture in Germany and in Prague, but we may wonder why he did not consider Austrian classicism and baroque. With the exception of Turnovský (although he may have been unaware of his contribution) all authors overlook Wittgenstein's high

The Kundmanngasse, spring 1971.

regard for Viennese baroque, in particular for the work of Johann Bernhard Fischer von Erlach, and only Kapfinger mentions Loos's, and possibly also Wittgenstein's, appreciation of the simplicity of Viennese Biedermeier classicism.

Kapfinger also makes a valuable comparison between Engelmann's, and subsequently Wittgenstein's, plan of the Kundmanngasse and Loos's conception of the three-dimensional *Raumplanung*, or 'spatial planning', and he stresses the importance of the nineteenth century *Palais Wittgenstein*, which belonged to Ludwig's parents, for the design of the ground floor. Still, as Amendolagine indicates but does not work through, much more can be said on plausible, also non-Loosian, influences on Engelmann's spatial concept of the house (for example, Otto Wagner) and on the relationship between the spatial plan and setting of the Kundmanngasse and the traditional Viennese aristocratic *Palais*-architecture. It is also useful to compare the materials used for the construction and finishing of the Kundmanngasse, which have only been listed in previous publications.

Furthermore, obvious differences between Loos's deliberate avoidance of pointless adornment and his treatment of decoration, and Wittgenstein's straightforward omission of any ornamentation (even that which is naturally present in the materials such as marble or wood), have only been sketched. Some authors connect both to the functionalism of the flourishing *Sachlichkeit* (New Objectivity) in architecture and design at the time, within which the 'psychological' approach of Loos is contrasted with the 'logical' approach of Wittgenstein. Others stress the classicist influence on Wittgenstein's supposed functionalism and interpret it as meaning that the idea of clarity and precision was more important to Wittgenstein than modernist functional design. Although a great deal can be said in favour of both viewpoints, the origins of Wittgenstein's non-ornamental and 'purifying' preferences have not been thoroughly investigated or compared to Loos's

16

anti-ornamental roots and conception of functionalism and classicist inclinations at the time of the inception of the Kundmanngasse. Did Wittgenstein pick up other influences during his study in England from 1908–13? What role did machine design play in his ideas as compared to those of Loos? He was, after all trained as a mechanical engineer in England, which profession and country Loos and possibly also Wittgenstein, in his years as a student, admired very much for their modernity? And, again, to what extent did Engelmann's ideas and sketches influence Wittgenstein's solutions in this respect?

A last unresolved problem is whether Wittgenstein applied some proportional system. We know from several anecdotes that harmonic proportions were of overriding importance to him. Though some geometric relations are easily recognizable and have been recorded as such, and some others are suspected, there has never been a thorough study of the presence, the nature and the extent of any proportional system underlying the Kundmanngasse in Engelmann's and Wittgenstein's plans and elevations.

The second point of view focuses on the connection, or supposed connection, between the Kundmanngasse and Wittgenstein's philosophical work. The reader of the *Tractatus logico-philosophicus* will inevitably be struck by the similarities to Wittgenstein's architectural achievement, characterized by the words of Hänsel: austere, ethereal, noble, rigorous. The most seductive interpretation would imply that the Kundmanngasse is a literal 'translation', 'materialization' or 'representation' of the philosophy of the *Tractatus* in glass, metal, and stone. Though none of the publications go so far as to make such simplistic claims, for example searching for the propositions of the book in the architecture of the house, some authors come very near to it. In the same way any suggestion that the Kundmanngasse can be taken as an intentional physical representation of Wittgenstein's philosophy cannot be justified. As will be explained later, approaches like these contradict Wittgenstein's own conceptions of philosophy and of aesthetics. The first consideration is how the relationship between an architectural object and a conceptual structure can be established meaningfully and convincingly. Giacomini attempts to bridge the gap by reference to Wittgenstein's character traits. It is certainly true that psychological or even psychoanalytical explanations can be found that attribute both his philosophical–ethical ideas and his aesthetic preferences to underlying common psychological factors. These factors would account for the perfectionism and perseverance and the inclination to austerity and frugality which are obvious in everything he produced. However, to make such a connection between psychological factors and Wittgenstein's conceptual and architectural constructions would be almost as feeble, and as dependent on the willingness of the single reader to accept it, as to make a direct connection between philosophy and architectural design. The danger becomes even greater when, as Amendolagine seems to attempt, psychobiography, logic and architectural analysis are forced together into the straitjacket of the idea of 'historical necessity'.

The second connection which has been proposed is the presumed stylistic similarity or even identity of both the Kundmanngasse and, in particular, the *Tractatus logico-philosophicus*. Establishing such an identity is fraught with problems: can formal categories ascribed to one material form of expression, such as architecture, be transposed to other material forms of expression such as philosophical language? Again, terms such as classical, monumental, unadorned, which may have precise meanings in each domain of artistic expression, are too vague if used across both contexts.

The semiotic interpretation of Rentschler, based on his interesting morphological observations with regard to the Kundmanngasse, seems unconvincing in this respect. He indeed 'identifies' abstract common tendencies in the articulation of the building material of the house on the one hand, and of the linguistic-conceptual material of *Tractatus* on the other. These are expressed by the concept 'attempt at precision', to be realized by 'striving for autonomy of syntactical elements', which ought to explain the 'structural analogy' between both, to be expressed finally by the stylistic denotation 'classicist'. However, to avoid tautological play with these terms, the abstract 'attempt at precision' should not be presented as the conclusion of the analysis of the stylistic relationship between house and philosophical text, but rather as its starting point. What exactly are 'syntactical elements', and what does 'precision' mean, either in architectural construction or in linguistic-conceptual construction? Why is 'precision' in late baroque architecture formally different from, or more imprecise than, 'precision' in neoclassicism, as Rentschler seems to imply? How can architectural precision, which consists in visual–spatial–tactile relationships and in a certain use of building elements, be identical or analogous to, or reflect philosophical precision, which consists in semantic relationships and in the precise use of words and concepts?

A third way to evaluate the relationship between the Kundmanngasse and Wittgenstein's philosophy is to start from the material at our disposal. Close examination may provide more tangible links with the results of the analysis of the Kundmanngasse as an architectural object, and thus give a clue to Wittgenstein's 'implicit conception' of architecture. His ideas about philosophical aesthetics and more general aesthetic conceptions which he most likely held during the building period of the house should be considered first. It is true that he neither formulated nor intended to formulate a systematic aesthetic, but we do possess a proposition in the *Tractatus* (1922), a number of remarks in his preliminary *Notebooks* (1914–16), and in the text of a lecture (1929) that touch upon the subject of aesthetics and which span the building period (1926–28). Though these are summary, they are so intimately connected with his philosophical method of 'clarification', that it is surprising that before now this connection has only been suggested or indicated briefly. We should determine the extent to which this conception is consistent with, or reflected in, the principles that guided Wittgenstein's design of the Kundmanngasse.

In this context we should remember that Wittgenstein was trained as a mechanical engineer, which influenced, in the spirit of the time, his ideas on design, as is clear from remarks that have come down to us. His philosophical approach, especially in the case of the *Tractatus logico-philosophicus*, is also strongly influenced by his understanding of the functioning of machines. The ethical–aesthetic connection that Wittgenstein made implies an interesting continuum comprising the activities of the engineer, the designer and the artist. Moreover, his philosophical ideas account for the decisive role he attributed to intuition in engineering, in thinking as well as in designing which may, by the way, also throw light on the design and proportioning of the Kundmanngasse, as well as on his own opinion on being an amateur architect.

Finally, we possess a number of diary entries on architecture and recollections of former students and friends on the subject. Almost all were written after the completion of the Kundmanngasse and can, for that reason, only be useful as an *ad hoc* corroboration and qualification of what may be concluded from the abovementioned approach.

The third perspective from which the Kundmanngasse may be viewed is that of the cultural context in which it originated, in particular the context of Viennese cultural and intellectual history from the *fin de siècle* until the 1930s, when the rise of Nazism drained Austria of its cultural and intellectual resources including Ludwig Wittgenstein himself who, in 1939, saw no other choice than to become a British subject. Questions arising from this perspective have been dealt with by Engelmann in his *Memoir*, and touched upon in the books by Johnston and Janik and Toulmin. Johnston mentions the supposed influence of Loos's ideas on architecture. Janik and Toulmin point to the apparent correspondence between the meaning of functionality in design adopted by both Wittgenstein and Loos, and subsequently refer to Leitner's appreciation of the originality of the non-professional aspects of the house's architecture, in which they recognize Karl Kraus's conception of the artistic personality. A comprehensive assessment of these problems would require careful study of the influence of Kraus's ideas on Wittgenstein, and probably also of the mutual influence of Kraus and Loos, who knew each other well, together with a study of the origins of Wittgenstein's conception of aesthetics in the works of Goethe, Schopenhauer and Weininger.

It is beyond the scope of this book to examine these matters in depth and we shall restrict ourselves to a discussion of Wittgenstein's 'implicit conception' of architecture *vis-à-vis* Loos's ideas on architecture and design set against the background of the modernism of the time. In so far as references will be made to other cultural and intellectual disciplines, they will only be conjectural or, particularly in chapters 2, 3 and 4, serve as a background to the story being told.

This background is, however, being extended in a way that may not be connected directly with the Kundmanngasse so far as Paul Engelmann is concerned. Enquiry into his role as Wittgenstein's co-architect resulted in the discovery of a number of facts about his life. As his friendship with Wittgenstein has often been mentioned but never been given sufficient attention, and as it seems unlikely that these facts could fill a book, a more elaborate account of his life and his character seems justified within the context of one of the main events of his life, the design and construction of the Kundmanngasse, which resulted in the tragic ending of his friendship with Ludwig Wittgenstein.

Ludwig Wittgenstein 1

From mechanical engineering to philosophy

Ludwig Wittgenstein was born on 26 April 1889 in Vienna, the youngest son of the Austrian steel magnate Karl Wittgenstein and his wife Leopoldine. Karl Wittgenstein came from Germany and his family was of mostly Jewish origins; during the nineteenth century the Wittgensteins had completely assimilated into German culture and acquired considerable wealth in trade. As an adolescent, Karl ran away from home and wandered around the United States, earning his own living. There he came to know about the large scale industrialization of the time. On his return to Europe he was trained in economics and mechanical engineering. After he moved to Austria, he worked his way up to become one of the wealthiest and most influential industrialists in the Hapsburg Empire.

Ludwig Wittgenstein.

When Ludwig was still young, Karl withdrew from active business and devoted himself to the role of Maecenas. Ludwig grew up in surroundings which were not so much commercially but culturally and artistically oriented, splendidly isolated from the everyday world because of his father's wealth. The composers Johannes Brahms, Josef Labor, and Gustav Mahler were friends of the family; Bruno Walter and Pablo Casals more than once gave performances in the neo-Renaissance *Palais* Wittgenstein in the Alleegasse, or at the Hochreith, the large country estate in the Alps south of Vienna. With the assistance of his eldest daughter Hermine, Karl started to collect art; works by Klimt, Klinger, Moser, Puvis de Chavannes, Rodin, Carpeaux and Mestrovic found places in the Alleegasse. Gustav Klimt used to call Karl his 'Minister of Fine Art'. He also acted as a patron of the Viennese Jugendstil movement, the *Wiener Secession*; their exhibition building in the Friedrichstraße, designed by Joseph Olbrich, was almost entirely financed by him. Karl paid for Klimt's mural *Philosophie*, which depicted a sensual naked woman, after the scandal which led to its rejection by the University of Vienna, which had commissioned the work.

As for Karl's involvement with architecture, a few small buildings on one of his estates were designed by Josef Hoffmann. In 1903 Hoffmann's *Wiener Werkstätte* designed and executed the wooden 'hunting lodge' on the Hochreith, the private dwelling of Karl and his wife set apart from the main building, for which no trouble or expense was spared. The walls and ceilings were covered with hand-painted or gilt-bordered mahogany panelling, the lamps were made of gold plated silver and crystal, the taps were of gold, the chairs and tables were inlaid with mother-of-pearl and ivory, and stained glass depicting hunting scenes filled the windows. But in spite of the expensive materials the modestly sized rooms do not strike one as pompous, rather as tasteful and intimate.

Karl Wittgenstein.

Although Ludwig Wittgenstein's interest in art originated in these surroundings, the first of his talents to manifest itself and that which became fundamental to his philosophical and aesthetic ideas, was of a technical nature. Hermine Wittgenstein relates in her *Family Recollections:*

By the age of ten, for example, Ludwig was already so familiar with the construction of a sewing-machine that he was able to build a small model of one out of pieces of wood and bits of wire, which actually sewed a few stitches. Of course, in order to build his model he had to make a detailed study of each part of the full-sized machine and the movements of the mechanism required to produce each stitch, watched all the time with suspicion and displeasure by the old family seamstress.

Max Klinger, *The Squatting Woman.*

Ludwig's considerable technical ability, undoubtedly inherited from his father, profited from the private education of the Wittgenstein children which Karl arranged according to his own ideas. Ludwig got his own construction workshop in the basement with a lathe adapted to his height. He could amply satisfy his fascination with apparatuses and the principles of mechanics by reading the books of his father's library. Among the books he brought with him to England as a student were a beautifully made facsimile edition of Leonardo da Vinci's technical inventions, the mathematical work concerning the mechanics of Galileo Galilei, the sixteenth century *Machinae novi* by the Italian Veranzio Fausti, a number of seventeenth century German *Theatri machinarum* on mechanical and hydraulic engineering, and eighteenth century French and Italian studies on the aeronautics of ballooning. He had two works by Gottlob Frege, the logician whom he so much admired, bound in one volume with a cover of saffian leather designed by the *Wiener Werkstätte* and provided with new titles that pleased him better.

Though unlimited as far as culture was concerned, Ludwig's upbringing was extremely puritanical from a moral point of view, as his friend Paul Engelmann recounted later. Having an iron will himself, Karl demanded the utmost of his children in respect of clear judgment and perseverance. Only the best was good enough and, thanks to his wealth, the best was always available. The family was encouraged to show an extremely critical attitude not only towards art and music, but also towards each other's conduct. In life, and in art, a person ought to aim at 'genuineness' (*Anständigkeit*), which meant that, under all circumstances, each person should show merciless honesty towards themselves as well as towards others. A person should set about a piece of work for the intrinsic value of the work itself and the attainment of self-set goals, not for the sake of personal prestige. Attempting to satisfy these self-imposed demands meant relentless perseverance; failure gave rise to devastating feelings of guilt and worthlessness. Throughout his life this perfectionist view would make it hard for Ludwig to come to terms with the dreariness and pettiness of everyday life; on the other hand, without his perfectionism and almost naive straightforwardness his philosophy, his technical inventions, and not least, the architecture of the house he was to design and build for his sister would have been inconceivable.

In 1906 Wittgenstein graduated from the *Königliche und Kaiserliche Oberrealschule* ('Royal and Imperial High School') in Linz, where he had been sent after the suicide of two of his brothers; his father feared that their isolation from the everyday world had played a decisive role in these tragedies. Ludwig wanted to study physics with Ludwig Boltzmann at the University of Vienna, for his technical abilities had led him, after reading the work of Boltzmann and of Hertz, to a philosophical interest in the foundations of the natural sciences. He had started to write down philosophical thoughts. That same year, however, Boltzmann committed suicide and Ludwig decided to study mechanical engineering at one of the leading institutions in that field, the *Technische Hochschule* in Berlin-Charlottenburg.

Two years later Wittgenstein left for England to follow his interest in aeronautics, without doubt in those years of the first motorized flights the greatest challenge for a young student of engineering. He conducted aerodynamic experiments with new types of kites for meteorological research at the Kite Flying Upper Atmosphere Station in Glossop, Cheshire. A second reason for studying in England may have been the admiration for English upper class culture prevalent at that time in the German-speaking countries. In autumn Wittgenstein continued his studies at the famous Department of Engineering at the University of Manchester where he developed a jet engine which formed a whole with the propeller it drove. The principle had already been described by Heron of Alexandria, whose work Wittgenstein had encountered in his father's library. A variable volume combustion chamber was built into the propeller's shaft, while reaction jets were attached to the tips of its blades. The prototype which he constructed eventually worked and he patented it, but the problem of sealing off expanding gases proved insurmountable. (Incidentally, the principle was put to use in the Second World War by the Austrian engineer Doblhoff in the rotor of a helicopter and was later adapted by an American aircraft factory.) The optimal aerodynamic form of the propeller blade was a problem that could be approached mathematically and Wittgenstein started to fol-

Gustav Klimt, *Philosophy*, 1905.

Far left: Joseph Olbrich, exhibition building of the *Wiener Secession*, 1898-1899.

Left: the *Palais* Wittgenstein (about 1872), Alleegasse 16, after 1918 Argentinierstraße (demolished in the early sixties).

The Hochreith. Pencil drawing by Hermine Wittgenstein.

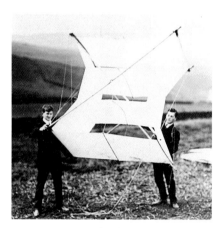

Ludwig Wittgenstein (right) and William Eccles with a kite on the moors of Glossop.

The young Ludwig Wittgenstein working at his lath.

low lectures in mathematics. This subject, however, reawakened his philosophical interests; at that time the work of Bertrand Russell and Gottlob Frege had made the foundations of mathematics and logic the focus of philosophical research. In 1912 Wittgenstein decided to discontinue his research in Manchester and to study mathematical logic with Russell in Cambridge.

By this time he must have realized that the machine, that is, the efficiently functioning mechanical system, could be the paradigm of the philosophical explanation of the world, the good and the beautiful that he was striving for. He then felt that the strict efficiency with which a well-designed machine had to comply corresponded with the principle of parsimony underlying exact logical–mathematical demonstration. It formed the criterion of its truthfulness, which coincided with its rightness and beauty. He told Russell, for example, that studying logic improved one's aesthetic judgment, a conviction that certainly influenced his aesthetic preferences and ideas.

According to C.M. Mason, who was the Assistant Director of the laboratory where Wittgenstein worked on his prototype aeroplane engine, architecture and design were subjects to which he returned in conversation almost daily. Wittgenstein abhorred ornament and stressed the importance of simplicity in furniture design. When Wittgenstein furnished his rooms in Cambridge he could not find any furniture he liked in the shops and drove the shopkeepers mad with his demands. In the end he ordered specially designed furniture that met the degree of simplicity that he required. Although the colours applied in his interior – blue, black and yellow – reflect a sobered down *Wiener Werkstätte* palette, his preference for functionality and simplicity was undoubtedly influenced by the writings of the foremost Viennese innovator of architecture, Adolf Loos, who had published his pamphlet *Ornament und Verbrechen* ('Ornament and Crime') in 1908.

Design was also an important theme in Wittgenstein's friendship with William Eccles, whom he had come to know in Glossop and who studied engineering with him in Manchester. In 1914 Eccles and his new wife furnished their new house in Manchester and he and Wittgenstein exchanged letters on the subject which refer to the canon of beauty they adhered to. Note the attention paid by Eccles to the mechanical and electrical aspects of the house, it was obvious that these should be treated in the same way as furniture design and decoration:

Josef Hoffmann and the *Wiener Werkstätte*, corridor (left) and living room (centre and right) of the Wittgenstein hunting lodge, 1903.

Sunday, 28-6-14
15 High Lane
Chorlton-Cum-Hardy
Manchester

Dear W[ittgenstein],

I know it is a very long 'fortnight' or so since I wrote last but it was because I have been very busy with work and important things about the house. At last I have got up to date with reports, letters, bills etc. The house is about equipped now electrically except for a motor to drive a washing machine and a vacuum cleaning arrangement. The furnishing is complete (partly thanks to you for many items). The decorating has been designed or rather planned by Ada except for the drawing room which is a copy of your Cambridge room (blue carpet, black paint, yellow walls) except that the ceiling and about 2 ft down the walls all around is white and the lighting which is indirect, i.e. reflected from the ceiling.

All the other rooms are on the same simple scale but with different (plain) colours of walls and woodwork (the ceilings in every case are the same as the drawing room).

The effect is greatly admired by everyone and is certainly good to live with but we are looking forward to your criticism when you come here.

The electric fittings, especially the cooking which is really fine, are so clean and handy. The radiators too are excellent and we have no need of fires at all so that when we are without a maid - as is the case at present - there is very little inconvenience.

In all we have apparatus of an aggregate capacity of about 15 kilowatts!

Now I want your advice about a suite of bedroom furniture which I would like to have made sometime when enough cash accumulates to pay for it. The enclosed sketches [regrettably lost, P.W.] are just about what I want.

I have considered only

1. *Utility*

We have not a separate room for clothes, hence the large size of everything, but as the room is

Impeccably dressed Ludwig Wittgenstein, about 1912.

Postcard from Ludwig Wittgenstein to William Eccles, sent during his first trip to Skjolden and showing his rooms in the local boarding house.

large (being 18 ft x 13 ft which is just about the same size as the room you slept in when staying in Coleraine).

2. *Construction* (giving preference to the easiest method of construction).

3. *Absolute simplicity*

Unfortunately my sketches are only working drawings and require some imagination to see the articles.

The manufacturer's *sketches* are better in this respect but I would rather have my own designs. Now please let us have your opinion and, I must say, soon, as I have left this too long and now we need the Medicine Chest quite soon.

W. Eccles

Wittgenstein answered:

XVII Neuwaldeggerstraße 38
Wien.

Dear Eccles,

As you will observe I am in Vienna again for a holiday. Thanks for your letter, your designs are splendid as far as I can judge. I will make a few remarks: *re* wardrobe - why is the horizontal cross-piece on the doors not in the middle (from top to bottom), such that top and bottom panels are of the same length? 2. I think it might perhaps be more convenient to rest the wardrobe on a low (3") V at the base as is done on the manufacturer's design instead of the doors opening right on the carpet.

MEDICINE CHEST: Splendid.
DRESSING TABLE: „

Patent registration of the propellor engine.

I cannot see any drawing of a bed, or do you wish to take the one which the furniture manufacturers submitted? If so *do* insist that they cut off all those measly fancy ends. And why should the bed stand on rollers? You are not going to travel about with it in your house!? By all means have the other things made after *your* design.

Yours ever,
L.W.

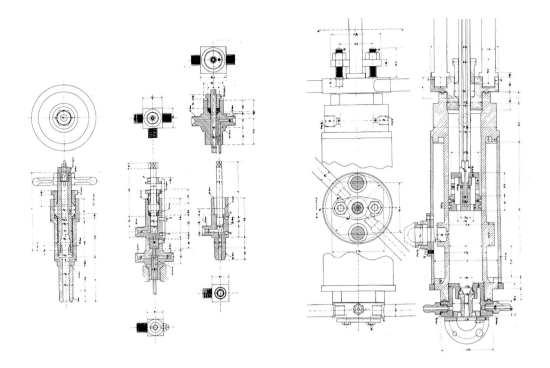

In January 1913 Karl Wittgenstein died and Ludwig inherited a 'child's portion' of his wealth, which was still immense. In spring 1914 he built his first and only house near the Norwegian village of Skjolden on the shore of the Sognefjord, where he had found the peace necessary to work on logic. The house was constructed of wood in the local fashion. It was modest in size, with a basement, a ground floor with a few rooms, and an attic. Although it is no longer in existence and any plans or other documentary material have been lost, friends of his remember that it had ingenious details reminiscent of those to be found in the house he later built for his sister. Because it was situated against a steep slope high above a lake (one could only reach it by rowing over) there was, among other things, a winch and cable mechanism which enabled a bucket to be lowered to hoist water.

At the beginning of July 1914 Wittgenstein had returned to Austria to arrange a gift on the occasion of the inheritance, as was customary, in favour of destitute artists. This amounted to 100,000 Crowns (its present value would be £40-50,000, or US$ 75,000). He approached Ludwig von Ficker, editor and publisher of the cultural magazine *Der Brenner* ('The Burner'), requesting him to divide the money between artists of his choice without revealing the name of the benefactor. Among the beneficiaries were the poets Georg Trakl and Rainer Maria Rilke, the painter Oskar Kokoschka and the painter and poet Else Lasker-Schüler, and the architect Adolf Loos whom Wittgenstein so much admired and to whom von Ficker would introduce him that same month.

Construction drawing of the variable volume combustion propellor engine.

Wittgenstein's wooden house at the lake near the Sognefjord.

Ludwig Wittgenstein and Adolf Loos

Adolf Loos.

The ideas on design which the young Ludwig Wittgenstein cherished demonstrate a strong affinity with those of Adolf Loos at the time. Shortly before the turn of the century Loos had set out his ideas for the first time in a series of articles published during 1897–1900 in the leading Viennese newspaper *Neue Freie Presse*. During the years that followed he was strongly supported by the satirical writer and moralist Karl Kraus in his magazine *Die Fackel* ('The Torch'), which had a far-reaching influence in Viennese intellectual life for more than 30 years. Both the *Neue Freie Presse* and *Die Fackel* were read in Wittgenstein's parents' home in the Alleegasse. Karl himself had published articles on political and economic subjects in the *Neue Freie Presse*; *Die Fackel* had attacked him for shadowy financial transactions when he retired from business. His youngest daughter Margarethe, seven years Ludwig's senior, was a keen reader of Karl Kraus and probably brought his magazine to the attention of her younger brother as she did with a number of writers. It is certain that Ludwig read *Die Fackel* before 1910, and when he stayed in Norway in 1914 the magazine was sent to him there. Wittgenstein had learned the name of Ludwig von Ficker from *Die Fackel*, for in it Kraus had mentioned von Ficker's *Der Brenner* as the only honest Austrian periodical. Wittgenstein wrote to von Ficker:

I choose you as the executor of this matter [the gift of 100,000 Crowns] trusting the words that Kraus wrote about you and your magazine, and trusting the words you wrote about Kraus.

On 27 July 1914, on the eve of the outbreak of the First World War Ficker introduced Wittgenstein to Adolf Loos. Ficker had told him that he knew Loos personally and Wittgenstein showed great interest in meeting him. The meeting took place in Café Imperial where the two entered into a somewhat stilted (partly because of Loos's deafness) but nonetheless exciting conversation, of which regrettably no further details are known; it resulted in a friendship that would last till Loos's death in 1933. Loos, by the way, never knew that Wittgenstein was the anonymous donor of the 2,000 Crowns that reached him at the end of that year. In his letter of thanks to von Ficker he said:

Your kind letter deeply moved me and gratefully I accept the gift in these cursed times, realizing that everything will change for the better and that I shall then be able to repay the sum to its original destination.

Christmas postcard written by Ludwig Wittgenstein from the front, 1915.

We may safely assume that Loos was never in a financial position to fulfil his promise.

Wittgenstein readily volunteered for service in the First World War. During the next four years, whenever Wittgenstein was on leave in Vienna he visited Loos. It was Adolf Loos who, in 1916, gave him an introduction to one of his pupils, Paul Engelmann, living in Olmütz (now Olomouc in the Czech Republic), when he was sent there to be trained as an artillery officer. They became friends and thanks to this friendship Wittgenstein's sister would later commission Engelmann to design the Kundmanngasse. In his *Memoir* Engelmann wrote that Loos once exclaimed in front of Wittgenstein: 'You are me!', so much did he recognize of his own ideas in Wittgenstein's, who while at the front, when he did not have to fight, worked on the manuscript of 'Logico-Philosophical Treatise' (*Logisch-philosophische Abhandlung*, which was published in 1922 as the *Tractatus logico-philosophicus*). Engelmann recounted:

They valued each other highly. Loos had a sure instinct for genius, although he certainly did not understand W[ittgenstein] in many respects.

Loos would have imbued Wittgenstein with the conviction that the unifying force of the times one lived in should find expression through one's thoughts and deeds. Wittgenstein himself indeed mentioned the great architect among the persons whom he believed had a decisive influence on him.

Adolf Loos (1870–1933) maintained that his conception of modern, *sachlich*, 'objective', architecture found its origin in his journey to America and England, which he undertook immediately after finishing his training as an architect in Dresden and Vienna. During his stay in the United States he was confronted with the building activity of an industrial society which developed, unimpeded by tradition, on a scale unknown to an inhabitant of the Old World and making a daring use of construction techniques in steel. He was certainly impressed by the skyscraper architecture of the Chicago School, but perhaps more by the practical, straightforward, individualist and liberal mentality of a civilization based solely on business, which contrasted strongly with the aristocratic class society and the bureaucracy of the Austro-Hungarian monarchy. Loos himself said that the moment when the essence of architecture became clear to him was in New York. In a shop his eye was caught by a solid leather cabin trunk with brass fittings, the travel accessory of the businessman of his time. He instantly realized that its aesthetic value lay in its well-considered functional design, or, reversing a statement by his teacher Otto Wagner, that something impractical could not be beautiful, *Das Praktische ist schön!* – The practical is beautiful.

On his way home Loos spent some time in England, the country in which the nineteenth century discussion on the status of ornament and craftsmanship had begun, which had attracted so much attention from Viennese architects and designers. It was stirred up by the Industrial Revolution,

Robert Scheu on Adolf Loos in Karl Kraus's *Die Fackel* of 26 June, 1909.

Das Haus am Michaelerplatz, drawing by Paul Engelmann on the cover of his brochure on Adolf Loos, 1946.

Adolf Loos, view from the music room into the
dining room of the Villa Moller, 1927-1928.

which made possible the mechanical reproduction methods that brought
cheap kitsch ornament within the reach of everyone, and resulted in the
condemnation of the machine by such artists and designers as John Ruskin
and William Morris. Loos, however, was struck by another consequence of
the Industrial Revolution: the intrinsic beauty of steel construction applied
on a large scale in bridges, railway stations and exhibition halls, which
came to be characterized as the *Maschinenstil* ('machine style'). These were
not designed by architects trained in art schools, but by engineers whose
sole aim was to achieve reliable and functional constructions. Loos also
came to appreciate the layout of the English country house with its rooms
practically arranged around a central living hall, and to admire the craftsmanship developed from longstanding tradition with which these houses
were built and finished. It inspired the emphasis on the severe application
of beautifully worked natural materials in his interior design and his abhorrence, expressed in his pamphlet *Ornament und Verbrechen* ('Ornament and
Crime', 1908), of unnecessary ornament in architecture, which had its cli-
max in the *Haus am Michaelerplatz* (1911), which caused a scandal. Later
on he developed the idea of the *Raumplanung* (literally 'spatial planning')
from the plan of the English country house.

After his return to Vienna, Loos found a justification for his functionalist
conception in the architecture of antiquity, in particular of the Romans.
Roman architecture should have developed from the basic human needs for
shelter and convenience, and from the demands generated by living in
groups. The use of ornament in antiquity – column, frieze, architrave, cornice, pediment – resulted from natural functionality and possessed therefore eternal validity. For this reason, later architectural styles in western

history had time and again revived the principles of Roman architecture. The nineteenth century parade of neo-styles, however, had put an end to sound classical tradition. In addition, the generation of architects and designers like Otto Wagner, Joseph Olbrich and Josef Hoffmann, who wanted to develop a truly modern style, ignored the lessons antiquity could teach in modern times. Still under the influence of Romantic ideas, they pretended to practise a liberal art in which the spirit of their times could be expressed by way of ornamentation and decoration for, after all, these elements could be freely designed and styled without any serious effect on the construction of a building. Loos stated — not without calculated hyperbole — that architecture was not one of the liberal arts, but a craft bound to its characteristic methods and techniques. Only in its capacity to serve, typical of any craft, could architecture produce great results. In the Industrial Age this meant serving the aims of *Sachlichkeit* — matter-of-fact building, constructional efficiency, the expression of reserve in exterior design and of practicality and privacy in interior design.

We may therefore imagine that Adolf Loos and the young engineer Ludwig Wittgenstein found a great rapport between their ideas on design, the more so since Wittgenstein had been studying in England which for Loos, as for many of his German-speaking contemporaries, was the best example of modern industrial society, and Wittgenstein knew the English 'machine style' from his own experience. Equally important must have been their shared appreciation of English traditional craftsmanship which for both, by the way, went further than building and finishing techniques: they greatly admired British tailoring and clothing and Wittgenstein, as a young man, was quite as well-groomed and elegant as Loos; both feared that the craft of tailoring would become extinct. (In later years, when Wittgenstein dressed extremely simply and, for that reason, made a shabby impression on those who could not recognize the intrinsic quality of tailored clothes, he still ordered the few garments he possessed made to measure from the best tailors in Cambridge.) As for Loos's classicist inclinations Wittgenstein must have felt a strong affinity with them, for it will become clear in later chapters that Wittgenstein's aesthetic creed of clarification, fundamental to the house he would later design for his sister, should with reason be identified as 'classicizing'.

Although initially Loos and Wittgenstein believed they recognized in each other a common attitude to aesthetics it soon became apparent that their characters and the underlying motives for their ideas differed considerably. If Loos was an artist before all else (or, at any rate, a skilled designer), whose functionalist style was deeply rooted in his feeling for the practical and his love for all earthly things, for Wittgenstein, the thinker and searcher for truth, 'functionalism' was most literally represented in the functioning mechanism and entailed an ethical principle; as far as the aesthetic aspect of design was concerned, it was still meant to satisfy a basic need for moral justification. The aim of Loos's architecture was convenience, to make a person feel at home after a day's work. Compared to the lavish furnishing of late nineteenth century interiors Loos's designs at first sight seem frugal, but they do instil a sense of shelter and convenience and the materials, though applied unobtrusively, are often costly, not to say luxurious. Wittgenstein's ideas on design, however, aimed at moral relief from the wickedness of everyday life. This relief had to be brought about by rigorous elimination of any form, any architectural attribute that was not of itself necessary, that was merely a diversion and was, therefore, insincere. Simplicity was for him as much a moral as an aesthetic tool.

These differences between the characters of the two men soon came to light. On a postcard to Engelmann, dated 25 December 1916, Wittgenstein vented his annoyance at Loos's negligence in keeping to appointments. When Wittgenstein met Loos again for the first time after his return from captivity in Monte Cassino in 1919, he reported to Engelmann disappointedly:

A few days ago I looked up Loos. I was horrified and nauseated. He has become infected with the most virulent bogus intellectualism! He gave me a pamphlet about a proposed 'fine arts office', in which he speaks about a sin against the Holy Ghost. This surely is the limit! I was already a bit depressed when I went to Loos, but that was the last straw.

Adolf Loos, *'Directions for a Ministry of Art'*, 1919.

This pamphlet, *Richtlinien für ein Kunstamt* ('Directions for a Ministry of Art', 1919), is regarded, together with *Architektur* ('Architecture', 1910), as Loos's main theoretical work although we should not underestimate the deliberate propagandist purport of all his writings. It was written as the result of the profound changes that took place immediately after the First World War: Austria changed from being a vast empire under Hapsburg rule into a small republic. The apparatus of government had to be adapted to the new order, which for Loos was a pretext to formulate an outline for the establishment and policy of a new Ministry of Cultural Affairs. He based these directions on the historical role of the artist in society. It was through the artist that Providence – the 'Holy Ghost' – realized civilization and cultural flowering in man. Now that the monarch, who had traditionally fostered the arts and protected artists from the natural philistinism of the man in the street – 'the sin against the Holy Ghost' – had gone, the responsibility for art and artists fell to the state. The state, as the general representative of the common citizen, had to educate that citizen to appreciate the arts:

The State, therefore, has the duty to bring the people to the artist as near as possible. No other method of government support for the arts can be achieved.

Loos went on to propose a programme to achieve this aim for each of the domains of art, among which, for the sake of convenience, he now also included architecture. The programme for music was signed by Arnold Schönberg, whose musical compositions were despised by Wittgenstein; the other collaborators remained anonymous.

Wittgenstein would not have disagreed with Loos about the idea of literally bringing the populace to the arts for, during the following years while he was teaching, he himself more or less put the idea into practice by making trips with his classes to Vienna to show them historical buildings of architectural importance and to visit the Museum of Art History and other museums. However, his concept of the relationship between language and world and its consequences for leading a moral life, which had led him immediately after his release from captivity to part with his fortune and to earn his living as a school teacher in the poorest parts of Austria, made it impossible for him to regard Loos's pamphlet as anything but idle talk. The austere language of the *Tractatus logico-philosophicus*, with its resigned conclusion that what can be said at all can be said meaningfully and what cannot be said meaningfully can only be shown, with its tacit emphasis on acting, contrasted sharply with the gratuitous and propagandist belief in progress manifest in Loos's writing. The *Richtlinien* could only have strengthened Wittgenstein's doubts about Loos's moral character.

Almost nothing is known about later contacts between Adolf Loos and Ludwig Wittgenstein. It seems likely that they continued to see each other during Wittgenstein's school holidays, which he spent in Vienna or at the Hochreith. In 1924, when Loos prepared to leave Vienna to take up residence in Paris, he made Wittgenstein a gift of his collected articles from the *Neue Freie Presse*, published in 1921 under the title of *Ins Leere gesprochen* ('Spoken into the Void'). It was dedicated:

To Ludwig Wittgenstein, gratefully and most affectionately, grateful for his inspiration, most affectionate in the hope that he will return this feeling.

From these lines we may infer that Wittgenstein maintained a certain deliberate reserve towards Loos, though he still felt friendship towards him, as is clear from a postcard he sent to Loos in Paris in September 1925, in which he announces that he is going to try one more year as a teacher as he did around the same time in postcards to his friends William Eccles and John Maynard Keynes in England:

Dear Mr Loos!

I returned to my old village to try once more. If it doesn't work out – and that is very likely – then I'll quit. I have had a good trip. I thoroughly examined your instructions concerning the Basel jam and pastry and have approved of them. Yours, Ludwig Wittgenstein.

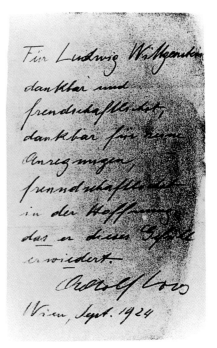

Adolf Loos's dedication in Ludwig Wittgenstein's copy of *Ins Leere gesprochen*.

Postcard from Ludwig Wittgenstein to Adolf
Loos, showing the village and its school where
he was teaching, September 1925.

The fact that one year later Wittgenstein agreed to design and build the house for his sister aroused Loos's indignation. He must have resented Wittgenstein's acceptance of the commission when he had no training in architecture and while two of Loos's pupils, Paul Engelmann and Jacques Groag, only played a background role. From Loos's professional standpoint Wittgenstein was a bungler.

During the construction of the Kundmanngasse, Loos and Wittgenstein met at least once on the occasion of one of Loos's sojourns in Vienna. Wittgenstein visited him, with Margaret, and undoubtedly the Kundmanngasse was the subject of discussion. He may have tried to convince Loos that he was serious about practising architecture; on the other hand it is very unlikely that Loos exercised any significant direct influence on the design of the house. During his stay in Vienna from mid-October 1926 to January 1927 the design phase had been completed and the actual construction had already begun. Moreover, Wittgenstein's alterations to Engelmann's preliminary classicist design already deviated from the path Loos had followed since 1922, and only stressed the contrast between the latter's interpretation of modernist functionalism and the former's classicizing concept of modernity. During Loos's stay in Vienna from mid-April to mid-May 1927 the construction of the house was well under way and no significant changes were made afterwards.

When, in September 1928, Loos returned to Vienna Wittgenstein had just taken the first steps to enable him to go to Cambridge to take up philosophy again. We may only conjecture that in the five years before Loos died, during one of Wittgenstein's holidays in Vienna, they inspected the Kundmanngasse together, but time has erased any remembrance or record, if such ever existed, of Loos's opinion on Wittgenstein's architectural gesture.

Ludwig Wittgenstein, *architect*

In spring 1926, an incident occurred which resulted in Wittgenstein's departure from the teaching post he held in one of the poorer areas of Lower Austria. Wittgenstein was a rather irascible teacher, as is instanced in a pupil's record of an architecture lesson:

Yes, that was my best memory because it was very disagreeable to me, for I didn't get done what Master Wittgenstein wanted of us, or at least wanted of me. Again and again we had to draw Corinthian columns. We were only rubbing out and rubbing out again and we never got the columns done as he had imagined it, actually we hadn't even imagined anything. Then he became very angry and he seized us by our hair and then of course we finished and didn't get anything more done.

So when Wittgenstein boxed the ears of one of his pupils, a sickly boy, and forced him to stand in a corner of the classroom where he subsequently fainted, the villagers seized the opportunity to bring about Wittgenstein's removal from the school. They not only distrusted him because of his manner and speech, which immediately betrayed his background, but also because of his unorthodox teaching style. This aroused their suspicions and increased their feelings of insecurity. A charge was brought against him and he felt compelled to resign. Morally, he regarded himself as an utter failure in life and although he was exonerated by an official enquiry, he did not change his decision to tender his resignation. In fact he had been thinking of changing his profession for some time and had even visited Cambridge the year before to see whether he could take up an academic career. He was officially discharged from his teaching post on 28 April.

Even before the formal date of dismissal he had found employment as a gardener in the monastery of the Brothers of Charity in the Viennese suburb of Hütteldorf. For his lodgings he took the shed in which the gardening tools were kept. Just as in summer of 1919, when he had also experienced a profound moral crisis he saw no other way, apart from suicide, to restore his inner peace than by performing strenuous physical labour in the open air. About this time his *Wörterbuch für Volksschulen* ('Vocabulary for Public Schools') was published, a book designed as an aid to learning spelling and grammar and based on the typical mistakes made by his former pupils in the village of Trattenbach; Wittgenstein, however, showed no interest in it. On 3 June his mother died. It was in this period of personal crisis that his sister Margaret Stonborough and his friend Paul Engelmann agreed to suggest that he act as co-architect in the design of her city mansion, an undertaking in which he had shown a great interest from its inception. As we know from the testimony of his colleague teacher Josef Putré, he had been seriously considering the profession of architect earlier; now the opportunity arose for him to practise the profession and to see if he would be suitable for it.

Page from Ludwig Wittgenstein's *Vocabulary for Public Schools*, published in 1925.

Working model of a steam engine built by Ludwig Wittgenstein to demonstrate to his elementary school pupils.

Cover of the building permit for the
Kundmanngasse, November 1926.

Jacques Groag, around 1927.

In autumn 1926, after much hesitation in which lack of self-confidence after his failure as a teacher and doubts about the feasibility of such an undertaking in cooperation with Engelmann may have played a part, Wittgenstein left his job as a gardener and moved into number 18, Parkgasse, a small house which formed part of the lot his sister had bought and which was to serve as architectural office. The first plans for the building permit, dated 13 November 1926, were signed by both Engelmann and Wittgenstein. Subsequent plans were signed by Wittgenstein alone, although the stamp continued to bear Engelmann's name. There was, however, a third architect involved in the project. Because Engelmann's experience as a architect was limited to interior design work and because Wittgenstein's training as a mechanical engineer was inadequate for the task, Jacques Groag was charged with supervising the constructional specifications and the calculations concerning the building costs. Engelmann knew Jacques Groag from Olomouc; he, like Engelmann himself, had been a pupil and assistant of Adolf Loos.

With regard to Engelmann's preliminary plan Wittgenstein enlarged the plan of the ground floor, revised the proportions of the building and removed all ornament. He designed the mechanical components of the house, selected the materials used in the interior and exterior finishing, including the fastenings, latches and locks, as well as the electrical installation and the plumbing system. The dimensions of the rooms and the division of floor- and wall-planes were determined by their proportional harmony only; colours were chosen for their unobtrusiveness and transparency, and materials were selected for their durability and inconspicuousness. The house was to be a tacit framework for its furnishings, for the precious objects placed in it, and, of course, for its inhabitants. Its beauty had to derive from the purity and clarity of architecture.

The beauty of the house, therefore, necessarily came into being during the process of construction. Decisions about the design of windows and doors had to be made on the basis of prototypes. Wittgenstein's ideal demanded that there be no skirtings, covering plates, superfluous rings or similar devices designed to compensate for constructional irregularities, so the building had to be finished with an unprecedented accuracy. The use of steel for the windows and doors necessitated the invention of entirely new principles of construction that expressed Wittgenstein's ideas of good mechanical engineering. His sister Hermine relates in her *Family Recollections:*

Ludwig designed every window and door, every window-lock and radiator, with as much care and attention to detail as if they were precision instruments, and on a most elegant scale. And then, with his uncompromising energy, he ensured that everything was carried out with the same meticulous care. I can still hear the locksmith asking him, in connection with a keyhole, 'Tell me, Herr Ingenieur, does a millimetre here or there really matter so much to you?' Even before he had finished speaking, Ludwig replied with such a loud, forceful 'Yes!' that the man almost jumped with fright. Indeed, Ludwig had such a sensitive feel for proportions that half a millimetre often mattered to him.

That Wittgenstein managed to get the workmen and contractors to accept such an unusual degree of perfection was due to a great extent to the politeness and courtesy with which he treated them. His friend, Marguerite Respinger, remembers how he would greet each of them 'as if he were a prince', the reason being that for Wittgenstein these men were craftsmen whose workmanship he held in high esteem. Many details had to be corrected repeatedly and orders filled by suppliers were returned more than once until the precise requirements were met. Hermine continues:

In such cases time and money were never allowed to matter, and I admire my sister Gretl for giving Ludwig a completely free hand in this respect. Two great people had come together as architect and client, making it possible to create something perfect of its kind. The same attention was devoted to the most inconspicuous detail as to the main features, for everything was important. Nothing was unimportant, except time and money.

Wittgenstein's high standards may have been the cause of disputes between him and Jacques Groag, who at one point early in 1927 was close to withdrawing from the undertaking. In a letter to his brother Emo he wrote:

Dear Emo, I come home very depressed with a headache after a day of the worst quarrels, disputes, vexations and this happens often. Mostly between me and Wittgenstein. One can think so differently on matters of business and construction that when both have a sensitive nature there will continuously be frictions. I am terribly sorry for this because mostly they are misunderstandings and I don't want it like that and I see where this may lead to: either there will be a clash and I give up the whole thing or I become even more nervous than I am, or I have to take the whole thing completely coolly and put up coolly and uncaringly with the high overspending that will probably occur. And all this because we can't get along with each other.

The rising structural work, early spring 1927.

In a first outline for his *Memoir* Engelmann quotes what seems a sigh issued by Baumeister Friedl at a delay caused by Wittgenstein's perfectionism: 'A third winter in the fields...'

Although Wittgenstein had parted with his estate to be able to live 'unburdened', he never showed any qualms about the luxury in which his sister wished to live, which was to be reflected in the design of the house. He regarded his own inability to live with wealth as a strictly personal matter and believed that, insofar as wealth in itself was wrong, forced redistribution in favour of the poor would only increase injustice; mankind was simply incapable of determining its own fate. He respected the way Margaret spent money on art, on cultural and intellectual affairs and in charitable deeds, as corroborated by Engelmann:

Furthermore, during this period of his own very proletarian way of life as a teacher in Otte[rthal] he stayed time and again with Mrs Stonborough of whose *extremely* luxuriant way of life he on principle never took offence (apart from occasional kindly ironical remarks); indeed, shortly thereafter he designed and executed, with unchanging attitude to life, the house in the Kundmanngasse wholly in *her* style, however much in most ascetic spirit and austerity. Since parting with his own wealth his attitude to these matters was so unequivocally clear and certain that for *this* reason it never caused him any more inner conflicts.

Finishing the exterior, probably summer 1928.

Wittgenstein became so totally absorbed in his architectural undertaking that at night he would be completely exhausted. He found, however, that unpretentious American motion pictures, especially westerns, relaxed him. Paul Engelmann, and later Marguerite Respinger, usually accompanied him to the cinema in the working-class district of Margareten where the films were shown. Engelmann relates that what delighted Wittgenstein most was the uncomplicated and enthusiastic way in which the public was captivated by what took place on the screen. (At that time motion pictures were still silent. With the advent of the sound-film, which through its spoken dialogue introduced an intellectual aspect with all its dangers and deceptions, Wittgenstein's pleasure was spoilt.) The films, usually composed around the theme of the wild chase and subsequent punishment of the criminals, convinced him of the importance of the 'happy ending'. This was, after all, in keeping with remarks made in his *Notebooks* a decade earlier in which he maintained that good art was not only unaffected and candid, but also brought a 'solution' that made one happy. For the rest of his life Wittgenstein would unwind in cinemas.

He found another refuge from work in his friendship with Marguerite Respinger, the young daughter of a wealthy Swiss merchant. While she was studying at Cambridge she had become acquainted with Margaret Stonborough's son, Thomas, and she was subsequently invited to spend the summer in Gmunden. Later on she broke off her studies to become a pupil of the Viennese sculptor Anton Hanak, whom Margaret patronized. Marguerite stayed with her in the *Palais Batthyány-Schönborn*. Eight days after her arrival, however, she was obliged to give up her room, temporar-

ily, to Wittgenstein, who had sprained his ankle at the construction site and had to rest. It was decided that the habitual *salon,* which took place on Saturday afternoons, should be moved to Ludwig's room to entertain him. Ludwig decided to read from his favourite author's book, J.P. Hebel's *Schatzkästlein* ('Anthology'), but suddenly broke off to enquire whether their guest, Marguerite, who was seated next to his bed, found it boring. She replied that she did not, and from that time on he showed a growing interest in her.

At the time of their acquaintance, in the winter of 1927, the structural work on the Kundmanngasse was almost completed. Each night Marguerite would pick Ludwig up after working hours and accompany him to the cinema or, in summer, go for a walk in the Prater with him. Afterwards they would have a meal in a *Kaffeehaus*; Wittgenstein's ascetic dinner consisted of two soft-boiled eggs, a few slices of dark rye bread and a glass of milk. When the doors and windows of the Kundmanngasse were ready to be hung, Marguerite had to help him adjust them before they left the construction site. She was obliged to open and close the same door or window again and again for hours while Wittgenstein made endless adjustments until they hung exactly perpendicularly and closed flawlessly — 'as one constructs a watch', Marguerite remembers. Wittgenstein urged her never to discuss the house — or for that matter the *Tractatus* — with him, nor to try to understand them. He did talk to her about the difficult period he had gone through, about his suicidal thoughts and the interruption of a suicide attempt by a chance meeting with his uncle which saved his life. He told her that the design and building of the house had rescued him from the deep moral crisis caused by his failure as a teacher.

Wittgenstein considered it his duty to ensure that Marguerite was devoid of artificial affectations and to make an *anständige* woman of her. She had to abandon her ambition to become an artist at his instigation, for in his opinion her drawings and watercolours lacked any real value. Her flower arrangements for the Hochreith provoked his criticism, they strove too

Finishing the structural work, probably autumn 1927.

Michael Drobil, *Ludwig Wittgenstein*, pencil on paper, about 1927.

much for effect. He commented on the way she dressed and his approval – a 'good' dress, not a 'beautiful' dress – or disapproval implied a moral judgment. Any comment made by him was meant to reform her life. He confessed to her that he wished he had more money in order to be able to dress her and travel with her. A few years after the Kundmanngasse was finished they still continued to see each other during his holidays and they exchanged letters. In summer 1931 she stayed in Skjolden and Wittgenstein found her accommodation in the village (he himself stayed in his house on the lake). There Marguerite was obliged to perform humble work intended to make her think about the way in which she ought to live her life. *'Du mußt gut sein und wahr'* – 'You must be good and truthful' – was the directive of which Wittgenstein constantly reminded her. As a result she entered a child care school in Bern in the early 1930s. Later her marriage to the brother of Ludwig's close friend Arvid Sjögren caused a breach between them.

As an architect Wittgenstein was still leading the modest life he had adopted when he was teaching. He used his money sparingly; when he needed money he would collect it from Margaret Stonborough's private cashier. On one occasion he borrowed money from Engelmann. At the building site he invariably wore workman's clothes – grey trousers and a flannel coat. In his leisure hours the latter was replaced by a Norfolk tweed jacket, the elbows of which Marguerite patched more than once. 'The fact that he never wore a tie and that the collar of his shirt was always unbuttoned was extremely offensive in those days', Engelmann recalled. Wittgenstein's simple, sturdy shoes were not polished for some considerable time; Marguerite knitted stockings for him. Wittgenstein's eccentric appearance was exaggerated by a facial tic and his unnaturally high-pitched voice, symptomatic of his extremely nervous disposition, which had also been observed previously by his colleagues and pupils at his former school in Lower Austria. An incident recorded by Engelmann confirms this portrait. Wittgenstein often visited Engelmann's brother, Peter, and his wife, whom he liked very much. One evening Peter read from a satirical sketch he had written, entitled *Ein Abend im Hause Stonborough* ('An evening at the Stonboroughs'), in which Tolstoy entered the scene as a horrible chained monster named *Lew Fuchs Nikolajewitsch Tollhaus* ('Lev Fox Nikolaevitch Madhouse'). Paul Engelmann, who expected a furious reaction from Wittgenstein because of Peter's twisting of the truth, was astonished to see him tumble from his stool splitting his sides with laughter: 'Obviously it was a kind of relief, a release of obviously long suppressed inner tensions that found a way out — something that may be an extremely beneficial relief for the one struck by it.'

While he was still teaching, Wittgenstein had become fascinated by another artistic profession. When he was in Vienna for a holiday he frequently visited the studio of his friend Michael Drobil, the sculptor he had come to know during his captivity at Monte Cassino between 1918–19. Wittgenstein was one of his most vehement critics. An example of that criticism is contained in a letter to his sister, Hermine, where he mentions one of Drobil's pieces:

I hope that Drobil has not spoilt anything by enlarging the breast!!! The highly concave breast was *necessary*. It is *quite* easily possible that he has done something stupid! It so happens that the breasts and upper arms should not together form four equal shaped swellings which subsequently, taken as a whole, become an undulating oblique stage before which the rest takes place. Nor should the space between the right lower arm (the vertical one) and the breasts be reduced, since the former then will become expressionless and — so to speak — adventitious. Please, tell Drobil my objections, he will understand them (if he wants to!). That the breast was not all right is correct, but it is more than likely it cannot be corrected by enlarging it and Drobil himself has, as you will recall, told me in your presence that he will *not* at any rate show the breast *in public. I believe it is not that simple.*

During his work on the Kundmanngasse, Wittgenstein decided to try to work in plaster himself, because one of Drobil's sculptures — possibly *The Squatting Girl* — did not please him. He modelled the head of a young woman. It is turned slightly to the right and its sympathetic, attentive gaze is directed towards some point far away below. To obtain some frame of reference he measured Marguerite's head, though the sculptured head reveals no further resemblance to her, rather to other sculptures of young women by Drobil. During these years Wittgenstein also tried to learn to conduct music. He had already learnt to play the clarinet when he was a teacher.

On 1 October 1928, the permit to occupy the Kundmanngasse was granted, on condition that an alarm was installed in the lift and that the gap between the doors of the lift cage and the wall of the shaft was narrowed.

Ludwig Wittgenstein, *Head of a Young Woman*, about 1927.

A friend of Thomas Stonborough, Ludwig Wittgenstein, and construction supervisor Friedl on a balcony of the Kundmanngasse.

Margaret Stonborough and her family moved into the house that same month. Margaret's sons, who did not get along well with their difficult *Onkel Luki*, and who had been forbidden by Margaret to visit the construction site to avoid them being a nuisance to Wittgenstein, showed reserve in their opinions about their uncle's creation. In a letter to his friend John Maynard Keynes not long after the house was finished, in which he also mentioned that he would like to visit England for a holiday, Wittgenstein anticipated reservations:

Enclosed you will find a few photos of my house and [I] hope you won't be too much disgusted by its simplicity.

'À la Corbusier' was Keynes' reaction to the photos in a letter to his wife – a reaction that almost certainly would have infuriated Wittgenstein had he been familiar with the work of Le Corbusier.
A letter of thanks he wrote to one of the contractors has been preserved:

Construction Palais Stonborough
Vienna
10 November 1928

To the firm of
M. Weber & Co
in Vienna

Since your work on my building is now approaching its end it is my duty and my desire to express my gratitude and appreciation for your excellent management. I have to say that without your work it would have been impossible to achieve the precision and correctness necessary for this type of building. I am convinced that no other firm in Vienna would have been as competent to do what I had to ask. It is true on the one hand that this is thanks to your outstandingly trained and skilful workmen which no other firm of locksmiths could have placed at my disposal in this quality and number, but, secondly, thanks to the exemplary achievement of Herr Ingenieur Ferdinand Kunz on behalf of your firm, who uses his extraordinary knowledge and ability to achieve the objective set with an equally extraordinary willingness. - Also exceptional, especially on Viennese soil, are the *conscientiousness & dependability* of your company, two characteristics which bring fame to you and benefit to your clients.

Expressing my highest esteem,
I remain
Yours faithfully
L. Wittgenstein

Wittgenstein arrived in Cambridge in January 1929 after a delay caused by illness, probably due to exhaustion. Keynes picked him up at the station and Wittgenstein told him that he had no intention of returning to Vienna. Throughout the following ten years, though interrupted by periods of tormenting doubt, Wittgenstein came to regard philosophy as the only calling to which he, by temperament, was really suited.

After the Second World War Wittgenstein was involved in the limited renovation of the Kundmanngasse, when the commandeered house was no longer required as a shelter for repatriates and was returned to Margaret Stonborough. During the war it had served as a military hospital (30 beds could be accommodated in the *Saal*) and at the time of the Allied occupation it had been used by the Soviet Army. The Russian soldiers stabled their horses in the dining room, damaged the built-in cupboards with their bayonets and, because the heating system was out of order, installed coal stoves, the pipes of which projected out of the windows. The coal for the stoves was kept in the bathtubs. When Margaret Stonborough left Vienna in 1939, the family cook, Mrs Milli Vogl, and her husband remained behind in the gardener's lodge (the former architectural office) and tried her best to keep the commandeered house in order. When, however, a bombing raid damaged their home they were forced to leave the lot. On the arrival of the occupying Soviet Army Mrs Vogl tried to prevent the soldiers from taking possession of the Kundmanngasse, carrying her baby in her arms to arouse their pity, but her efforts were in vain. She accompanied Wittgenstein and his friend, Rudolf Koder, when they inspected the house early in the autumn of 1948. Wittgenstein was upset by the condition of the house and deeply moved by Mrs Vogl's story; he took her hand and called her a brave woman: 'Milli, I understand what you have been through' — words that made a deep impression on her, for in the past he had seldom spoken to her.

Wittgenstein's letter of thanks to the firm of Weber.

Serie
Серия
Serie
Serial } № 000212

Befehl

Dieser Besitz und sein Inhalt steht unter
Kontrolle der Militärregierung
Nichtbevollmächtigten ist der Zutritt verboten

Wenden Sie sich nötigenfalls an das Amt für Eigentumskontrolle

Приказ

Это владение и содержимое находятся под
контролем Межсоюзной Военной Комендатуры
Посторонним
лицам доступ запрещен

В случае необходимости обращаться в бюро
Имущественного Контроля

Ordre

Cette proprieté et son contenu se trouvent sous le
Contrôle du Gouvernement Militaire
L'accès est interdit aux personnes nonautorisées

En cas de nécessité s'adresser au Bureau du Contrôle des biens

Order

This Property, with its contents, is under
the control of Military Government
unauthorised entrance is forbidden

In case of necessity refer to Property Control Office

Office Adress: PROPERTY CONTROL
AMERICAN MILITARY GOVERNMENT SEC.
Porzellangasse 51
Tel. A 17580 Kl. (Ext) 191

Telephone No:

Österreichische Staatsdruckerei. 1300 45

Confiscation bill posted up the Kundmanngasse
during the allied occupation.

44

Paul Engelmann

Architecture or *belles lettres*

Paul Engelmann was born in 1891, in the old cathedral city of Olmütz, Moravia (now Olomouc in the Czech Republic). At the end of the nineteenth century most of its inhabitants were descended from the German colonists of the middle ages, who had governed the city for centuries and made the city great through trade and commerce. The rich architecture of its buildings, Romanesque, Gothic, Renaissance, baroque, Biedermeier and *Wiener Secession*, still testifies to its glorious past. Its minority groups were the indigenous Czechs and the Jews, but they were forbidden to live in the centre of town until late in the nineteenth century. When the Jews were allowed certain privileges within the Hapsburg Empire, they sought careers in business and in the legal and medical professions, and assimilated completely into German culture. It was in this German speaking Jewish milieu that Engelmann grew up. His father was a small businessman, his mother the daughter of a physician; both brought their children up with great enthusiasm for German literature, art and music, which was fertile soil for their talents. Paul's brother Peter was an accomplished draughtsman and became a well-known satirist in Vienna under the pseudonym of *ENG* (German for 'narrow' as in narrow-minded, 'cramped'); his sister Anne achieved a certain fame as a painter and illustrator.

Paul Engelmann, Tel Aviv 1937.

As a young man Paul had literary and philosophical ambitions, but like his brother and sister his strongest sensibility was of a visual-spatial nature. After he graduated from the *Deutsches Realgymnasium* in Olmütz in 1909, he decided to study architecture at the *Technische Hochschule* in Vienna, which was one of the most important cultural and intellectual centres in the world. Within a few weeks he became acquainted with two of the most influential spirits of his time, the architect Adolf Loos and the commentator and satirist Karl Kraus; he probably met them in the Café Pucher at the Kohlmarkt, where early in the evening both held court. When Loos founded his private *Adolf Loos Bauschule* ('Adolf Loos School of Architecture') in 1911, Engelmann left the *Hochschule* and became one of Loos's first regular students. That same year Engelmann showed his admiration for Loos's revolutionary architecture by publishing a sonnet on the occasion of the completion of the controversial *Haus am Michaelerplatz*. The sonnet was printed in *Die Fackel*, the satirical magazine published by Kraus, for whom Engelmann now acted as a secretary. He was entrusted with the task of cutting articles from newspapers which were used for Kraus's satirical *Glossen* ('glosses') on the press. From the beginning *Die Fackel* had sided with Loos's ideas on architecture and Engelmann's sonnet concluded the defence of the house by Otto Stoesl. Wittgenstein, who read *Die Fackel*, told

Paul Engelmann's poem on the *Haus am
Michaelerplatz*, in *Die Fackel* of 28 February,
1911. Literally translated:
'From the scroll work of vacant brains
a true deed rises, as sharply outlined,
as beautiful and pure, as a clean conscience,
as among frauds a free brow.
The chastity of all glaciers shines on it,
to be kissed on smooth masonry!
And marble, that they do not lack the splendour:
unaffected and voluptuous, almost like a maiden.
That though is a masterpiece, and it will stay!
And each who fought and versed,
knows that the mob spits at all true deed.
They may continue their clamour and scribbling:
You stand by yourself, powerfully erected
as first sign of a new age!'

Engelmann later that the poem had made a bad impression on him, possibly he had been irritated by its rapturous tone; he had almost written to Kraus, telling him that he should not include pieces by contributors in his magazine.

As a regular student ('irregular' students only attended special lectures) Engelmann was trained while working on the daily activities of Loos's architectural office. The most important subjects within the curriculum were interior design, history of art and knowledge of materials. These were essential to Loos's concept of architectural design as a process from the inside out to arrive at modern functional form, and to his idea of architecture as a craft based on a long tradition of skilled craftsmanship, and not as one of the 'romantic' liberal arts. It was during the years of Engelmann's apprenticeship that Adolf Loos fully developed the idea of the *Raumplanung* basic to the architecture of the private house, that is a plan developed three-dimensionally as opposed to the common two-dimensional floor plan. As will be elaborated in the chapter on his design for the Kundmanngasse, Engelmann would in fact draw the first known design for a house planned in three dimensions. Furthermore, he worked on Loos's city regulation plan of Vienna.

A few months after the outbreak of the First World War Engelmann was called up but the primitive living conditions in the barracks caused a recurrence of the lung disease for which he had been in a sanatorium when he was young. He was sent back to Olmütz on sick leave for the rest of the war. There he did some voluntary work in the city's building office and from time to time visited Kraus and Loos in Vienna. Incidents during this period throw some light on Engelmann's highly strung and idealistic character that would mark his friendships and occupations and, in fact, would tragically influence the course of his life. Like most young men of his time, and unlike his master Kraus, he had been carried away by the general euphoria following the declaration of war, but early in 1916 the atrocities of the war brought about a moral crisis and nervous breakdown, which he could only overcome by converting himself, like many young men of his time, to a Tolstoy-inspired pacifism. His first act was to call on soldiers marching through Olmütz to lay down their arms. Later on he regarded it as his task to submit detailed peace proposals to the government which, incidentally, show his engagement in the Jewish problem for the first time: he suggested that a Jewish State be founded in south-east Europe or in the Middle East. In January 1918 the Minister for Foreign Affairs, Count Czernin, thanked him in a personal letter and Engelmann naively believed that his efforts had not been in vain. More important from a historical point of view, however, was the work he did for Karl Kraus. At his request Engelmann compiled a manuscript from *Glossen* from the volumes of *Die Fackel*, which Kraus later refashioned into his anti-war drama *Die letzten Tage der Menschheit* ('The Last Days of Mankind', 1919).

It was during the war years that Paul Engelmann and Ludwig Wittgenstein became friends. Early in September 1917 Wittgenstein was promoted to corporal and went on leave to attend the artillery training school in Olmütz. Before he left he paid a short visit to Vienna, where Loos had given him the address of his pupil Engelmann and asked him to look him up. Wittgenstein, impeccably dressed in the chocolate-brown and vermilion artilleryman's dress uniform introduced himself to Engelmann's mother saying '*Gnädige Frau*, I am an evil person', which left a deep impression on Engelmann:

We said goodbye with the customary invitation on my part to call on us again as soon as possible and as already said I was seriously interested in continuing our acquaintanceship. I was, however, in doubt whether this would also be true of him. But he came back soon. Already those first conversations with him made it, of course, clear to me that he was truly an extraordinary person.

The tower of the city hall of Olomouc.

One of the extraordinary things that struck Engelmann was Wittgenstein's desire to take lodgings in the tower of the Renaissance city hall because of the magnificent view from the gallery, 170 feet up. To his regret the watchman did not let out rooms and he rented a primitive room in a suburb not far from the artillery school.

Wittgenstein visited the Engelmanns almost daily during his five month leave. He enjoyed the homely atmosphere after the hardships of two years of life at the front, and the warm and attentive personality of Engelmann's mother became very important to him. He was also adopted by Engelmann's circle of friends who formed a sort of young Jewish-German cultural elite of the town. They gathered almost every evening in the *Berlinerzimmer* ('Berlin Room') in the Engelmann family home to discuss literature and art, make music, or even to perform a play; on occasion of the latter Wittgenstein remained a critical spectator. They indeed respected Wittgenstein's critical judgment on any subject, which inspired Peter Engelmann to draw a caricature described by his brother:

Max Zweig is sitting in uniform, just like Fritz Zweig and Wittgenstein, the latter facing the other two, who are listening silently and plunged in thought, with the caption 'Is Wittgenstein an angel after all?'

This alludes to a parable by Tolstoy, a writer highly revered by most young people of that time, in which an angel is banned from heaven and takes up, incognito, an apprenticeship with a shoemaker. Wittgenstein's behaviour within the circle of friends reminded Paul Engelmann of Prince Henry's attitude towards Falstaff and his companions:

S. Exc. Dr. C. Lueger's letzter Besuch im Hotel Panhans 24. Februar 1909. — Semmering.

Postcard from Adolf Loos to Paul Engelmann, 2 November, 1912(?). Carl Lueger, son of the concierge of the *Technische Hochschule* and Christian Socialist Mayor of Vienna from 1897 to 1910, modernized the public services of the city.

The irresponsible manner in which matters of intellectual interest were done with, was at that time more tolerable and certainly more amusing to him than unctuous academic talk, which he found exasperating throughout his life.

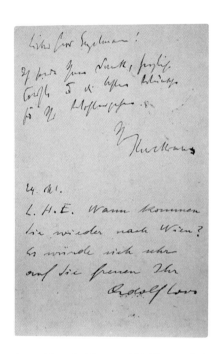

Postcard from Karl Kraus and Adolf Loos to Paul Engelmann, 26 October, 1915.

Engelmann, who until then hardly had any interest in philosophy, acted as a sounding board for the philosophical ideas that Wittgenstein had worked on at the front when he did not have to fight and which, during the next two years, took definite shape in the *Tractatus logico-philosophicus*. 'When I cannot bring out a sentence, then Engelmann comes with the forceps and pulls it out of me!' was the way in which Wittgenstein once characterized his role during their long conversations while Engelmann accompanied Wittgenstein to his rooms late at night, which journey they sometimes repeated three times in order to continue talking. They also discussed art, poetry, and fundamental questions about life and ethics. In fact it was during this period that Wittgenstein formulated his thoughts on ethics and aesthetics, and though Engelmann contributed little if anything to these he was a good listener; his account of Wittgenstein's thoughts in his *Memoir*, published after his death, played an important part in the reinterpretation of the *Tractatus* as an ethical philosophy.

The differences in their characters, however, were considerable and these accounted for the complete failure of their cooperation as architects on the Kundmanngasse ten years later. While Wittgenstein was a man of tremendous willpower who made high demands on those around him because of his almost childlike straightforwardness and unwillingness to compromise, Engelmann hid behind his sympathetic modesty, his understanding nature and his proverbial sense of humour a degree of vacillation that sometimes bordered on an inability to act at all. These differences were reflected in their different ethical outlooks and, because both felt that matters of the Good and the Beautiful were closely related to each other, in their different aesthetic attitudes. Engelmann believed that human suffering had worldly causes and that individuals were obliged to change the world for the better despite human inadequacy. Engelmann thought architectural design should serve this ideal by creating better living conditions, or at least providing for a human and comforting atmosphere. He may have been influenced by the ideas of the philosopher Tomáš Masaryk (who after the war became the first president of Czechoslovakia), with whom he shared an aversion to collectivism and socialism and an abstract mystical attitude to life which placed

48

great store by scientific solutions for social wrongs; this also motivated his endless theorizing on the construction of the ideal Jewish state.

For Wittgenstein the origin of human misery lay within the individual, in his inability to live without expectations and to accept the world as it is together with his own place in it. Man's task then was to restrain himself, to live humbly at the service of others, who faced the same difficult task, and to abandon the arrogant effort to change one's lot. Wittgenstein never understood science as a sign of moral progress or even as instrumental to moral progress, and his mysticism was fundamentally indifferent to the world. In such a world view architectural beauty, or beauty in general, was fundamentally of an unworldly nature and, as we shall see later, was never meant to improve life in a material sense or to be a relaxation after everyday exertions.

At that time, however, Engelmann's modesty, his capacity to listen and the warm-hearted atmosphere of his family home provided the basis of a friendship which Wittgenstein affirmed by giving him the collected work of his favourite author Wilhelm Busch and, later, as a remembrance of their stimulating conversations, one of the typescripts of the *Tractatus*. Engelmann summed up the correspondence between his three great teachers and friends, as he perceived it, as follows:

Loos separates the object of use from art and kills their common bastard, ornament. Kraus separates life from language and kills their common bastard, the empty phrase. Wittgenstein separates science from mysticism and kills their common bastard, philosophy.

Paul Engelmann, interior of Neuwaldegg, about 1919.

After the First World War Paul Engelmann became Adolf Loos's first assistant and, because Loos fell ill, he took over the design of the reconstruction of a castle and a country house for Prince Sapieha in Poland. Thanks to his introduction to the Wittgenstein family in Vienna, during 1917-19, Engelmann also renovated the interior of Neuwaldegg, their house in the Viennese suburb of Neuwaldegg. Wittgenstein's (oral) criticisms of Engelmann's first drafts and Engelmann's insecure defence did not bode well for their future cooperation as architects:

I regret very much that you do not like my work for Neuwaldegg, as appears from the letter of your Fräulein sister; although I did the best I could and though nothing false can be found in the plans, I am not sure whether I succeeded. I look forward to hearing your opinion and hope that then something can be made that is satisfactory to all.

In the summer of 1919 he informed Wittgenstein, who was in captivity in Monte Cassino in Italy, that everybody was content with the result, but he added, in similar vein to that which he would later use when he ascribed the architectural merit of the Kundmanngasse to Wittgenstein, that it had been reached thanks to the good offices of Wittgenstein's sister Hermine. Engelmann soon decided to apply himself to literary and philosophical activities and to leave Loos's office; from now on he would only accept commissions when he needed the money. On 12 September 1921 he received a reference in which Loos praised his gift for architectural design; Engelmann was also presented with a copy of Loos's *Ins Leere gesprochen* ('Spoken into the Void') with the dedication: 'For my beloved pupil Paul Engelmann, my most beloved!' Commissions, mainly for interior design, came from Olmütz, now Olomouc, but in the early 1920s Engelmann also renovated Hermine Wittgenstein's rooms in the Alleegasse, and built in its courtyard an exhibition room for the porcelain collection belonging to Wittgenstein's brother, the pianist Paul Wittgenstein (the display cases were designed by the *Wiener Werkstätte*).

Engelmann became a close friend of the Wittgenstein family and was invited each year to the Hochreith or to Toscana Park, the magnificent country estate of Wittgenstein's sister Margaret near Gmunden. He was highly respected because of his modesty and his conscientious way of living. Ludwig Wittgenstein, his friend Arvid Sjögren, the family friend count Schönborn-Buchheim and Engelmann were regarded as exemplary moral minds whose judgments were regarded as authoritative by the family. The friends gave advice on problems of life, shared a preference for simple and honest work (the immensely rich Schönborn-Buchheim worked for some time as a roof-builder and as a shop-assistant in a department store in an attempt to give meaning to his life), and read together Thoreau's *Walden, or Life in the Woods*. Engelmann was also appreciated for his sense of humour and his mimicry of other people, among them Adolf Loos, which even made 'Luki' shriek with laughter.

Paul Engelmann (fourth from the right) as a guest of Margaret Stonborough (seated behind the table).

Engelmann spent most of his time in Olomouc where he was rarely without work. The few photographs that survive show interiors strongly reminiscent of the work of his teacher Adolf Loos, although it was less luxurious and expensive. He applied natural materials such as wood in furniture, panelling and exposed floor joists and ceiling beams, and bare brick for the construction of the fireplace. The atmosphere of neat middle-class cosiness is enhanced by warmly but not lavishly decorated textiles for upholstery, carpets and curtains. One wonders whether Wittgenstein, or for that matter his later client Margaret Stonborough, ever saw these designs which were such a far cry from the austere simplicity favoured by the former and the semi-aristocratic way of life of the latter. In his spare time Engelmann wrote some poetry and a short play, and embarked on theoretical work of which one of the most curious projects concerned the composition of a *Psychologie graphisch dargestellt* ('Psychology Represented in Graphical Form') composed in the manner of Wittgenstein's *Tractatus logico-philosophicus* around the same basic triad of logic, ethics and aesthetics.

Engelmann earned such a good living that he started to doubt his own motives and got scruples about working for clients who could afford interior design instead of being at the service of the poor like his friend Ludwig. Although privately he was also doing charitable work for which he more than once appealed to Margaret to pull some strings, he seriously considered changing his life radically by emigrating to Palestine. For some time he had been supporting the cause of a Jewish homeland by sending sums of money, though he abhorred the socialist and nationalist aspects of Zionism. Like many Jews from Moravia and Bohemia he may have felt himself alienated since the creation of the Czechoslovakian State, for his moth-

Paul Engelmann, the Palais Stonborough, sketches from an intermediate design phase (above) and for his final design (right).

er tongue and the culture he identified with was German-Austrian, not Czech. The alternative he considered was to move to Vienna, but he did not expect any moral improvement from that course. In Palestine, where there was large scale building activity in Tel Aviv, Haifa and Jerusalem, he might be needed as an architect and interior designer; there he might also find a response to his ideas on building a better society and he could undertake the moral task of bringing the best products of German and European culture to Palestine.

In February 1925 he informed Wittgenstein of his plans. Wittgenstein suggested that he might accompany him, as his own efforts to lead a moral life as a schoolteacher in the poorest parts of Austria also seemed doomed to failure. Wittgenstein seriously considered finding another profession and that same summer, while he was in Cambridge exploring the possibility of an academic career, Engelmann suggested that he take a job in the Brno law firm of his friend Heinrich Groag, whom he and Wittgenstein knew from Olomouc. It is certainly not inconceivable that Wittgenstein meant to accompany Engelmann to Palestine as an architect. Around the same time he and Engelmann discussed an architectural topic that might have been related to the problem of modern architecture in the Middle East, in response to which Engelmann had written to him: 'Stimulated by your thoughts on Egyptian architecture, I am, after a long time, in the mood again for modern architecture. I did some drawings and should like to show them to you.' For both, however, the radical change of life had to be postponed until after the completion of an architectural enterprise they did undertake together, the building of the Kundmanngasse; but this common enterprise also made it clear to each of them that they had to continue their lives separately.

The design of the Kundmanngasse

Early in November 1925 Margaret Stonborough invited Paul Engelmann to Toscana Park and told him about her plans to build a large house for herself and her family in Vienna. As he wrote to Wittgenstein: 'We had long conversations on the question as to whether such an undertaking is still possible these days. I believe no rather than yes; I should, however, when I receive the commission, venture to make the attempt. I should very much like to discuss this matter (...) with you.' It was to this letter that Wittgenstein enthusiastically answered: 'I should also be very interested in the building of a house.' Engelmann was commissioned and, while staying in Vienna during the months of April and May 1926, drew a series of sketches in close cooperation with Margaret Stonborough, which received comments from Wittgenstein. These formed the beginning of the basic design of the ground floor and of the spatial disposition of the Kundmanngasse.

Engelmann later described Wittgenstein's gradual involvement in the design in a letter to Friedrich von Hayek:

L[udwig] W[ittgenstein], who was teaching at that time, was very interested in this project and, when he was in Vienna, gave such excellent advice that in the end I had the feeling he understood Mrs St[onborough]'s intentions much better than I did; she herself actively participated in the elaboration of the plans. Her accomplishment was of great taste and of perfect culture, yet the result of this cooperation was not truly satisfactory. For that reason, and because he found himself in a deep emotional crisis after giving up his teaching post, I proposed to him that he carry out the building plans together with me and, after a long hesitation, he accepted. This solution proved to be a very happy one, for him as well as for the building. From that moment he was the actual architect, not I, and though the plans were ready when he joined the undertaking, I regard the result as his achievement, not mine.

Paul Engelmann, interior, before 1934, whereabouts unknown.

Dedication of Adolf Loos in Paul Engelmann's copy of *Ins Leere gesprochen.*

These words, however, conceal the disappointment that this, the most ambitious commission he had ever received, had now become for him.

The first setback must have been that he could not meet his client's wishes regarding the design of a modern city mansion of aristocratic proportions. Margaret Stonborough was a strong-willed woman and it is more than likely that she chose Engelmann not only because he had already done some work to the satisfaction of the Wittgensteins, but also because his modest and pliant nature would enable her to realize her own ideas. The commission explicitly stated that throughout the design phase he should work in close collaboration with her: '(...) Your mother commissioned me to draw the plans for her house after her own wishes and ideas, *together with her.*' The preliminary sketches do not show very much relationship to the architectural ideas Engelmann had learned from Loos, or to designs he made for other clients. There is, for example, no trace of a *Raumplanung.* Right from the start Margaret wanted something quite different and Engelmann's initial doubts about the possibility of such a design expressed in the letter quoted above to Wittgenstein concerned a modern embodiment of a scale and style that in the view of most contemporary architects belonged to the world before the First World War. He must have felt that his freedom to give shape to his ideas on architecture was severely restricted.

He may have hoped that Wittgenstein's participation would help to overcome the differences between him and Margaret, because on the one hand his friend understood his sister's lifestyle and character so much better than he did, and on the other he had shown himself to be an admirer of Adolf Loos. If so, the partnership must have proved even more disappointing. From the first day Engelmann was completely overpowered by the perseverance and dedication with which Wittgenstein accomplished his duties as an architect. He hadn't expected this and realized later that he had an idealized image of his friend, nurtured by infrequent contact during the preceding five years:

While, until that time, I had come to know and to admire his intellectual and emotional sides, I came to know him now as a man with a strong will. During those two years of continuing collaboration I could only bear his superiority and the uncompromising manner in which he pushed his own plans through with the greatest difficulty.

Though incomparable in scale and cost, Engelmanns's own ideas about architecture are revealed in the house he built during the same period for Vladimir Müller in Olomouc. Within a cube placed on a high base (a precaution against flooding from the nearby river Morava), measuring 26 by 32 feet, he realized a *Raumplanung.* It manifests itself, as in the Rufer House in Vienna (1922) designed by Loos, in the use of different levels on each floor. The austerity of the cubic exterior is, however, relaxed by slightly projecting wall-planes which create a plastic tension. The house stands at a street corner, and on both street aspects windows are placed more or less symmetrically within these wall-planes; the garden elevation shows how-

Paul Engelmann, Müller House,
Olomouc, 1926-1928.

Paul Engelmann, the *Raumplanung* of the Müller
House. The stove to the left originally was a fire
place.

55

Paul Engelmann, garden façade of the
Müller House.

ever, in exact opposition to the teachings of his master, the reserved aspect
and asymmetrical layout that is to be found in street elevations in Loos's
designs. One may wonder whether this was a intentional humorous *homage*
to his former teacher.

Like his earlier interior designs the interior of the Müller house is of distinctly Loosian intimacy, an impression given by the application of natural
materials, reduced in size and luxury to bourgeois standards. It is a far cry
from the combination of monumental austerity with period and *Wiener
Werkstätte* furniture that characterized the interior of the Kundmanngasse.
Typically Loosian too is the built-in sitting area near the three windows in
the front elevation. Typically Engelmann, however, are the shallow built-in
cupboards with glazed doors, lined with wall-paper showing floral motifs.
The ingenious heating system, consisting of a series of channels hidden in
the walls which transported hot air into every room, was also Engelmann's
invention, but it did not work very well.

Engelmann's diaries show that he left Vienna regularly to work on the
Müller house or on other commissions in northern Moravia. For example,
he did interior architecture for Jacques Groag's mother. Between
Engelmann's notes are a number of sketches of private houses, but it is
uncertain whether any of them, apart from the Müller house, were ever

realized. After a short stay with Margaret Stonborough in Gmunden in February 1928, Engelmann went to Olomouc and did not return until after the Kundmanngasse was completed. It was during this period that the interior of the Kundmanngasse was finished, a matter which should have required Engelmann's skill as architect, but which Wittgenstein had wholly appropriated; and he had to admit that Wittgenstein's un-Loosian and completely original solutions to design problems were superior to his. There are strong indications that Engelmann now felt himself so superfluous at the building site that he preferred to stay away from Vienna in order to avoid a rift with Wittgenstein. During this time he continued his work on the *Psychologie graphisch dargestellt*, but did not succeed in revising his notes to form a coherent structure.

Late in November 1928, after the Stonborough family moved into the Kundmanngasse, Engelmann returned to Vienna. Wittgenstein would already have been in Cambridge had his health not prevented him from going to England. During the next weeks they met a few times and certainly inspected the Kundmanngasse; as was their way they went to see a movie together. Engelmann also sent Wittgenstein his *Psychologie*-manuscript, requesting him to do with it what he thought best when he died, either publishing or destroying it. He added: 'I hope you have sincerely forgiven me for anything that ever happened between us, just as I have forgiven you.' This farewell, presumably on the occasion of Wittgenstein's departure, is evidence of the change in their relationship brought about by their cooperation as architects, as well as the continuing respect of Engelmann for his friend, who even as an architect had proved superior to him. On the other hand it also suggests a certain reserve towards Engelmann on Wittgenstein's part. During the time of their collaboration Wittgenstein must have thoroughly realized his friend's abilities and preferences and found that they differed substantially from his. This was later implicitly confirmed by Engelmann:

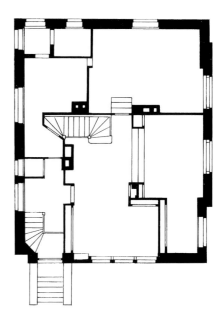

Plan of the Müller House. The stairs leading from the entrance to the vestibule and making a rather awkward turn are not executed in accordance with Engelmann's plans.

Several times during the years 1928-30, after the completion of the house, I was the guest of his family at the Hochreith. I still had conversations with him that proved very fruitful for me [Wittgenstein visited Austria during holidays]. Yet we were both changed since the time of our correspondence. His need to express himself completely in my presence was not there to such an extent any more.

Later years

During his last years in Europe Paul Engelmann was awarded a prize for the design of a public park and open-air swimming pool in Opava (1929). He also continued to do interior design and worked with his brother Peter on a theory of caricature. He emigrated to Palestine in 1934 and thus became the only member of his family to escape the Holocaust. He found a job as an interior designer in Tel Aviv and accepted commissions as a self-employed architect. In 1937–38 he built a house for Dr Yadlin in Haifa, in which he brought together aspects of Loosian architecture with typical characteristics of the flourishing International Style in Palestine such as the curved façade and the concrete canopies over balconies and windows. At the same time he collaborated with Yehuda Kurt Unger, another pupil of Loos who had emigrated, on the design for the market place, the Shuk, in Haifa, but this project was never completed. Engelmann's estate includes a number of designs which may never have been executed. One shows a partly enclosed terrace which is strongly reminiscent of sketches of one of the preliminary design phases of the Kundmanngasse. In 1947 he drew the throne hall and throne for the King of Jordan; his last known commission was the design of the lobby and restaurant of the King David Hotel in Jerusalem in the early 1950s.

Yadlin House, bird's-eye view to the north. Later windows in the curved wall of the lower floor and a canopy awning above the balcony were added.

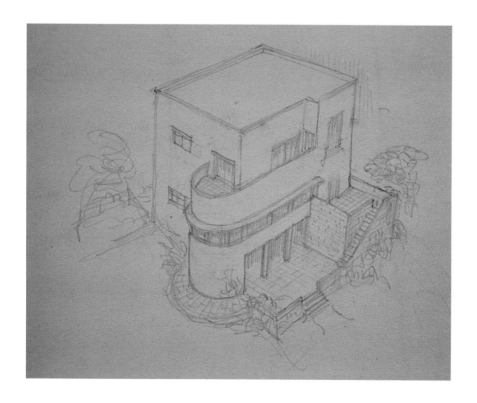

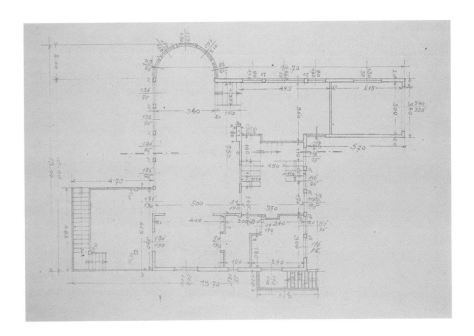

Yadlin House, plan of the main floor.

In Palestine Engelmann more and more devoted his time to literary and philosophical activity and only worked when he needed the money. To reduce the costs of living he shared rooms at the top of a house with a friend who also came from Olomouc, the playwright Max Zweig, who happened to be visiting Palestine when the Second World War broke out and decided to stay. During these war years Engelmann put together, from memory, an anthology of 400 years of German poetry because he was convinced that the Third Reich was the end of German culture. He participated in a literary salon of Jewish emigrés from the German speaking countries in Europe which existed in Tel Aviv since 1943. Here he met the poet, essayist and Kraus scholar Werner Kraft, who encouraged him to publish his writings, but he lacked the necessary confidence. He privately edited two small literary magazines, *Bei der Lampe* ('Under the Lamp') and *Prozdor* ('The Porch') and also privately published small brochures, among them one on the ideas of his teacher Adolf Loos and their consequences for Israeli architecture (1946), and one on the philosophy of his former friend Ludwig Wittgenstein (1948). In fact, Engelmann probably delivered the first lecture on Wittgenstein in Israel, in 1953, for which he translated the seven basic propositions of the *Tractatus logico-philosophicus* into Hebrew.

The last contact between Engelmann and Wittgenstein had been in 1937, when the latter had sent him a 'confession' concerning his supposed 'vileness'. Engelmann forgave him: 'You are spiritually the most important person I ever met.' Shortly after the Second World War he exchanged a few letters with Paul Wittgenstein, Ludwig's brother, after they had met on the occasion of a performance by the latter in Tel Aviv. Engelmann asked him for Ludwig's address in Cambridge, but although he more than once seriously considered renewing their contact, he did not have the courage to write. He was afraid that Wittgenstein would strongly disapprove of his way of life. Another short correspondence took place between Engelmann

59

Paul Engelmann, Yadlin House, Haifa, 1937-1938.

and Richard Neutra, another of Adolf Loos's pupils who had become an influential architect in California. He remarked respectfully but a little exaggeratedly that Wittgenstein, in the design of the spatial structure and the interior of the Kundmanngasse, had 'already anticipated the tendencies of contemporary architecture in many respects around 1930.'

High, and somewhat idealized, esteem for his former friend is also characteristic of the countless notes, written on loose pieces of paper and meant to bring order into his remembrances. He started this undertaking in the late 1950s, after he discovered that Wittgenstein, since his death in 1951, had gradually became recognized in the Anglo-Saxon world as one of the greatest thinkers of the century. He realized that he could interpret

60

Wittgenstein's philosophical thinking against the background of the intellectual milieu of Vienna around the turn of the century, something that was completely absent from the then prevailing understanding of his work. Again, as was the case with earlier theoretical projects of some scope, he did not succeed in composing a complete manuscript and could not overcome his hesitation to negotiate a final contract with a publisher. He died in destitute circumstances in February 1965.

Two of his intellectual friends arranged the *Memoir* from the collection of notes in Engelmann's estate. It was published in 1967 in exchange for the gift to the Bodleian Library in Oxford of the typescript of the *Tractatus logico-philosophicus* which Engelmann had. The *Memoir* began with the letters Wittgenstein had written to Engelmann. The chapters which Engelmann had planned on Wittgenstein's teaching career, on the design and construction of the Kundmanngasse and on the relationship between the *Tractatus logico-philosophicus* and the *Philosophical Investigations* remained in note form; the last two were meant to form one part under the aptly chosen title of *Eine neue Lebensform* ('A New Form of Life' — 'form of life' is an expression borrowed from the *Philosophical Investigations*, in which in one place it is also used to refer to friendship). There are hardly any notes on the chapter concerning the Kundmanngasse. It may still have been too painful for Engelmann to write about this difficult period; for Wittgenstein it has represented the beginning of a new life, but for Engelmann it culminated in the loss of his most respected friend.

In a note written in 1954 Engelmann characterized his life in the shadow of three of the great minds of the first half of the twentieth century with whom he had once maintained such close ties:

If I can claim credit for anything with regard to my own intellectual pursuits, then it is for the fact that I availed myself of the opportunity, with which fortune favoured me, to have had the best teachers my generation could possibly have, and that I learnt something from them: from Kraus not to write; from Wittgenstein not to speak; from Loos not to build. If I, nonetheless, occasionally write and speak and build, then it is because at times I play truant; and because, as Homer too sometimes sleeps, at times even these teachers did not act in accordance with their own teachings.

Invitation for an intellectual evening on which Paul Engelmann lectured on the *Tractatus logico-philosophicus*.

Gustav Klimt, *Margaret Stonborough-
Wittgenstein,* 1905. Oil on canvas, 180 x 90 cm.

Margaret Stonborough-Wittgenstein

3

Modern lady of the Old World

Margaret Stonborough-Wittgenstein, born in 1882 as Margarethe Anna Maria Wittgenstein, was seven years older than her brother Ludwig. She was the youngest daughter of Karl and Leopoldine Wittgenstein and in her own way was at least as independent and eccentric as Ludwig. Hermine Wittgenstein relates in her *Family Recollections* of a self-willed nature that became manifest when Margaret was still a girl:

Even in her youth her room was the embodiment of the revolt against everything traditional and represented the opposite of a so-called young girl's room, such as my room had been for a long time. God knows where she got all those interesting things with which she embellished it. She brimmed over with ideas and, what is even more, she could do what she wanted and she knew what she wanted. Because she could not buy modern paintings she very skilfully copied good drawings, using coloured pencils, from the first modern magazine, Jugend ['Youth'] – which in those years was still excellent – and framed the copies. And although womenly needlework was not her forte, she designed for herself most original pieces of embroidery; e.g., to mention only one, the anatomical representation of a human heart with coronary arteries. This was, however, not naturalistic, but seen from a purely ornamental point of view.

Anton Hanak, bust of Margaret Stonborough-Wittgenstein.

As a young woman Margaret took a serious interest in cultural matters and read contemporary writers as well as the classical ones in her father's library. She also studied mathematical and physical theory and read writers on psychology and sociology, which was still exceptional for a woman of her time. Her intellectual and aesthetic preferences were to exert a considerable influence on her youngest brother and it was she who introduced him to the works of such thinkers as Lichtenberg (whom she liked to quote), Schopenhauer and Weininger, and of the physical scientists Mach and Hertz, without which Wittgenstein's philosophical thinking cannot be understood. She also subscribed to Kraus's satirical magazine *Die Fackel* and her encouraged her brother to read it.

In 1904 she married an American, Jerome Stonborough, from which time she called herself Margaret. Jerome Stonborough was trained as an industrial chemist and had become an advisor to the United States government regarding the application of statistical techniques to government finance. He also applied these techniques privately on the stock exchange and amassed a large fortune, after which he retired to follow his personal pursuits. He went to Vienna to study medicine, and met Margaret. After further study in Berlin he became a very competent surgeon. Later in life he

Josef Hoffmann and the *Wiener Werkstätte*,
Stonborough apartment in Berlin, drawing room,
about 1905.

applied himself to Egyptology and at his own expense took part in several excavations. The marriage, however, did not prove to be a happy one. Around 1923 he and Margaret decided to live separately and Jerome moved to Paris into an apartment which was furnished and decorated for him by Margaret. They continued to visit each other, and although Jerome preferred to stay at the Toscana Park in Gmunden, Margaret also provided rooms for him in the Kundmanngasse.

Shortly after Margaret's marriage Gustav Klimt, one of her father's protégés, painted her famous full length portrait. She was not satisfied with the resemblance and did not hesitate to repaint the mouth (the present owner, the Pinakothek in Munich, restored the original), but even so she preferred to keep it out of sight of visitors. In the Kundmanngasse it used to stand in the corner of the study on the first floor, and after the Second World War, it stood almost hidden in an annexe to the library of Toscana Park.

During the First World War Margaret's money, which like Ludwig's was invested in Holland, had increased in value; it enabled her to continue living in the style of the *belle époque* and acting as a patron of the arts like her father. Before the war, when she and her husband were living in Berlin, she had their apartment furnished by the *Wiener Werkstätte* under Josef Hoffmann. In 1912 she acquired the country estate Toscana Park (built between 1870-77 and formerly in the possession of the Grand Duke of Tuscany) and commissioned the young architect Rudolf Perco to redesign most of the rooms. She also had the sculptors Anton Hanak and Michael Drobil work for her (the latter having been introduced to her by Ludwig). Furthermore she collected porcelain and chinoiserie, and a number of plaster copies of ancient Greek statues which later found their way into the Kundmanngasse. At Toscana Park she built greenhouses in which she grew

64

Josef Hoffmann and the *Wiener Werkstätte*,
Stonborough apartment in Berlin, dining room,
about 1905.

exotic flowers and plants. Between 1924-26 she was president of the *Werkbund Wien*, a movement initiated by Josef Hoffmann which temporarily broke away from the *Wiener Werkstätte*. Like all the Wittgensteins she had a great love of music and frequently arranged performances at her house which would be subject of serious discussion afterwards, according to the accepted practice among the Wittgensteins. Composers such as Schubert, Mendelssohn, Brahms and Beethoven, frequently mentioned by Ludwig Wittgenstein in his private notebooks, were her favourites.

Margaret also maintained close ties to Sigmund Freud – her brother Ludwig often compared and contrasted his philosophical method with Freud's psychoanalytical method. She maintained a correspondence with him (still unpublished) and underwent 'didactical analysis' as she called it, intended to help her to understand other people better. With Ludwig she shared a strong urge to influence other people's lives which, as in her brother's case, was not always appreciated by the other party. In 1938, after the *Anschluß* of Austria with Nazi Germany she arranged Freud's emigration to England, in close collaboration with her friend Princess Marie Bonaparte and thanks to her connections in the leading circles of the Anglo-Saxon world. On a previous occasion she had played a diplomatic role when, after the First World War, she acted as the special representative of the Secretary of Commerce (later President) Hoover entrusted with the supervision of the American Relief programme for her impoverished country of birth.

Johann Bernhard Fischer von Erlach, *Palais* Batthyány-Schönborn, 1698-1705.

Around 1925 Margaret, who had been living since 1921 in the Renngasse in Vienna, in the early eighteenth century *Palais* Batthyány-Schönborn designed by the great Viennese baroque architect Johann Bernhard Fischer von Erlach, decided to build a modern city mansion for herself and her family. The house was to be constructed on the eastern half of a park-like lot, completely enclosed by buildings, behind her parents' home in the Alleegasse. It had once formed part of the former *Palais* of the Archduke Carl-Ludwig, and would provide close contact with her eldest sister, who now occupied the Alleegasse, and rural quiet and strict privacy in the very centre of the aristocratic fourth district of Vienna. She commissioned Paul Engelmann to draw up the plans in close collaboration with her.

Villa Toscana, Toscana Park, Gmunden.

In late summer or early autumn of 1926, shortly before construction on the house began with both Engelmann and her brother Ludwig as architects, she became charmed by a slightly undulating piece of land with old chestnut trees in Landstraße, Vienna's middle class third district near to the Donau-Canal. Until then it had been a nursery-garden and it was the only land which had not been built on following the erection, during the latter half of the 19th century, of large apartment blocks in the former park of the neighbouring early nineteenth century *Palais* Rasumofsky. As her sister Hermine relates:

She had bought a curious piece of property in the Kundmanngasse, which just suited her purposes. It was somewhat above street level, and had an old house on it, which was fit only for demolition, and a small garden with beautiful old trees. It was surrounded by simple, inoffensive houses and, above all, it was not situated in an elegant, cosmopolitan district, in fact quite the opposite. Contrasts are very much part of my sister's make-up.

Margaret Stonborough painting.

In fact it was situated opposite the Teacher Training College in the Kundmanngasse, which Ludwig had attended during 1919–20, and it is quite possible that he suggested the site to her when he was drawn into the undertaking in August–September 1926. He had worked as a temporary gardener after he finished his teacher training, and he may well have visited the place out of curiosity. Her brother's idea of living in humble surroundings seems also to have been reflected in Margaret's choice of this neighbourhood. She acquired it on 24 November 1926 and the construction of the house started immediately.

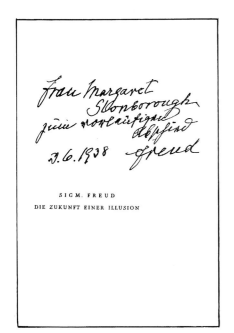

Dedication of Sigmund Freud to Margaret Stonborough, in a parchment-bound copy of 'The Future of a Illusion', as a gift of thanks for mediating in his departure for England in 1938: 'To Mrs Margaret Stonborough, a temporary farewell. Freud. 3 June, 1938.'

Map from the late 18th century *franziszeisches Kataster*, showing the lot bordering the park of the *Palais* Rasumofsky, presently within the third District of Vienna.

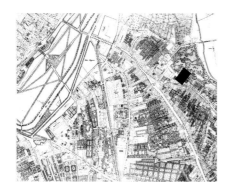

The joint enterprise of sister and brother

Designing and building the Kundmanngasse played a fundamental role in renewing the ties between Margaret and Ludwig. They had been drifting apart following her marriage to Jerome Stonborough. It must have been difficult for Ludwig to accept their way of life, which seemed to be aimed solely at fulfilling their personal interests and pursuits; moreover, Jerome's morose nature certainly did not help him make friends with his exacting wife's brother. It is also true that, like Hermine, Margaret seemed unduly anxious about what she saw as a certain weakness in Ludwig's character. She used to refer to the problems he had in adapting himself to new surroundings when he was sent to school in Linz and for a long period she could not take seriously his decision to divest himself of his wealth. She often disagreed, perhaps not wholly without reason, with his choice of friends – 'All Luki's swans are geese,' she used to comment. During the time he was teaching Ludwig had felt himself to be under pressure from his sisters and he tended to avoid prolonged contact with them.

When his mental condition worsened he again went to stay with Margaret during holidays; possibly her *separatio a mensa et toro* from Jerome made a better relationship between them possible. She was seriously concerned about her brother's state of mind after he left his job as a teacher and she hoped that having him design her house would help him to recover his self-confidence. Ludwig overcame his reluctance to accept her gesture of support and they regained their mutual respect by indulging in long 'intellectual' conversations, as Marguerite Respinger described them, just as they had had 20 years before. There were also, of course, the endless deliberations about the design of the house. Though Ludwig's 'terrible fussiness and total lack of practical sense' as Margaret thought of his meticulousness and perfectionism, got on her nerves, it did not lessen her appreciation of his work and she gave him a free hand in all matters concerning the house. Indeed, her respect bordered on adoration and she kept at bay anyone whom she thought might disturb him, not least her own sons.

Margaret not only played an important part in Wittgenstein's regaining his self-confidence, she also mediated in his subsequent return to philosophy. A group of neopositivist philosophers known as the *Vienna Circle* had come to see the *Tractatus logico-philosophicus* as possibly the best articulation of their ideas on the relationship between language and the world, and the group therefore tried to contact him. Moritz Schlick, the physical scientist and philosopher at the University of Vienna, had written to Wittgenstein in December 1924 while he was still teaching in Lower Austria saying he wanted to meet him to discuss the philosophy of the *Tractatus*. Wittgenstein replied that he would welcome a visit from Schlick, but two years later when the latter finally made the journey to Otterthal with some of his students he found that Wittgenstein had just left his post to take up the job as gardener in the monastery at Hütteldorf. Later that same year Schlick sent some of his articles to Margaret to pass on to her brother and

repeated his wish to meet him. Margaret pressed her brother to agree to the request. He asked her to write to Schlick stating that he wished to see him alone, as only then would he be able to ascertain whether he would still be capable of formulating any significant philosophical thought. In February 1927 they met at the *Palais* Batthyány-Schönborn in one of the salons which housed the beautiful Schönborn art collection. Margaret had also invited the *Gestalt*-psychologists Karl and Charlotte Bühler for tea, after which Schlick and Wittgenstein withdrew. Wittgenstein told Engelmann the following day that they must have thought each other completely mad, having talked the whole time at cross-purposes. Moreover, Engelmann added, Wittgenstein's appearance within these elegant surroundings must have made a strange impression, as though the rich lady had a half-idiotic brother whom she would like to do a favour; his stammering way of formulating philosophical thoughts, vacillating between modesty and rudeness, did not produce the effect the hostess had hoped.

Yet this meeting led to regular gatherings, usually on Monday evenings. However, Wittgenstein was not always receptive to philosophical discussion, if only for the reason that his work on the Kundmanngasse used up most of his energy. In such instances he preferred to read poetry, in particular that of Rabindranath Tagore, seated with his back towards the others in the room. He did not participate in formal gatherings of the *Vienna Circle*, but on one occasion at least he attended a lecture given by Schlick; the other students thought he was a tramp because of his tattered and patched clothes. On 10 March 1928, the Dutch intuitive mathematician, Luitzen Brouwer, gave a lecture in Vienna entitled *Mathematics, Science and Language*, which Wittgenstein was persuaded to attend. Afterwards a group from the audience went to a *Kaffeehaus* to discuss the lecture and

The 'picture gallery' on the beletage of the *Palais* Batthyány-Schönborn.

69

Wittgenstein joined in the discussion with great fervour. It has been suggested that on this occasion Wittgenstein was 'converted' to philosophy again, but this does not appear to be true. However, the incident does demonstrate his renewed involvement in philosophy. Many years later Wittgenstein told his student K.E. Tranøy that thanks to the discussions with members of the *Vienna Circle* 'I felt at that time that I had thought more, and more successfully, about certain problems than others had done.' The renewed intimacy between sister and brother is expressed in a letter, probably written around 1930 by Margaret to Ludwig in Cambridge, concerning the furnishing of the new house:

My dear Luki,

Imagine, the female torso is THE solution for the hallway (Yes, women!) and the classical youth THE solution for the library. Too silly of me not to have tried it out a very long time ago. When they stood in place I heard you say: 'Na, klar!' ['How obvious!'] – I must tell you about Kokoschka (...) Kokoschka made a very big impression on me. (Alas, I fear that I would not have hit on his quality myself) but he is at any rate outstanding & not even unsympathetic. Of course he only fits either into an anthology (like the collection in the Alleegasse) or a room for grand receptions. It has also become clear to me that in times in which architecture speaks an incisive language (or speaks the language of its times) one can, so to say, only hang on ones walls allegories in the style of these times and in certain dimensions. Allegories in the word's best sense. Such allegories could, when they existed, also hang on my walls, provided that the pictures spoke the same language as the house, i.e. subordinate to the house. The pictures in the Alleegasse are the masters of the walls upon which they hang & anthologies, that is to say galleries, are (& now Mining [Hermine Wittgenstein] explodes) the proof for a miserable period of architecture.

Stairs leading into the hallway of the Kundmanngasse. Pencil drawing by Hermine Wittgenstein.

A special human 'addition' to the Kundmanngasse was the multi-talented Heinrich Postl, porter, butler, gardener, and, when the family made music, singer. Postl had been a miner in Puchberg, one of the villages where Ludwig had been teaching. He had come to appreciate him because of his musical talent and his gentle nature. Together with Ludwig's colleague Rudolf Koder they often made music together, with Postl singing or playing the piano. When Ludwig was working on the Kundmanngasse, Postl visited him and asked if he could help him to find a job in Vienna. Ludwig recommended him to Margaret who employed him at the building site. After the Kundmanngasse was finished, she asked him to stay on and gave him a piano in his room. Postl worked for the Wittgenstein family until the Kundmanngasse was sold in 1971. His knowledge of the technical details of the house was enormous and, thanks to his recollections and the record he wrote shortly before his death, a number of details were saved from oblivion.

Margaret had to leave the Kundmanngasse in 1939 when the US government strongly advised Americans to leave Austria; she went to live in New York. The house was vacated and the furniture and precious objects were stored partly in the cellars of the St Peter in Vienna, partly in a depository

that was destroyed in the Second World War during a bombing raid. When the Allies occupied Austria she was able to return as far as Gmunden, which was in the American zone. In 1948 she was able to return to Vienna and started to make plans for a limited renovation and refurnishing of the Kundmanngasse, which had suffered from the war and its aftermath. Another letter to Ludwig about the house probably dates from this period:

Aerial photograph (1959) with the Kundmanngasse in the lower right. In the lower left corner the *Palais* Rasumofsky, with the former Teacher's Training School as its counterpart.

The house-affairs have partly been written down & will be discussed & completed tomorrow with the contractor. Only the absolutely essential repairs will be made. The stone flooring and the cracks in he walls will have to be mended. The glazier will have to replace the putty on several windows. Many rooms have to be painted. The question of the garage and the problem concerning the ventilation of the room next to the kitchen will depend on the price the contractor will set. Apart from that there are only all sorts of small matters that remain to be done. (...) What do you say? – If you want to make money then you would have to design furniture for the whole house. It cries out for decent furniture. One can, nevertheless, also let it cry out for a while. For a few years, if it can't be helped.

Not long before his death, just after his return from the United States where he had spent the summer with his former student Norman Malcolm and where his terminal illness had manifested itself, Ludwig wrote to Margaret that he had found the published letters of Frau Anderson to Wilhelm Busch in a London bookshop, which reminded him of the time that they read this peculiar and humorous correspondence together. He added in a postscript:

Yesterday I thought, I don't know why, of the Kundmanngasse & how delightfully you furnished it & how comforting. In these matters we understand each other.

Margaret survived her youngest brother by seven years; she died in 1958 at the age of 76.

Margaret Stonborough, about 1930.

The Kundmanngasse   4

Origins of Engelmann's design

At Christmas 1926 Paul Engelmann gave Margaret Stonborough a present of a number of his preliminary sketches for her house, which he had pasted in more or less chronological order on the pages of a self-bound booklet made of cheap coarse paper and cotton cloth. Thanks to this 'sketchbook' we are now able to study the origins and the development of the design of the Kundmanngasse, as well as to gain an insight into the list of demands made on its architect. According to the dedication, the sketches were drawn in April and May 1926; during those months Engelmann stayed with Margaret Stonborough in Vienna, for it was her explicit wish that the design should involve close collaboration between client and architect. Though Wittgenstein's interest in the project dated from Christmas 1925, it seems his involvement in the design cannot have started before he left his teaching post in Otterthal, that is before the second half of April. When he was teaching he used to visit Vienna only during holidays; Engelmann, however, suggests that Wittgenstein commented more than once on the design work, which would imply that he was already living nearby in the Viennese suburb of Hütteldorf, at the monastery of the Brothers of Charity.

The stylistic consistency of the sketches at their respective design phases, the fact that there is no evidence in the sketchbook of any other hand, not even in the form of examples or hints, and also the use of the same type of paper for series of sketches indicate that Engelmann worked alone, elaborating on a certain theme before presenting the sketchbook to Margaret and later on also to Ludwig, rather than drawing up plans and elevations in their presence. This is borne out by a letter he wrote to Margaret's son, Thomas Stonborough:

The drawings in your possession undoubtedly all stem from me, i.e. from the time before the participation of your uncle. At that time [the time of the involvement of L.W.] the definitive plans of the building were already completely finished after making many alterations. As far as I can remember these have hardly been changed at a later date.

Engelmann's final plan, which obviously was the starting point of Wittgenstein's revisions when he became Engelmann's co-architect in September later that year, bears the date 18 May 1926; it was the result of a design process which went through at least ten clearly discernible phases. The sketchbook originally opened with a copy from the cadastral map of the intended building site. It was a park-like lot directly behind the Palais Wittgenstein in the former Alleegasse, where Hermine and Paul

Aerial view of the lot (1959). The ruins of the beletage of the bombarded Alleegasse are just visible in the upper right part.

Wittgenstein then lived. (Since 1920 it has been called Argentinierstraße, but the family continued to refer to it as 'the Alleegasse'). It is possible that a rear entrance was intended, connecting it to the parental home. We do not know, however, whether Margaret ever actually owned this piece of land, for the land registry documents covering these years were destroyed during the fire of the Viennese Palace of Justice of 1927.

Originally the site was part of the gardens belonging to the former palace of archduke Carl-Ludwig, which was situated next to the place that was once the studio of the fashionable, and notorious, nineteenth century painter and aesthete Hans Makart. It had a peculiar perimeter and was completely enclosed by buildings and garden walls, which posed great difficulties for the architect. The lot had to be entered at the south-east side by way of the gate of the *Palais* four houses further up the Argentinierstraße from the *Palais* Wittgenstein; it had to be possible for Margaret's chauffeured car to be driven up to the entrance and turned around for parking in the garage or leaving again. The most favourable location for the house in terms of sunlight, of making an approach by car without spoiling too much of the gardens, and of a possible back door to the *Palais* Wittgenstein was therefore the northern corner of the lot, with the main entrance on the south-east or north-east (back) side of the house.

Furthermore, the house had to correspond to Margaret's grand style of living and be large enough to accommodate her family and household staff. Engelmann's plans reveal that, from the beginning, the ground floor was to include a drawing or music room, a library which would also function as an informal family living room, a dining room and pantry, a private living room and private rooms for Margaret Stonborough and for her husband. Later a breakfast room was added. It seems clear that right from the begin-

74

ning Margaret preferred to live on the main floor. The earliest plans of the upper floors contain three children's rooms, a governess's room, two or three guest rooms, one each for a secretary and a dressmaker, six servant's rooms, and a number of bathrooms. The kitchen and scullery, the servant's dining room and an additional servant's room and bath were in the basement. As the total number and function of the rooms hardly change during the design phases, one may safely assume that they correspond to the initial wishes of the principal. What Margaret had in mind was a city mansion surrounded by a park, a *villa suburbana*, though not built in a Viennese suburb but, thanks to the presence of a suitable lot, in the IVth, aristocratic, district of Vienna. As far as size and conception were concerned it was intended to continue the tradition of Old World aristocratic mansions rather than a twentieth century well-to-do bourgeois city house, though its architecture was to be in some, yet to be determined, way distinctly modern.

As a professional architect Engelmann was quite inexperienced when he received the commission. He had not yet developed his own style and one may even wonder whether his strength lay rather in interior design than in architecture. The sketches in the sketchbook, which are probably the best selected from a larger collection, are sometimes clumsy and certainly not the virtuoso imaginings in three dimensions of a gifted, unhampered architectural draughtsman. His weakness as an architect and his modest character must have made him a tool in Margaret Stonborough's hands.

Moreover, as a pupil of Adolf Loos, from whom he had acquired strong ideas on modern living and the architecture of private dwellings corresponding to it, Engelmann must have felt an inner contradiction in the commission; this is reflected in the doubts he expressed to Wittgenstein in his letter of 27 November 1925, 'whether such an undertaking is still possible these days.' Before examining the design phases in detail it may therefore be helpful to form an idea of what Engelmann had learned about designing mansions or villas at the *Adolf Loos Bauschule* and as Loos's first assistant.

One of his first designs at the *Bauschule* shows a variation on the theme of the Roman atrium-house. In his educational programme, Loos presented this as the seminal plan of the private dwelling designed for purely practical needs. It comprises a large, central, hall-like room with a high ceiling, the atrium, in which daily life took place and around which other, less important rooms – vestibule, bedrooms, servant's rooms, kitchen and storage rooms – were functionally grouped. The rooms of the upper floor there were situated along an gallery giving on to the atrium. The atrium-house also justified Loos's preference for plans inspired by the layout of the English country house, which was mostly determined by practical considerations and influenced many German and Austrian architects of the period (for example, Hoffmann). It is characterized by a functional, and usually therefore asymmetrical, arrangement of rooms around a high-ceilinged living hall with a gallery on the upper floor. Engelmann's early design also betrays the strong influence of the austere classicism of Karl Friedrich

Site plan. The outline of the intended building area, as derived from sketches GC 6, 9, 19, 17, and 39, is drawn into it (I).
The northernmost corner touches the rear of the coach house of the parental Wittgenstein Palais (II) in the Argentinierstraße (GC 1).

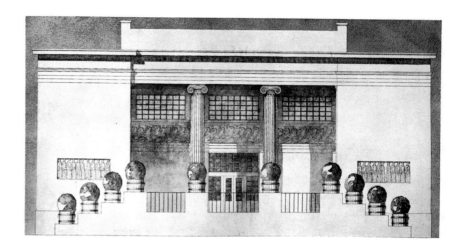

Paul Engelmann, study for a villa. Published as an illustration to Adolf Loos's article on his school of architecture, in *Der Architekt*, 1913.
Ground floor plan: *Zimmer* = room; *Halle* = hall; *Salon* = drawing room; *Speisezimmer* = dining room; *Küche* = kitchen; *Eingang* = entrance; *Vorzimmer* = vestibule.
Upper floor plan: *Schlafzimmer* = sleeping room; *Bad* = bathroom; *Dienerzimmer* = servant's room.

Schinkel (1781–1841), whom Loos held up as the last great architect who thought like a Roman master builder and who made functionality and simplicity of form the starting point of his neo-classicist designs. Engelmann's neo-classicism also comprises clearly defined building volumes and the sparing and simplified application of antique ornament, recognized and applied by Loos as the eternal, and therefore the only justified ornament. This restrained manner of ornamentation and the asymmetrical layout of the plan around a symmetrically designed hall form an interesting point of contrast between Engelmann's villa and the otherwise remarkably similar neo-baroque first villa of Otto Wagner (1888). On the one hand Loos greatly admired Wagner for his clarity of design, but on the other hand he reacted against him because of his eclecticism.

Loos's modernist elaboration of the principles of the atrium-house to enhance the functional nature of the private dwelling and the efficacy of its spatial design resulted in the *Raumplan*, or *Raumplanung* as Engelmann consistently names it, which was made possible by relatively new construction techniques, which employed reinforced concrete supports and ribs to make an open structural framework that allowed ample freedom for organizing space. To give Loos's own first, and germinal, characterization:

The projects [the assignments given at his *Bauschule*] had to be developed from the inside out. Floor and ceiling (parquet and coffering) were of primary importance; the façade was secondary. The subtlety of axes (in the ceilings and windows) and the correct furnishing was given the greatest weight. In this way I made my pupils think three-dimensionally, in cubic space.

This led to the idea of placing rooms, according to their function, on different levels and of giving them different heights. 'Decentralized' connecting stairs force a passage through them which is functionally ordered as well. Initially the *Raumplanung* was done around a central living hall, but soon the hall became subordinate to the functional arrangement of rooms. The whole design should be enclosed within a cube or composition of cubes. Furthermore, to accommodate the needs of modern man who worked in the city during the day and needed a suburban residence for relaxation and family life, the house should reflect privacy and seclusion on the street side and be open to the private garden. The device of the *Raumplanung* and the double aspect of the exterior culminated in the design of the Villa Moller (Vienna, 1928), with which we shall compare the completed Kundmanngasse in a later chapter.

What is less obvious from Engelmann's early designs was the importance of acquiring a thorough knowledge of building materials, including those applied in decoration of the interior and exterior. This reflected Loos's predilection for craftsmanship. It comprised:

General knowledge of geology and mineralogy. The varieties of stone used for construction purposes (sandstone, limestone, granite, etc.). The decorative and luxurious stones (marble, syenite, porphyry, etc.). Semiprecious stone, agate, precious stone. – Materials from the animal kingdom: pearl, mother-of-pearl, tortoiseshell, horn. – Artificial materials: lime, plaster, cement, concrete, reinforced concrete.

One may, however, safely assume that these were to be applied in these first houses, just as they were in most of Loos's designs, and it is more than likely that Engelmann had them in mind for the villa Stonborough.

During Engelmann's years as an assistant to Adolf Loos a number of projects had been comparable to Margaret Stonborough's commission. The city-*Palais* Bronner in Vienna (1921, not realized) is closest to the Kundmanngasse in size and intent although it has a much smaller garden at its rear only. The project for a mansion in Vienna (1921, not realized) is considerably smaller and known only from plans. Another house of the same sort of size as the latter is the house designed by Engelmann himself for Dr Hermann Konstandt in Olomouc (1919, not realized). The Konstandt House was the first to show a more elaborate *Raumplanung* without a central hall. The *Palais* Bronner and the project for a mansion both have different levels on the main floor: in the first the rooms are grouped around a central hall. The latter's plans reveal columns in its interior and exterior. The exteriors of both the Konstandt House and the *Palais* Bronner have antique ornamentation: Ionic order, herms and friezes in the former case, the Doric order in the latter. Both also show the double exterior aspect with regard to the street and the garden façades.

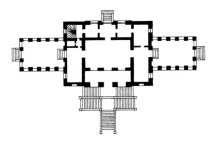

Otto Wagner, 'first' Villa Wagner in the Viennese suburb of Hütteldorf, 1885.

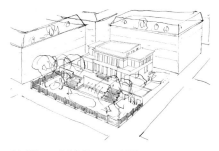

Adolf Loos, *Palais* Bronner, 1921. Perspective sketch.

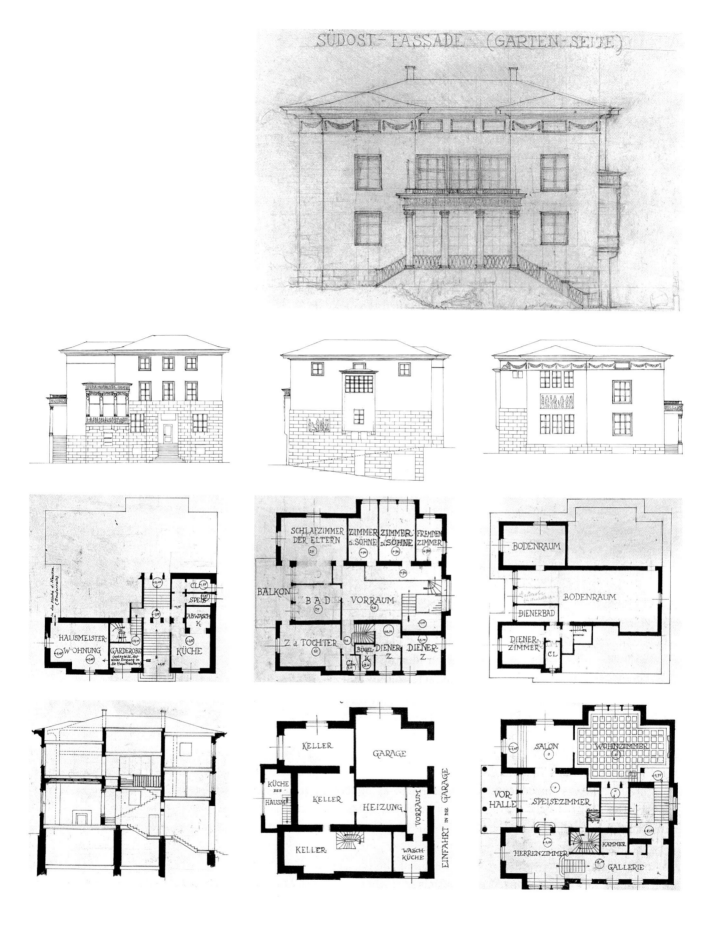

SÜDOST - FASSADE (GARTEN-SEITE)

78

A garden-*Palais* Stonborough

The sketches of the first phase of Engelmann's designs for the villa Stonborough – for a house surrounded by a park and entered by way of a terrace certainly conforms to the features of the neo-classicist villa – show an exterior strongly reminiscent of the atrium-house which he drew in the *Adolf Loos Bauschule*. The outline of its plan is a symmetrical **H** and as such is almost a classicist cliché (for example, in 1885 Wagner designed the Villa Hahn with almost the same outline): the main floor, including a terrace which can be reached by two symmetrically placed flights of steps, rests on an elevated base. The façades are symmetrically arranged; the windows have mouldings and on the main floor they are taller than on the upper floor, the walls are topped by a slender cornice. However, the fact that the sketch of the ground floor plan has neither stairs nor a central living hall does not imply a *Raumplanung*, though its asymmetrical layout is strongly reminiscent of the asymmetrical *Raumplanung* of Loos's *Palais* Bronner. Indeed, at no stage of the design process did Engelmann even try to introduce a *Raumplanung* or central living hall. We must assume that Margaret Stonborough rejected both the idea of a *Raumplanung*, which was so dear to him, and the concept of the atrium-house. Because the lot did not face on to any street a Loosian double aspect for the exterior was irrelevant; the north-west and north-east façades of the house face the wall surrounding the lot and make them relatively uninteresting from an architectural point of view. These circumstances may very well account for Engelmann's indecision and the fact that he tried a number of alternative designs.

In the second phase a partly enclosed terrace is introduced with an opening to the south. This forms an intermediate space connecting house and garden which continued through all the design stages, ending up as the south terrace of the Kundmanngasse. By refracting the cross of the **H** at an angle of 90 degrees, Engelmann breaks out of the stereotype of tradition into a much more modernist theme: a house arranged around a terrace, in which the south-east is given prominence as a two-storeyed main wing, which connects with a garage, or a portico with entrance, against its north-east wall. The plan of the lot also gives an idea of the layout for the garden, which here and in later phases is characterized by stately avenues bordered by trees and hedges. Its geometrical forms seem to have been inspired by the same tendency towards classicism as that which is recognizable in the house.

In the third phase the main wing is extended along two sides of the inner terrace and two of its façades are curved. The curved line as a deliberate design element was introduced by expressionist architects, such as Erich Mendelsohn (1887–1953), through whose influence it became a main feature of Jewish immigrant architecture in Palestine in the 1930s. However, it is very difficult to find modernist designs based on the curved line that obviously could have influenced Engelmann before 1926. Moreover, Engelmann's façades are concave, for which no earlier modernist example

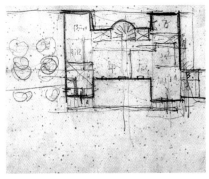

Paul Engelmann, design for the *Palais* Stonborough. Phase 1, south-east (front) elevation (top) (GC 3, 94 x 105 mm) and ground floor plan (above) (GC 4, 97 x 121 mm).

Büro = study; *Bibl* = library; *Sp* = dining room; *Z(zimmer)* = room; *Saal* = drawing room; *Salon* = (Margaret Stonborough's?) living room; *Schl Z D* = Margaret Stonborough's sleeping room; *B* = bathroom.

Translation drawings oppositie page:

Bad = bathroom; *Vorraum* = landing; *Bügel-K.* = ironing room; *Zimmer d. Tochter* = daughter's room; *Diener-Z.* = servant's room; *Bodenraum* = attic room; *Dienerbad* = servant's bathroom; *Keller* = basement; *Küche des Hausm.* = butler's kitchen; *Heizung* = central heating; *Vorraum* = hall; *Wasch-Küche* = scullery;

Salon = drawing room; *Wohnzimmer* = living room; *Vorhalle* = portico; *Speisezimmer* = dining room; *Herrenzimmer* = gentleman's room; *Kammer* = closet; *Gallerie* = gallery.

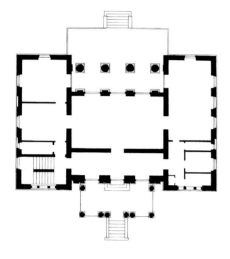

Otto Wagner, *Villa Hahn*, 1885.

Above, Villa Hahn, plan of the main floor, 1885.

seems to exist, with the exception of the façades of apartment blocks curved around a square, for example, by Bruno Taut in Berlin (1925). A concave south-west frontage to the Kundmanngasse would have given all the main ground floor rooms a view of the garden, placing the entrance on the south-east or on the north-east side, and providing an elegant solution to the problem of the driveway: the car could be driven up to the door, turned and then parked in the garage. It seems, however, that Margaret Stonborough did not want to pursue the curved line: in the next phase it disappeared never to return.

The fourth phase shows perhaps the most harmonious blending of neo-classicist and modernist design. It is neo-classicist in the sense that its plan and its axial structure are strictly symmetrical and its severe exterior employs the same austere classicist vocabulary as that which characterizes the first phase. It is modernist in the arrangement of cubic volumes, recessed at the second floor, around a central terrace, which causes the axis of symmetry of the plan to cut through its axial structure at an angle of 45 degrees instead of being parallel or perpendicular. It is the most elaborated design phase and it contains almost the very rooms that were eventually realized in the Kundmanngasse. The number and function of these rooms betray the influence of the English country house, which by then was the norm for villa design in the German-speaking countries and which was most probably suggested by Engelmann. It could have been the definitive design were it not, as we shall see below, for the insurmountable problems raised by the positioning and plan of the entrance.

The music room (or large drawing room), dining room, library and small drawing room (most likely meant to be Margaret Stonborough's private living room) are arranged around the central terrace in such a way that the longitudinal axis of each room is at a right angle to the longitudinal axes of the adjacent rooms; it looks like a broken-up enfilade typical of Viennese *Palais*-architecture. This arrangement re-establishes views of the garden from all these rooms (not to say the most advantageous views) and makes it possible to enter the garden by way of the terrace. The fact that it is partly enclosed guarantees an aspect of intimacy despite the openness of the rooms. The plans of the first and second floors and of the basement are clumsy and not very well thought out. To some extent this is also true of the ground floor plan where it becomes muddled by idle attempts to find a functional and elegant design for the entrance, hallway and stairwell.

From this fourth phase it appears that a more formal and monumental, more *Palais*-like function for entrance and hallway must have been important to Margaret Stonborough in this villa. The sketch of the ground floor plan and one of the perspectives still show a simple entrance at the north-east rear side of the house comparable to the unpretentious nature of the entrances and modest vestibules of the Konstandt House, of Loos's project for a mansion in Vienna, and of the Palais Bronner. However, starting with a sketch on the back of the basement plan, which places the entrance and vestibule in the north corner of the house, there are successive sketches that elaborate this alternative into a more prominent entrance and hallway.

In this phase Engelmann stubbornly adheres to the idea of a hallway at the back of the house, as if holding on to Loos's principle regarding the double aspect of the street and garden façades. It is placed diagonally in relation to the wings of the house, creating problems with regard to the doorways on all floors and, consequently, further difficulties with the plans for the rooms near the north corner on both sides of the symmetry axis of the house. The location and structure of the stairwell, initially a semi-cylindrical addition against the diagonal wall of the north corner, also remains unclear. All variations of the entrance plan have an interior flight of steps in its axis leading to the hallway on the ground floor. In its axis also stands the pedestal for a sculpture against the blind wall facing the stairs which did eventually appear in the hallway of the Kundmanngasse. Elevations of both the simple and more prominent entrance versions show the simple neo-classicist exterior Engelmann had in mind from the beginning, complete with columns on both sides of the doorway.

The solution, however, was to break with Loos's principle and move the entrance from the rear of the house to the front, that is, the south-east side; this constitutes the fifth phase. A large hallway was placed between the music room and the terrace so that the centre of gravity of the design shifted from the terrace to the hallway, thereby placing the design somewhere between the classical *villa suburbana* and the city *Palais*. In the subsequent intermediary phase part of the block in the west corner disappeared while a small block is added in the north corner, which contained a sleeping room and the library.

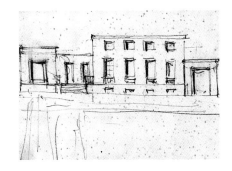

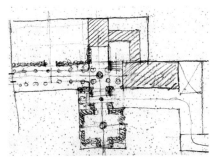

Paul Engelmann, design for the *Palais* Stonborough. Phase 2, south-east (front) elevation (top) (GC 5, 102 x 146 mm) and site plan (above) (GC 6, 102 x 145 mm).

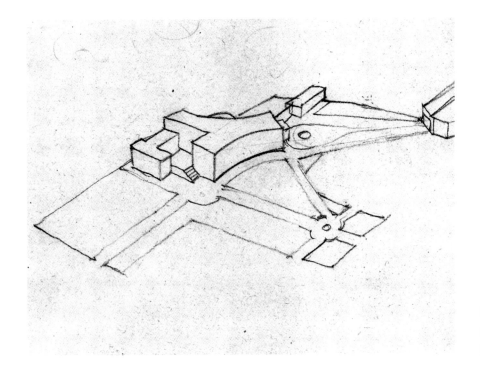

Paul Engelmann, design for the *Palais* Stonborough. Phase 3, bird's-eye view to the north (GC 10, 98 x 100 mm).

81

The ground floor plan of the sixth phase shows the basic lay-out of the Kundmanngasse as it was eventually built: a second terrace was inserted in the corner created by the above-mentioned additional block, which was enlarged by the addition of a perpendicularly placed oblong room. The east terrace was therefore partially enclosed. A new room was added to the left of the stairs to the hallway. This would eventually become the breakfast room, but on the plan it was indicated by 'WZ' which may mean anteroom *(Wartezimmer)*. It is also interesting to note that a proportional ratio – 9:6 – has been assigned to the dining room. The grid drawn inside the room, however, does not agree with this ratio. The façades of the south-east entrance block belonging to the fifth phase have large square windows with checkered window panes on the ground floor reminiscent of Loos's design for the windows of the *Palais* Bronner. The windows of the sixth phase, however, show the verticality that would eventually be realized by Wittgenstein.

The seventh phase reduces the depth of the building by one bay; it also expands the upper block into a gigantic cubic volume with almost sky-scraper-like aspirations (its previous narrowness would have been inadequate for any well-proportioned rooms). Traces of rubbed out pencil marks show that Engelmann seems to have contemplated raising both wings to the height of the central section. The ground floor plan pasted in the centre of the sketchbook is almost identical to the layout of this perspective, while the line drawing of the ground floor plan that was loosely inserted in the sketchbook shows the slightly projecting part of the front that is also found in a second perspective of this phase. These plans formed the basis of his final design phase and would become the starting point for the plan of the Kundmanngasse as built. The rooms are arranged around a central hallway in such a way that each room stands crosswise to the adjacent rooms. The entrance and central hallway have a formality and impressive-

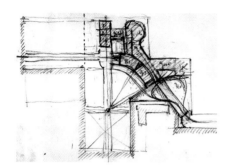

Phase 3, site plan (GC 9, 135 x 212 mm).

Paul Engelmann, design for the *Palais* Stonborough. Phase 4, main floor plan (GC 17, 135 x 222 mm).

Schl = sleeping room; *Bi* = library; *Sp* = dining room; *MZ* = music room; *KlS* = small living room; *Gar* = garage.

Presumably, the western sleeping room, directly above the study in the basement, was Jerome Stonborough's; the eastern one, directly above a bathroom, dressing room and maidservant's room in the basement, Margaret Stonborough's.

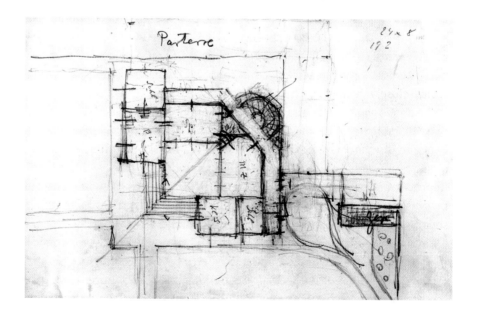

 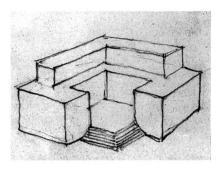

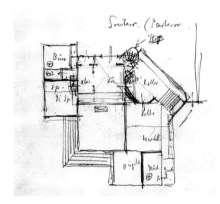 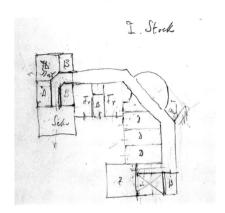 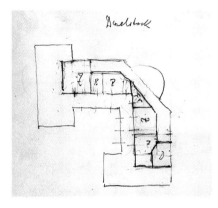

ness borrowed from the baroque city *Palais*; on the other hand, the plan embodying a main building volume of three bays with wings, the arrangement of a single layer of rooms around the hall, a main axis connecting the south terrace, the hallway, the music room or *Saal* and the east terrace, although it has been turned 90 degrees, and finally, the possibility of also entering the hall via a terrace with steps suggest the Palladian prototype of the *villa suburbana*. What makes it different from both is the asymmetric plan and composition of building volumes, which can only be understood as a last remnant of what Engelmann learned at the *Adolf Loos Bauschule*. Before Engelmann achieved his goal he made an unexpected turn that makes it even more clear that thinking from the exterior to the interior had, by this time, ousted the Loosian approach 'from the inside out'. The eighth phase seems to have been inspired by Engelmann's becoming aware of what he had actually arrived at during the preceding phases and what seems closely related to the contemporary designs of such constructivist architects as the Hungarian Forbat (the House Stadthagen, Berlin, 1921–22), or of functionalists like the Germans Mies van der Rohe or Mendelsohn (for example, the latter's Sternfeld House, Berlin, 1923): exploring the plastic qualities of compositions of super- and subordinated cubic volumes. This impression is strengthened by the fact that the outlines of rooms and terrace-levels in the ground floor plan are determined by a modular grid of squares, in which the rooms are regrouped around a central terrace having different levels. The plan still occupies about the same area. Although initially the façades show the same classicist elements as the previous designs, on the ground floor of the second version Engelmann introduces large glass screens between columns separating the interior from the exterior; the

Paul Engelmann, design for the *Palais* Stonborough. Phase 4, bird's-eye view to the north (top right) (GC 13 recto, 73 x 74 mm) and south-west elevation (top left) (GC 15 recto, 71 x 118 mm).

Phase 4, above from left to right, plans of the basement (GC 18 recto, 152 x 163 mm), first floor (GC 19, 135 x 114 mm) and second floor (GC 20, 135 x 116 mm).

Büro = study; *B* = bathroom; *Sp* = dining room; *Di Sp* = servant's dining room; *Kü* = kitchen; *Aufz.* = lift (here dumbwaiter?); *Stiege* = stairwell; *Keller* = cellar; *Mäd* = maid-servant's room; *Waschk.* = scullery; *Bügelk* = ironing room; *Gard* = dressing room; *Bad* = bathroom. *Nah* = dressmaker's room; *D* = servant's room; *Sekr* = secretary's room; *Fr* = guest-room; *Auf* = lift; *Z* = room.

83

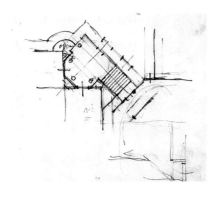 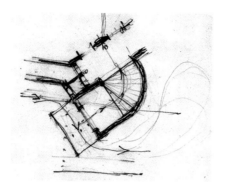 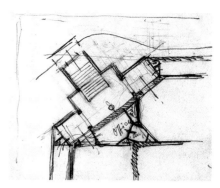

Paul Engelmann, design for the *Palais Stonborough*. Phase 4. Above: Plans of the hallway, from left to right, second version (with section) (GC 22/22*, 106 x 135 mm), fourth version (with curved flight of steps) (GC 24, 127 x 116 mm) and third version, in which the hallway partly encloses the stairs, anticipating the definitive design of the hallway (GC 23, 139 x 126 mm). The latter plan implies that the car should be driven around the house (or backwards) to be parked in the garage.

Below from left to right: East perspective with entrance in the northeast façade (GC 16, 72 x 131 mm).
East perspective with entrance moved to the north corner (GC 26, 147 x 177 mm).
West perspective showing the semi-cylindrical stairwell in the north corner (GC 28 recto, 80 x 117 mm).

SpZ = dining room; *Off* = pantry; *Vorr* = hallway; *MZ* = music room; *Aufz* = lift.

result is strongly reminiscent of the spatial effect and articulation, albeit on a much smaller scale, of Loos's project for developing the Horticultural Association Grounds (1916–17).

During the penultimate phase Engelmann abandoned his detour to apply the same play of cubic volumes to the ground floor plan of phase seven, adding one or two small intersecting cubic volumes to the front end of the main cuboid. Now the final contours of the Kundmanngasse become discernable: a tall, dominating block sitting on a rectangular block that forms wings, with terraces fitting into the corners. The transition to the final design seems to have been triggered by a tiny sketch made during the seventh phase and showing the – still lower – central block overstepping the terraces. The main block is extended and widened so that the lower east block at the front is absorbed; the entrance now leads directly into the main block. As a consequence it oversteps the east terrace. On the south-west side part of the second lower front block still protrudes from the enlarged main volume. By connecting it to the north-east wing on the upper floor only it in its turn crosses over the south terrace just as envisaged in the little sketch of phase seven.

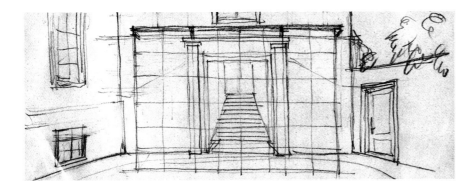

Paul Engelmann, design for the *Palais* Stonborough. Phase 4, elevation of the entrance (above) (GC 29, 73 x 176 mm) and elevation of an earlier version of the entrance, presumably in the south-east façade (below) (GC 21, 201 x 118 mm).

Engelmann's final design, the tenth phase, is shown in the last six sketches of the sketchbook and is quite close to the Kundmanngasse as eventually built. The general layout of the rooms seems to correspond with the line drawing of the ground floor plan of phase seven, although the north-east wing has been completely redesigned: it now has two bays instead of three, while the north-west elevation shows an entrance on this side of the building. The exterior with its tall windows emphasizing verticality, its attic storey and crowning balustrade, and its base, follows the same decorative scheme as in earlier phases. The large window screens between columns of phase eight reappear beneath the canopy over the terraces, separating the hallway and music room from the south and east terraces respectively (but a similar glass wall between hallway and south terrace already existed in phase five).

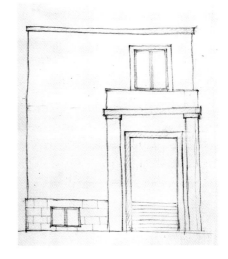

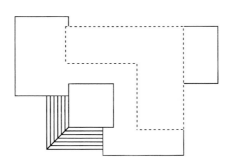

Left: Phase 5, schematic reconstruction of the plan (upper floor projected on to the ground floor).

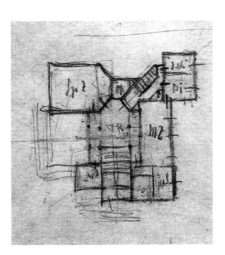

Paul Engelmann, design for the *Palais* Stonborough. Far left: Phase 6, plan with east terrace added. *B* = library; *M* = music room; *Kl* = Margaret Stonborough's living room (GC 30/30* recto, 113 x 109 mm).
Left: Intermediary phase between phases 5 and 6. *Sp Z* = dining room; *Of* = pantry; *VR* = hallway; *WZ* = antechamber (or living room?); *Schl* = bed room; *Di* = servant's room; *MZ* = music room; *KIS* = Margaret Stonborough's living room; presumably the small room to the left of KIS is Margaret Stonborough's bed room (GC 31, 105 x 86 mm).

Paul Engelmann, design for the *Palais* Stonborough. Above: Phase 5, south-east (front) elevation (GC 34, 63 x 96 mm). Note that the entrance seems awkwardly low. Above right: Phase 6, south-east elevation (GC 36, 130 x 152 mm).

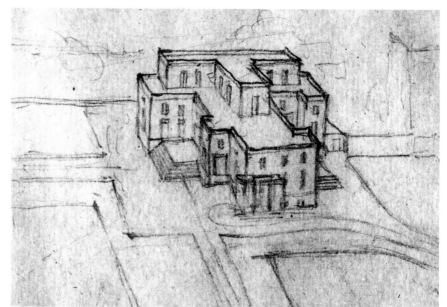

Phase 6, bird's-eye view to the north (right) (GC 39, 103 x 187 mm) and south-west perspective showing the south terrace (below) (GC 40, 123 x 130 mm).

Phase 7, east perspective (right) (GC 55, 135 x 129 mm). This version shows a slightly projecting frontispiece and a narrow flight of stairs leading to the terrace.

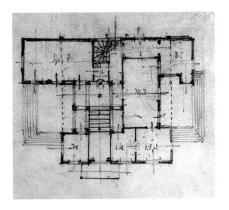

Plan pasted in the exact middle of the sketch-book (left) (GC 38, 137 x 162 mm).
SP Z = dining room; *Fr* = breakfast room; *Bi* = library; *MZ* = music room; *Schl* = Margaret Stonborough's sleeping room; *KL S* = Margaret Stonborough's living room.

Phase 7, bird's-eye view to the north (far left) (GC 52, 112 x 90 mm).

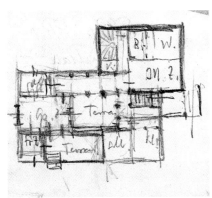

Phase 8, south-east elevation of first version (far left) (GC 58, 64 x 74 mm) and ground floor plan of first version with entrance at the north-east side (left) (GC 59, 62 x 80 mm).

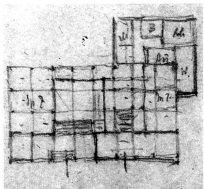

Above: ground floor plan of second version with entrance at the south-east side (GC 61, 80 x 91 mm).

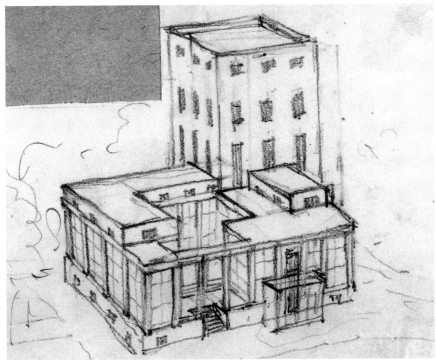

Left: Bird's-eye view to the north of second version (GC 60, 87 x 124 mm)

87

Paul Engelmann (1946), drawing of Loos's project for the development of the Horticultural Association Grounds, 1916. Engelmann comments: 'An example of modern planning in classical building forms.' (below) Phase 9, south-east (front) elevation, first version (right) (GC 68, 135 x 88 mm) and bird's-eye view to the north-west of second version (far right) (GC 71, 120 x 91 mm). Middle row from left to right: Transitional phase, south-west elevation (GC 73, 72 x 67 mm) and north-east elevation (GC 72, 94 x 72 mm)., phase 10, north-east elevation (GC 76, 59 x 74 mm).

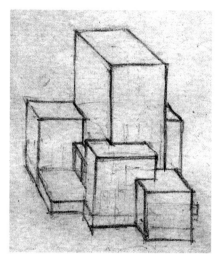

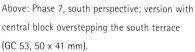

Above: Phase 7, south perspective; version with central block overstepping the south terrace (GC 53, 50 x 41 mm).

Right: Phase 10, north-west elevation (above left) (GC 77, 69 x 82 mm) and bird's-eye view to the north (far right) (GC 79, 60 x 71 mm).

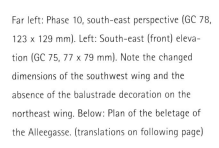

Far left: Phase 10, south-east perspective (GC 78, 123 x 129 mm). Left: South-east (front) elevation (GC 75, 77 x 79 mm). Note the changed dimensions of the southwest wing and the absence of the balustrade decoration on the northeast wing. Below: Plan of the beletage of the Alleegasse. (translations on following page)

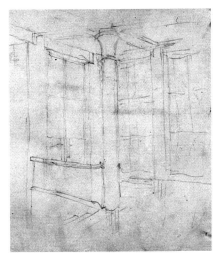
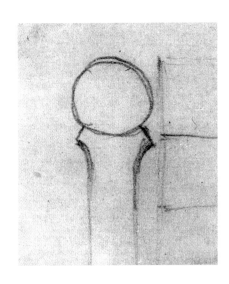

Paul Engelmann, design for the *Palais* Stonborough. Above left: Hallway, interior perspective towards the glass doors opening to the south terrace (GC 46, 135 x 175 mm). Above middle: Hallway, interior perspective towards the breakfast room (GC 47, 121 x 135 mm). Above: horizontal section of joint between staircase balustrade and column (GC 48, 67 x 80 mm) Far left: *The Galerie* of the Alleegasse. Pencil and ink drawing by Hermine Wittgenstein. Left: Paul Engelmann, design for the *Palais* Stonborough. Hallway, interior perspective (GC 45, 135 x 185 mm).

89

(translations of previous page)

Plan of the beletage of the Alleegasse.

Galerie = gallery; *Roter Salon* = Red Room;

Speisezimmer = dining room; *Musikzimmer* =

music room; *Hof* = courtyard; *Garten* = garden.

Between the sketches of the fifth and sixth phase there are five drawings of various aspects of the hallway which correspond closely to both plans of the seventh phase. Moreover, it was eventually realized in the Kundmanngasse without any change to its proportions. It bears no relationship at all to the atrium-like halls of Engelmann's early designs at the *Adolf Loos Bauschule* or to the much more informal halls of the projects encountered during his period as assistant to Loos. Though the likely origins of the representative kind of entrance hall she wanted will be discussed later on, there seems to be a precedent for the hallway Engelmann designed: the magnificent stairs and *Galerie* ('gallery') of the parental Wittgenstein house in the former Alleegasse, number 16.

The Alleegasse was built in 1871–73 and bought by Karl Wittgenstein in 1890 who adapted and redecorated its interior. It was a typical nineteenth century Viennese *Palais* designed at the height of the popularity of the architectural style of the buildings of the Ringstraße and its immediate surroundings which were constructed in the area of the former city ramparts after their demolition in 1857. The *Palais* was of medium size, though still immense compared to modern luxury dwellings, and built in a style reminiscent of Italian High Renaissance palazzi: a rusticated ground floor with portals on both ends, and a simple but dignified, clearly articulated *piano nobile* (referred to in Vienna by the French term *beletage*, or the German term Prunk-Etage, 'show floor' or 'best floor') as its only upper floor. Loos had called it 'one of the most sympathetic Viennese *Palais*' during one of his city walks with his pupils in 1913–14.

From the entrance in the passageway of the north portal a grand staircase led up to the hallway of the beletage, the Galerie, which, as in Engelmann's design for the villa Stonborough, surrounded the stairs on three sides. It gave access to the rooms of this floor which were situated as enfilades on both sides of the gallery, facing the street and garden respectively. Though the gallery is rectangular (real width to length ratio approx 11:15), its walls are partitioned by pilasters (suggesting a width to length ratio of 3:4) as in Engelmann's square hallway and its plan shows the same axial structure. On the landing facing the staircase stood a sculpture by Max Klinger, the *Squatting Woman*, against a blind wall which was completely covered by a Gobelin. These features are echoed in Engelmann's sketches. There are folding doors on both sides of the blind wall, shoulder to shoulder with the folding doors of the side walls; the door on the left-hand side opens into a large drawing room – the 'Red Room' – instead of the one on the right-hand side as in Engelmann's design. As in the villa Stonborough, the arrangement of blind wall between doors is mirrored in the opposite wall on the other end of the gallery though in the Alleegasse a window in the blind wall connects the gallery visually with the room behind.

Engelmann, however, added columns on both sides of the staircase as part of the structural framework supporting the upper floors (the gallery of the Alleegasse was covered by a glass and steel roof). These are smooth cylindrical columns with no base or pedestal and with chalice capitals. They may be inspired by ancient Egyptian models; one year earlier Wittgenstein and Engelmann discussed Egyptian architecture, in response to which Engelmann had written:

Stimulated by your thoughts on Egyptian architecture I have, for some time, been in the mood again for modern architecture. I did some drawings and should like to show them to you.

Furthermore, Engelmann's sketches show a ceiling of beams and cross beams, a floor characterized by a pattern of joints between slabs, tall glass doors leading to adjacent rooms, and glass screens between the south terrace and hallway that were eventually realized, though completely redesigned by Wittgenstein. Regrettably, one cannot deduce from the sketches which materials were to be used for the finishing of the interior of the hallway, whether Engelmann intended to apply Loosian luxury materials like granite or marble, or panelling of precious woods, which would also have been closer to the decoration of the *Galerie* of the Alleegasse than the materials Wittgenstein eventually chose.

The failure

It is clear that Engelmann was severely restricted in realizing his conception of architecture while designing the Stonborough house. In the first place the house had to be exceptionally large, that is, larger than Loos's general idea of the modern residence would allow (although the unbuilt *Palais* Bronner is even somewhat larger than the eventual Kundmanngasse). Secondly, right from the beginning it seems clear that the idea of a *Raumplanung* around a central living hall was out of the question for Margaret Stonborough, even in the reduced fashion of the *Palais* Bronner, while the nature of the lot and the position of the house in it made a dual-

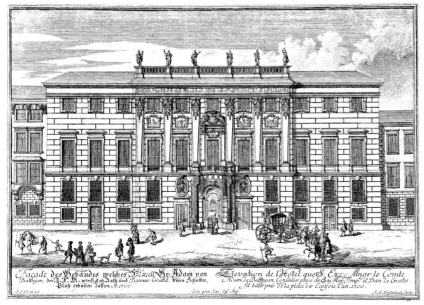

Johann Bernhard Fischer von Erlach, Palais Batthyány-Schönborn, 1698-1700.
(From *Wiener Ansichtenwerks Joseph Emannuel Fischers van Erlach*, 1715, Plate 11)

91

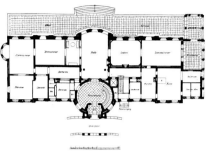

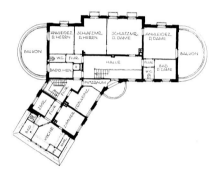

Examples of contemporary German historicizing mansion architecture: Hermann Muthesius, Haus T., Berlin, 1927 (top left), and Paul Baumgarten, Minoux House, Wannsee, Berlin, 1925 (top right).

Adolf Loos, *Palais* Bronner, 1921. South (garden) elevation.

istic Loosian conception for its exterior pointless. The fourth phase, from which the development of the design gained its momentum, seems to hark back to traditional grandiose dwellings, something in between a city *Palais* and a villa suburbana. Anyway, such a dwelling was much more suitable to Margaret Stonborough's semi-aristocratic style of life: until she moved to the Kundmanngasse she lived in the early eighteenth century *Palais* Batthyány-Schönborn in the Renngasse or, out of town, in the Villa Toscana in Gmunden, the former country estate of the Archduke of Toscana. It was, however, also in accordance with her lifestyle that anything that should express it, would have to do so in contemporary, 'modern', form, which was bound to create an inner conflict for Loos's pupil, Engelmann.

Just as Engelmann never succeeded in breaking loose from his teachers and friends, Ludwig Wittgenstein and Karl Kraus, he was too dependent on what he had learnt from Adolf Loos not to feel lost at the initial design stages. He saw no solution other than to return to the first designs he made in the *Adolf Loos Bauschule* and to start a new search from there following the wishes of his principal. The result is visually interesting as a sculpture of cubic masses and also as a marriage of the classical *villa suburbana* and the traditional Viennese city *Palais* adorned with extremely simplified classicist ornament. The only feature of the ground floor plan that can still be interpreted as having been borrowed from Loosian plans and which should be traced back to the possibilities derived from new building techniques is the deliberate asymmetry in the arrangement of the rooms and in the composition of cubic volumes. Engelmann's 'modern classicist' city villa, however, may not have been authentic enough for Margaret Stonborough, nor for Wittgenstein, as may become clear below: its reduced rather than reformulated vocabulary – the base, the window arrangement, the attic storey crowned by a balustrade, and furthermore, the fanciful choice of Egyptian

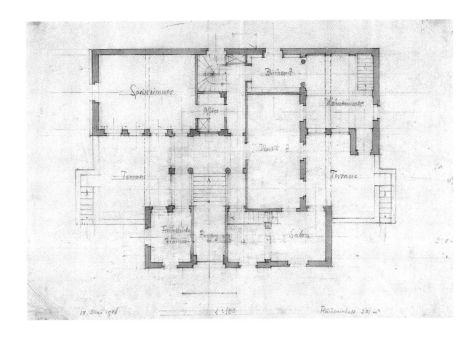

columns in the hallway — may not have been sufficiently 'modern' in their eyes and was perhaps too near to the empty pretentiousness of bourgeois villas and mansions built in the neo-styles that were again in vogue.

It is obvious that the design of the last phase closely resembles the eventual Kundmanngasse; however, it was to be altered in a more substantial way than Engelmann remembered in his account cited at the beginning of this chapter. Three years after the completion of the Kundmanngasse he was certainly aware of the discrepancy, as is revealed by a letter to Hermine Wittgenstein in response to a number of her drawings of the interior she sent to him:

Most respected Lady,

The pictures of the rooms in the Kundmanngasse pleased me extraordinarily and I thank you very much for that. As pictures they are truly exceptionally beautiful. That is your achievement. In addition, one can also see the achievement of your sister and your brother. So, even though I have no share at all in these pictures, I am satisfied with the thought that I had something to do with the origin of such beautiful things, regrettably more in a negative than in a positive way: at that time I wanted something different, something of myself. Now that the work of your brother can be seen in them in its final form, it is clear how much this something of myself would have paled in comparison to this accomplishment, which is better, and which at that time I barely understood. Unfortunately one only becomes wise after the event and therefore I then acted rather as a hindrance than a help. Anyway, I was there, if that can be said to be an achievement (...)

Most grateful to you,
Devotedly yours,
Paul Engelmann
Olmütz, 9.1.32

Paul Engelmann, design for the *Palais Stonborough*. Phase 7, plan corresponding to GC55, loosely inserted. (GC 80)

Speisezimmer = dining room; *Frühstückszimmer* = breakfast room; *Office* = pantry; *Terrasse* = terrace; *Eingang* = entrance; *Bücherzimmer* = library; *Wohnzimmer* = living room; *Musik Zimmer* = music room; *Salon* = Margaret Stonborough's living room (?); (rubbed out:) *Billiard Zimmer* = billiard room.

SITUATION

Site plan as submitted for the building permit, November 1926. *Neubau* = planned building; *Einfahrt* = entrance gate; *Abriss* = to be demolished; *Adaptierung* = to be adapted; *Schnitt* = section.

The architecture of Ludwig Wittgenstein

It is very difficult to determine the starting point and the extent of the influence of the advice which Wittgenstein gave before he oficially became Engelmann's co-architect in late summer 1926. If the omission of ornament in the exterior finishing, which Wittgenstein as co-architect was to enforce rigorously, is evidence of his involvement it may have been there from phase three onward. The perspective shows completely unadorned façades; only the base is clearly demarcated. This simple layout reappears in quite a number of perspectives and elevations of most of the subsequent phases. The suggestion becomes even stronger in the front elevation of the sixth phase which shows a vertical shading of windows reminiscent of Wittgenstein's designs for door and window frames. Furthermore, in the front elevation of the last phase, the balustrade of the north-east wing is missing while an earlier, rubbed out version of the main block in the same sketch does not seem to have had a balustrade. The east perspective seems to have been corrected in the same fashion and, in contrast to most sketches showing details of the façades, has windows without mouldings strikingly similar to those of the completed Kundmanngasse. Compared to the exterior of Loos's *Palais* Bronner it is obvious that Engelmann's final design is marked by its rigorously symmetrical window arrangement within each cubic volume and its exterior is also much more restrained in ornamentation. Finally, nothing can be deduced about the kind of finishing materials Wittgenstein might have suggested; to imply any influence by Wittgenstein on the ground floor plans of Engelmann's sketchbook, apart from what may be supposed to have been Margaret Stonborough's contribution, would seem unjustified for lack of any concrete evidence.

The first alteration in the building plans, which is immediately obvious from the documents submitted for the building permit signed by both Wittgenstein and Engelmann, is the change of building site. Shortly before the actual construction started, Margaret Stonborough acquired the lot bound by the Kundmanngasse, the Geusaugasse and the Parkgasse. It seems that the final plans for the new site were drawn up and submitted as soon as a positive decision of the City Council on selling the piece of land (it was owned by the City of Vienna) was expected. The decision was made on 22 October 1926; the actual date of approval of the building plans is 13 November, while the deed of conveyance is dated 24 November. The definitive plans of the foundation and the ground floor also date from before the actual purchase.

The lot was a piece of land with old trees in the IIIrd district. Though situated in a middle class neighbourhood, it had a number of advantages compared to the initial site behind the Alleegasse. It was a rectangular piece of land instead of a multi-cornered one; it was only partly, not completely enclosed by the rear walls of adjacent buildings; and the entrance could be directly on the street instead of via a passageway. Moreover, the northernmost corner still was the most favourable place to build the house, so the

94

original design hardly needed to be adapted to its new surroundings. The rear faced the Teacher Training School across the Kundmanngasse while the most important south-east and south-west façades faced the garden. The difference of orientation of the respective lots made it necessary to turn the house about 35 degrees counterclockwise, but that caused no substantial change in terms of sunlight: the sun reaches all the façades in the course of a day – the north-west, rear, and side had rooms of lesser importance, being the least favoured in this respect.

Originally the ground sloped downwards to the street level of the Kundmanngasse. However, an enclosing wall was built, while the building line on the Kundmanngasse was set back 6 1/2 feet to make room for a pavement. The space between the wall and the higher ground was then filled in, thereby raising the north-eastern section as a whole; thus the occupants could enjoy the view from the house unimpeded by the enclosing wall, while the garden remained hidden from the curious gaze of passers-by. A porter's lodge was built against the wall next to the main gate.

As the house was to be constructed in the north-western half of the plot of land, the south-western half was chosen for the garden and could be left in its original state. A wide gravel path dividing the garden area from the living quarters curved from the gate on the Kundmanngasse along the south-west façade to the main entrance of the house on its south-eastern side. The chestnut trees growing on the slightly undulating ground of the garden dated for the most part from the days when the Rasumofsky Palace grounds

Plan of the ground floor, first version, November 1926.

Eingang = enclosed porch; *Vorraum* = vestibule; *Garderobe* = cloakroom; *Waschraum* = restroom; *Halle* = hallway; *Terasse* = terrace; *Saal* = large drawing room (and music room); *Wohnzimmer* = family living room (usually referred to as 'library'); *Speisezimmer* = dining room; *Office* = pantry; *Diener Zimmer* = Servant's room; *Bad* = bathroom; *Schlafraum* = sleeping room (used as boudoir);

Wohnzimmer = living room (Margaret Stonborough's salon). *Stufenprofil* = profile of steps; *Eisenbeton* = reinforced concrete; *Stampfbeton* = (unreinforced) concrete; *Ziegelmauerwerk* = brickwork; *Scheidewände aus KB-Platten, Gypsschl. usw.* = gypsum dividing walls, etc.

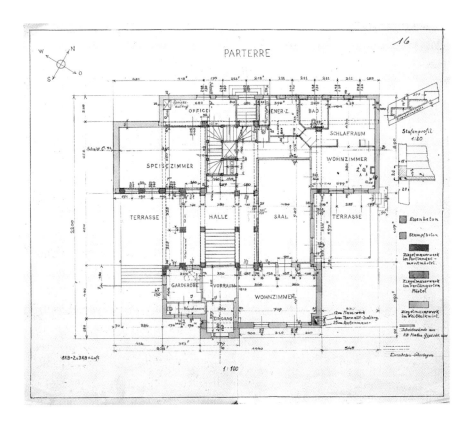

95

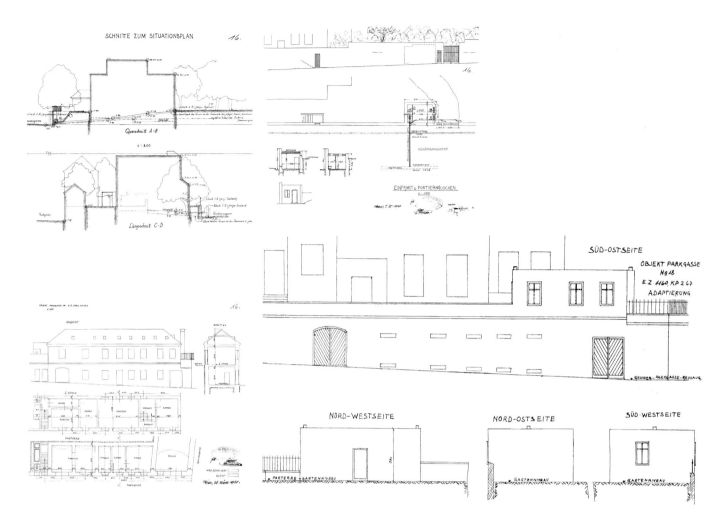

Top: Sections A-B and C-D through the building area with indications for filling up the sloping terrain between wall and street, November 1926, and plan, elevations and sections of garden wall with service entrance, main entrance gate and porter's lodge along the Kundmanngasse, second version, March 1928.

Above: Plans, elevations and section of the former warehouses on the corner of the Parkgasse and Geusaugasse, March 1928, and elevations of garage, fuel storage cellar, and gardener's house, November 1926.

were still intact. The trees in the north-eastern section — poplars behind the house, a nut-tree and some willow trees on the side and in front — ensured privacy. Azaleas and lilac bushes were dotted about the lawns.

Along the Parkgasse, at the corner with the Geusaugasse, stood some eighteenth century warehouses which belonged to the lot. It was decided to convert these buildings, or at least the ground floor (the ceiling of which was now level with the ground-fill surface) into a garage, kitchen cellar and fuel store. The upper storeys were demolished, with the exception of one part which was converted for use as gardener's quarters, the original saddleback roof being replaced by a flat roof in keeping with the style of the main house. An underground passage connected garage and cellars with the boiler room in the basement of the Kundmanngasse.

The exterior

Another, most dramatic, change concerns the general appearance of the building. Although the spatial arrangement of cubic masses of Engelmann's eventual design is instantly recognizable, the house is stripped of all ornament and reduced to an austere composition of lines, planes and volumes. The only spatial alteration which needs to be remarked on concerns the addition of a shallow block covered with a lean-to roof along the basement and ground floor of the north-west (rear) façade of the house. The bareness of the exterior and glass lean-to roof covering the added block is so unlike anything Engelmann designed that we are forced to assume that Wittgenstein is largely responsible for these changes. Other differences include: the lowering of the main building and the upper edge of the block overstepping the south terrace (the top of the parapet slopes down a little which is invisible from the garden and thus gives the impression of a well-proportioned block); the addition of a lower entrance portal projecting slightly from the south-east façade of the house which makes up a modest fifth block, and steps along the entire width of the south terrace which contrast with the small flight of stairs descending from the east terrace. Furthermore, the slightly recessed part of the north-east façade corresponding to the east terrace was limited to ground floor height only, a structure containing the lift hoisting engine and the stairs to the roof terrace was

Perspective drawing of the Kundmanngasse, November 1926.

97

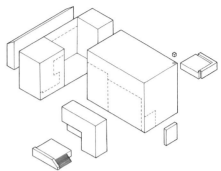

Above: The Kundmanngasse seen from the garden, April 1967.

Right: The Kundmanngasse seen from the corner of the Parkgasse and the Geusaugasse, spring 1929.

Top right: Volumetric composition of the Kundmanngasse.

Right: Elevations of the south-east façade.
Far right: Elevations of the south-west façade.

Right: Elevations of the north-west façade.
Far right: Elevations of the north-east façade, November 1926.

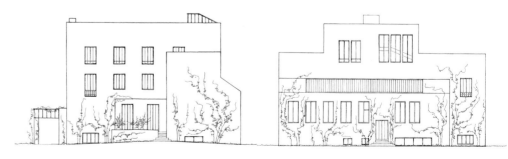

added, the mock windows in Engelmann's design suggesting an attic storey were left out, and some windows were omitted or changed. Because of the addition the north-west façade needed to be redesigned completely and later on three small basement windows in the north-west block were added to the two indicated in the rear elevation. The pergola adjoining the entrance, though still present in the front elevation and perspective submitted for the building permit, was not executed in the final building.

The tall, uniquely severe and almost white block structure of the Kundmanngasse forms a strong contrast with the shady trees in the sloping garden. The house gives an impression of uncompromising massiveness and austerity. The only inviting, more or less open, feature is the porch-like south terrace with its wide steps and glass wall adjoining the hall. Yet the Kundmanngasse is not a squat monolith in an elegant garden setting – quite the contrary. The monumental nature of the building is handsomely set off by the park-like surroundings, as a deliberate, complementary whole of culture and nature. The main block strides forward, as it were, overstepping the second crosswise block and the two terraces; the suggestion of dynamic movement is further emphasized by the third block which, on a more modest scale, repeats the same forward movement over the south terrace. This powerful surge forward comes to rest in the modest, flattened entrance block.

The surging movement sets off from the rear elevation, which is thus literally left behind by the house itself – since the back of the house is only a few yards away from the garden wall, it is virtually invisible from the garden. Only from the lower level of the Kundmanngasse are its proportions clearly visible, the upward thrust being further enhanced by the fact that the base is concealed by the garden wall. The push-off plane formed by the

Entrance gate and porter's lot, spring 1929.

The Kundmanngasse seen from the south, spring 1929.

The Kundmanngasse, south perspective,
present situation.

rear is emphasized by the fourth block with its high windows and lean-to roof suggesting a massive, wide buttress.

The force of the 'architectural gesture' – a term used by Wittgenstein to point at the expressive power architecture can have – which is realized in this building arises from its undisguised verticals and horizontals, its bare greyish white plaster planes, and, of course, the asymmetry of its cubic disposition. In contrast to Engelmann's design, wall-planes take priority over window-planes: the distance between the windows is consistently smaller than the distance between the windows and the edges of a wall plane, while the parapets of the roof terraces are extensions of the outer elevations – all this contributes to the impression of resolve. The windows are longer than they are wide, with vertical divisions only, and they diminish in height on successive levels to suggest height. The upward thrust which is thus implied is in turn tempered by the equally severe horizontals which mark the top of the wall planes; there are no roof gutters and the roof-edge had been pared down to the absolute minimum.

100

The only detail that has on occasion been described as decoration, to relieve the severity of the design, is the cavetto moulding along the base of the side and front façades. Photographs of the house taken in 1928 during the final stages of construction show that this was added at the last moment. Since it does not occur on the elevations it would appear that it is a functional detail, the necessity of which was not realized until the building was nearly completed, to drain rainwater off to the 1 foot 4 inch wide concrete collar which encircles the house. The same applies to the drip edge along the bottom of the front door that is also absent from these photographs.

The Kundmanngasse, east perspective, present situation.

101

Construction

As neither Engelmann nor Wittgenstein had professional experience in building, the responsibility for the technical drawings and the calculation of the building specifications rested with Jacques Groag. Indeed, it is certain that much of the preparatory work was done by him and his assistant. Given his thorough technical training at the *Technische Hochschule* where he studied for his engineer's degree, then at the *Adolf Loos Bauschule* and probably also in several construction firms closely associated with modern building, it comes as no surprise that the structure of the Kundmanngasse conforms to the latest building techniques of the time. Load-bearing outer walls of stuccoed brick enclose a framework of concrete supports, some of which are reinforced. Concrete ribs held up by concrete crossbeams resting on the supports and the outer walls underpin the floors. These pillars and concrete ribs form the structural framework of the main block and make possible the open, asymmetrical plan of the beletage and the arbitrary layout of the upper floors, for the inner walls, which are made of prefabricated wall elements, are not load-bearing. They also support the flat rooftops as well as the partial roofing of the south terrace by the third block. The stairwell and lift shaft are formed by a grid of 12 slender concrete pillars with concrete cross-ribs supporting the staircase, erected in the west corner of the structural framework.

Top: The cavetto moulding along the base of the side and front façades, 1971.
Above: Shoe-scraper beside the steps leading to the service entrance (the main entrance originally had the same type of shoe-scrapers on both sides).

The glass lean-to roof was constructed of thin steel V-girders (these were regrettably replaced by heavy steel H-beams during the renovation of 1976). The roof of the main block, which has three skylights over the corridor on the second floor, was covered with zinc; it sloped down from the centre to a gutter on the inside of the parapet which was inadequately constructed and leaked more than once. The terraces on the roofs of the wings and the overstepping block were flat and covered with square reddish-brown 'Czech tiles'.

The fine-grained plaster of the exterior walls showed a natural, very light grey colour. The interior walls are covered with off-white plaster in the hallway and with *stucco lustro* in very light shades in the rooms. The floor slabs which cover almost the whole area of the ground floor are made of artificial stone which gets its lustrous dark colour from coal tar. Stairs and landings are of finegrained grey granito. The rooms on the upper floors have parquet flooring; the kitchen and bathrooms had tiles. The ceilings were probably whitewashed in white or off-white. The doors on the ground floors and all the windows were made of steel and were designed during the building period, as were the cast iron radiators; the doors on the upper floors were made of wood.

The unobtrusive precision with which the construction work was executed contributed greatly to the powerful plasticity of the interior and exterior of the Kundmanngasse. Corners and edges were constructed with mathematical accuracy and were finished with knife-edge plasterwork. One may, by the way, wonder to what extent Groag's own feeling for perfection and

The Kundmanngasse as seen from the corner Kundmanngasse - Geusaugasse, present situation.

Far left: View from the south-east, spring 1929.

Left: South-west façade seen from the driveway, spring 1929.

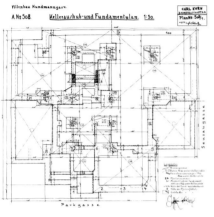 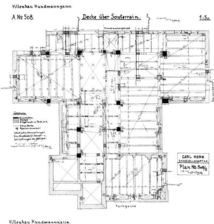

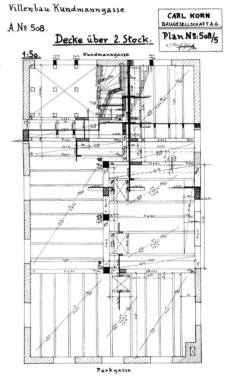

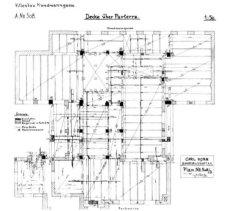 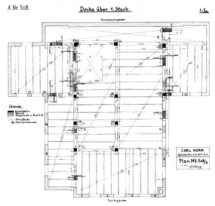

preference for visually elegant but technically difficult solutions, obvious from his later architectural work, enabled Wittgenstein to attain his goals. At any rate, the survey of 1976 made it clear that the dimensions and disposition of the windows and doors corresponded with the plans to the last quarter-inch, which meant that all symmetries were perfectly accurate too. The meticulous finishing must have demanded the utmost effort on the part of the builders and craftsmen involved — and have driven the building costs to astronomical heights.

Roof construction drawing (above), basement excavation and foundation plan (far left top) and floor construction drawing of the ground floor (middle top), November 1926.

Floor construction drawings of the first floor (far left) and second floor (middle), November 1926.

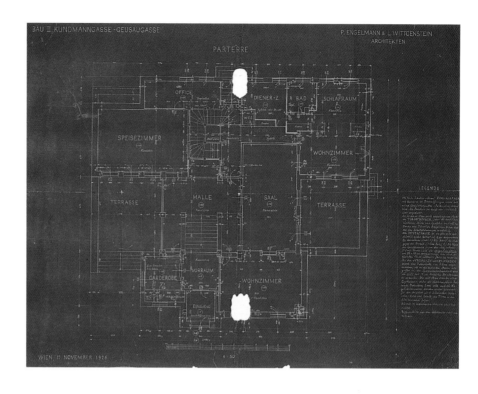

Plan of the ground floor, definitive version.
Eingang = enclosed porch; *Saal* = large drawing room; *Vorraum* = vestibule; *Garderobe* = cloak-room; *Waschraum* = restroom; *Halle* = hallway; *Terrasse* = terrace; *Wohnzimmer* = family living room (usually referred to as 'library');
Speisezimmer = dining room; *Office* = pantry; *Aufzug* = lift; *Diener Zimmer* = servant's room; *Bad* = bathroom; *Schlafraum* = sleeping room (used as boudoir); *Wohnzimmer* = living room (Margaret Stonborough's salon). *Kunststein* = artificial stone; *Tonplatten* = tiles; *Brettl* = parquet.

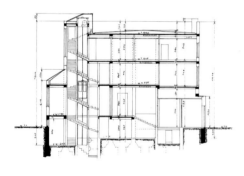

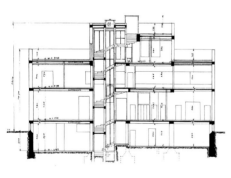

North-west - south-east section (far above) and south-west - north-east section (above), November 1926.

The plan of the beletage

The plan of the main floor, which is remarkably similar to the ground floor plan of the seventh phase loosely inserted in Engelmann's sketchbook, immediately reveals the purpose of the shallow block added to the rear façade: it creates the space necessary to situate Margaret Stonborough's private rooms on the beletage – as seems to have been the intention from the beginning – by reversing the position of Margaret's rooms and the family living room (referred to as the library by the family). Though we cannot be certain about the arrangement of rooms in the main floor plan of Engelmann's tenth phase, its outline implies that, as in the seventh phase, only Margaret's private living room was situated on the beletage while her other rooms, on the first floor, could be reached by way of a staircase. The plan of the seventh phase reveals two such staircases which are added as *ad hoc* elements rather at odds with the overall design, one in the *Salon* (probably meant as Margaret's private salon), the other in the family living room (this one lacks a landing which makes it awkward).

Wittgenstein's extension comprised a salon, a dressing room, a bathroom, and a servant's room – the last three connected by a corridor – and a second corridor leading from the salon to the stairwell which linked Margaret Stonborough's rooms as a separate apartment and gave a secondary, 'informal' plan, to the main, 'formal', plan of beletage. It also created space for a toilet (absent in Engelmann's plan), a large pantry behind the dining room, a separate service entrance at the rear of the house, and a spacious staircase erected around an open lift shaft, which receives full daylight through the glass of the lean-to roof. Further major changes to

104

c	closet
⊞	tiles
	door
⊢	light bulb on projecting pole
	cavetto moulding over concrete collar
–	shoesraper
-----	original situation uncertain
	parquet
	grid of flooring slabs
	door
—+—	window
	metal curtain
⊠	lift
	hot air outlet
	central heating radiator
•	location of light bulb on ceiling
	electrical switch or plug-socket

meter   yard

Engelmann's ground floor plan concern the subdivision of the entrance into a slightly projecting enclosed porch and vestibule, and the elevation of the breakfast room floor to mezzanine level in order to create sufficient height for a cloakroom and rest room adjacent to the vestibule.

By interchanging the family living room and Margaret's private salon the primary, 'formal', plan of the beletage encloses the representative and shared family rooms – vestibule, *Saal* (which is also the music room), dining room, south terrace, stairwell, the family living room (which is also the library), and breakfast room. Their interior layout is, even more so than in Engelmann's plan, strictly symmetrical but, as in Engelmann's plan, they are asymmetrically arranged around the central hallway. Their mutually asymmetrical ordering emphasizes the change of their identity when going from one room to the other; their internal symmetry reflects repose.

The rooms of the mistress of the house can only be reached by way of the *Saal* within the formal plan or by way of the corridor within the informal plan – they are rooms 'offstage', as it were, which guarantee a sufficient degree of privacy. Nevertheless, internal symmetry is as seriously maintained in her salon and dressing room as in the rooms of the formal plan.

A comparison of the measurements of the scale drawing of the ground floor plan of the seventh phase and those of the definitive plan of November 1926 lead to a number of interesting observations. The overall measures changed only little; the width by depth of Engelmann's plan is 23.65 metres by 17.20 metres, the final plan (excluding the shallow rear block which has a depth of 2.38 metres) measures 24.935 metres by 18.72 metres; the width

Reconstruction drawing of the ground floor plan as executed.

105

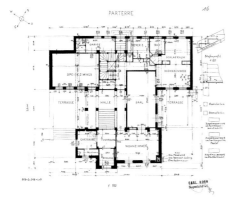

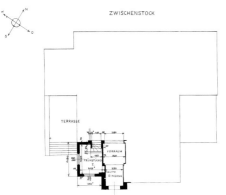

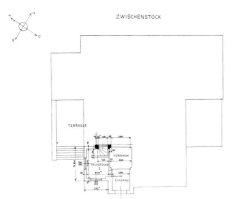

Above from top to bottom: Plans of the ground floor, second version and the mezzanine (breakfast room), first version and second version. November 1926

of both wings was hardly altered at all. Indeed, even the interior measurements vary little: Engelmann's *Saal* (referred to as music room) measures 9.10 metres by 4.40 metres while in the final plan its width by depth is 9.30 metres by 4.80 metres; the width by depth of the two dining rooms are 7.90 metres by 5.90 metres and 8.10 metres by 5.50 metres, respectively. The hallway, however, expanded: from the near square of 5.65 metres by 5.60 metres to the near square of 6.40 metres by 6.45 metres, causing the entrance and stairwell to be broadened and the terraces to be stretched. Furthermore, the front room, subdivided in Engelmann's design into salon and billiard room, became one shorter, deeper, room – the family living room.

Apart from the obvious practicality and the advantage of having more spacious corridors etc, the addition of the shallow rear block does not necessitate these changes and we may ask why they were made at all. As will be explained in the next chapter, there is a suggestion of the application of a geometrical proportional system, although in only two cases have either proportional section or ratio been found exact. Even the hallway is not an exact square. However, it is certain that the proportions of the hallway are subject to the same principle of symmetry which, in all the interior spaces, concerns the positioning of the windows and doors within the wall planes, the grids formed by the flooring-slabs, and the placing of the lamp sockets in the axes of the ceilings. Comparison of the subsequent plans of the ground floor that have come down to us and the survey of 1976 reveal that a small number of opportunistic alterations were made to restore symmetry even in those rooms in which proportional irregularities, caused by a symmetrical design of the other rooms, would necessarily accumulate.

These 'stop-gaps' in the overall plan are the library and, to a lesser extent, Margaret Stonborough's private living and dressing rooms, and the breakfast room. The position of the door between the *Saal* and the library is determined by its position in the axis of the *Saal*, which places it off any axis of the library. The elaborate solution was to suggest a symmetrical design of this wall in the library by adding a sham pillar mirroring the load-bearing concrete pillar next to the door between hall and library. It may even have determined the total length of the room, that is the exact placement of north-east wall of the main block. The painfully won symmetry of the room was, however, spoiled by the necessity of a flue in the east corner (the boiler room is directly beneath the library). Symmetry in Margaret Stonborough's salon was effected by partly thickening the wall between the door to the *Saal* and the glass door opening to the east terrace, thus demarcating the symmetrical part of the room, a division which was also reflected in the grid of the flooring-slabs (the projecting part of the wall is absent from the plans but was executed). In the dressing room the depth of the wooden cupboards which line the north-east wall, already drawn into the plans, has the same effect.

These adaptations prove that Wittgenstein did not hesitate to employ devices contrary to a strictly functionalist point of view to reach his aesthetic aims. Indeed, there are more such details: the sham second wall between the servant's room and the service entrance vestibule, the artificially thickened wall between the enclosed porch and the library, and the sham stretch of wall between the *Saal* and the library, inserted later, presumably to make a second set of two-winged doors on the library side at the same level of the wall plane. (Note also, in Section A-B, the artificially lowered ceiling of the enclosed porch and the vestibule, which creates an empty space above it with a height of 1.30 metre.)

The struggle for symmetry in the breakfast room has been amply described by Jan Turnovský. Obviously, Wittgenstein wanted the south-east window to be in the centre of both the exterior and the interior walls, which would have been impossible unless the wall between the breakfast room and the enclosed porch and vestibule were made twice as thick. Apart from the absurdity of wasting so much space for the sake of symmetry, an insoluble problem would have arisen regarding the placement of the door between hallway and breakfast room. The plans of the mezzanine, however, reveal a slight projection of a short stretch of the south-east wall towards its east corner so that the vertical symmetry axis of the window should coincide with the vertical symmetry axis of the south-east wall area thus shortened. In contrast to the thickened wall in Margaret Stonborough's salon, absent in the plans, this short stretch of projecting wall was certainly *not* executed, though the niche in the east corner was.

Small adaptations introduced in the approved plans include the removal of diagonal walls between the corridor, salon and dressing room reminiscent of Engelmann's designs which favoured straight walls that seem more consistent with the overall design and create more functional space. In the same way the straight staircase leading to the breakfast room which was actually built seems more consistent with the general axial structure and more space saving than the staircase with a turning of 90 degrees that was originally intended. A cupboard for china was split off from the pantry, which necessitated relocating the dumbwaiter.

The arrangement of folding glass doors and floorslabs. From top to bottom: The *Saal*, the dining room, the library and Margaret Stonborough's private salon.
Left: The problem of symmetrically proportioning both the exterior and interior south-east wall of the breakfast room. (After Turnovský 1987)

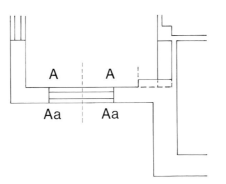

Entrance, vestibule and hallway

The low, slightly projecting entrance block is on the same level as the drive and provides entry to a quadrangular and bare enclosed porch that prevents the cold air from entering the house in winter. The vestibule behind it is slightly larger, also quadrangular, but has pilasters in its corners. The folding door to the cloakroom is placed in the symmetry-axis of the wall plane – the joint of the two-winged door meets the joint of the floor slabs exactly. A glass wall containing glass doors stands on the first step of a flight of stairs leading into the hallway and separates the latter from the vestibule. By climbing the stairs one rises from the relative darkness of the vestibule into the relative lightness of the hallway which receives daylight through its glass wall.

The characteristics of Wittgenstein's architecture are all evident in the interior design of the hallway. Upward thrust is stressed by the slender pillars and pilasters supporting the ceiling, by the tall doors, with glass panes partitioned vertically only, and by the height of the hallway itself (12 feet 6 inches). Symmetry in the ratio 1:2:4 marks the placement of pillars and pilasters, the width and the positioning of the doors in the wall planes, and the grid of the flooring-slabs with the sole exception of a hardly noticeable but intentional asymmetrical rhythm along the axis *Saal* entrance – south

Opposite page: Cross joint of the floor slabs in the hallway meets the floor slab of the *Saal* in the exact middle.

Below: View from the hallway towards the entrance, present situation.

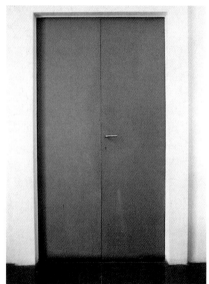

Top left: View from the vestibule into the
hallway, present situation.

Top centre: Hallway-stairs.

Top right: Hallway, view towards the south
terrace. Note the original silk lampshade
between the pillars.

Above: Vestibule, the folding door to the
cloakroom.

terrace entrance; joints meet the folding doors exactly in the middle. Austerity and anonymity, because of lack of any intrinsic structure, distinguish the materials used for the finishing: anthracite-coloured, shining artificial stone flooring, off-white plaster wall covering, a white plastered ceiling. The metal parts of the doors were painted a neutral grey or greyish-green with dull lustre. The double folding doors to the dining room and to the stairwell had clear glass on the hall side, but translucent milk glass on the other side so that, depending on which pair of doors was closed, an inviting or a reserved aspect could be achieved. The only opaque doors are those to the salon, thus emphasizing its status.

Extreme simplicity and perfection was practised in the details of finishing because Wittgenstein refused to use mouldings, skirting boards and thresholds. Walls, pillars and doors – the latter with a tolerance of about 1/16 inch, which is still intact after 50 years of use – join to the floor directly; window and door frames are anchored into the walls directly. Thanks to the cover provided by the overstepping tertiary block the hallway receives daylight indirectly rather than directly from the sky, which gives a softening effect of skimming light. At night it is lit from the centre by a single bulb placed between the two pillars.

Extreme simplicity also characterized its pre-war furnishing, which was limited to a plaster copy of the discus thrower in repose and vases of fresh flowers from Margaret Stonborough's country estate Toscana Park. There was only the contrast of the light lustrous walls, the shiny dark floors and the greyish-green doors.

As mentioned previously, the definitive plan of the hall is still Engelmann's. Wittgenstein did not, however, adopt Engelmann's columns crowned with chalice capitals and supporting crossbeams: he created his own 'order', stripped of any ornament. At that time the quadrangular pillar, not the column, was the most plausible form for the framework of the reinforced concrete support. It has no pedestal or base, its surface is smooth and it bears a slightly receding cushion. The width of the recess between cushion

Left: 'Wittgenstein's order'.

Centre: View from dining room through hallway towards breakfast room, 1975.

Above: View along the axis from the east terrace through the *Saal*-hallway door towards the south terrace, present situation.

Opposite page:

Pillar base on hallway floor, pillar and half-capital between glass wall-partitions separating the hallway from the south terrace, pillar base on stairs, pillar and half-capital against the northeast wall, pillar base between glass wall-partitions separating the hallway from the south terrace, pilaster and corner-capital in the north corner, detail of stairs leading to the breakfast room, and pilaster and corner-capital in the south corner.

perimeter and pillar perimeter is twice the width of the recess between the cushion perimeter and the even narrower cross-section of the ceiling beam it supports; the height of the cushion is half the pillar's width. The false ceiling beams extend lengthwise, parallel to the flight of stairs leading to the ground floor level; they thus suggest direction within an otherwise aimless cubic space.

Views across the hallway, present situation.

The *Saal*

The *Saal* (large drawing room) of the Kundmanngasse is the formal reception and entertainment room which has its precursor in the ballroom or
music room typical of the more grandiose *Palais*. Indeed the *Saal* was also
used for musical performances. The walls were covered with creamy white
stucco lustro that shone softly in the daylight, or at night in the even light
from three symmetrically arranged naked light bulbs in the axis of the ceiling. Emphasizing the formal importance of the room, all interior doors are
opaque; the folding doors to the library and to Margaret Stonborough's private salon are double, so that when closed no sound penetrated these rooms,
or *vice versa*. Between the double glass folding doors opening onto the east
terrace pink taffeta roller blinds could be lowered. Metal curtains could be
raised from the floor just between the inner pair of doors and the hot air outlets – the construction of these will be discussed in more detail below. Two
tall, specially made, rectangular mirrors in narrow gilt frames were hung
between the three two-winged doors in the north-east wall of the salon.

View from the library into the *Saal*,
present situation.

113

Above: Interior of the *Saal*, south corner, prewar.
Crayon drawing by Hermine Wittgenstein.

Wittgenstein did not allow carpets, wall-covering, drapery or chandeliers; in fact, anything that would detract from the architecture of the house or suggest the kind of interior design typical of the *fin de siècle*, as for example to be found in the Alleegasse. In the same spirit Margaret furnished the *Saal* sparingly. At first she was afraid that her *Wiener Werkstätte* and antique furniture, her plaster copies of classical sculpture, her Chinese scrolls and folding screens and her glass cases displaying valuable objects and bibelots would clash with the style of the house, but it happened that Wittgenstein's architecture formed a perfect subdued background for them. Moreover, she rearranged her furniture from time to time so that architecture and furniture could be experienced from different aspects. As a family friend put it:

I think the most stunning and liberating theme of the house was the absence of ornaments, wallpaper, painted walls, knick-knacks, etc. Thus the proportions of everything were important.

How important these proportions were to Wittgenstein will be explained later, but may be illustrated here by the story that when the house was virtually completed in autumn 1928, he was not satisfied with the dimensions of the *Saal*; the ceiling had to be pulled down in order to construct a new one just 3 cm higher.

Above: View towards the east corner of the *Saal* with door to the library. The chair on the lower right is by Kolo Moser of the *Wiener Werkstätte*. Charcoal drawing by Hermine Wittgenstein.
Right: Interior of the *Saal*, south corner, postwar.

114

Dining room, library and breakfast room

The dining room is equal in its proportional harmony to the austere beauty of the *Saal* and contained only those few pieces of furniture necessary to fulfil its function: a large table in the centre and some chairs against the wall ready to be drawn up if needed. On the walls, plastered with creamy white *stucco lustro*, hung panels of a Chinese folding screen painted with floral motifs. Margaret preferred to apply colours only in fabrics, for example in upholstery and the taffeta roller blinds, which in this room were a greyish-blue colour. An opaque metal folding door leads from the dining room to the pantry which contains the dumb waiter rising from the basement kitchen.

The large room at the front of the house, indicated in the original plans as the family living room (*Wohnzimmer*), was referred to by the family as the library because of the bookshelves covering its walls. It was the least consistently proportioned room and because of a less sparse, more convenient furnishing and the presence of books and a writing desk, it had a more informal, intimate atmosphere.

The breakfast room, furnished only with taut Hoffmann chairs around an elaborate Chinese table, was hardly used as such.

Top: South-east wall of the *Saal* with door to the library. The sculpture between the two discoboli is Jean Baptiste Carpeaux's *Pourquoi naître esclave*. Pencil drawing by Hermine Wittgenstein. Above: North-east corner of the *Saal* with closed door to Margaret Stonborough's private salon. Pencil drawing by Hermine Wittgenstein.

115

Top: The dining room, present situation.
Top right: Breakfast room and dining room
(above right)

Above: Interior of the library, prewar. Visible to
the left is a corner of the writing desk by Josef
Hoffmann. Crayon drawing by Hermine
Wittgenstein.

Right: Writing desk by Josef Hoffmann (chairs by
Kolo Moser), here in the Stonboroughs's Berlin
apartment furnished by the *Wiener Werkstätte*,
which found its way to the library of the
Kundmanngasse.

Margaret Stonborough's private rooms

Margaret's private rooms comprised a salon and a dressing room, a bathroom and a servant's room, and a private corridor connecting them; it did not have a separate bedroom. It was her idea that the salon and dressing room should be separated – or rather connected – by an open space in the partition wall into which her bed fitted exactly; during the day the bed was covered with a silk bedspread and used as a sofa. It was possible to get from one room to the other through one of the cupboards flanking the bed. In the living room these cupboards had mirror-doors; the holes for the door handle of the left door and the key of the right door were cut directly into the glass. The living room also had a mantelpiece made of the same artificial stone as the flooring-slabs.

The double folding doors between the *Saal* and private salon – opaque on the *Saal* side, clear glass on the salon side – permitted a similar double aspect as the doors to the dining room or stairwell in the hall: seclusion when the opaque doors were closed, invitation when only the glass doors were shut.

Top left: Interior of Margaret Stonborough's private salon, prewar. To the left the bed-sofa within the open space connecting salon and boudoir. Crayon drawing by Hermine Wittgenstein.

Top right: Library, postwar, showing the original bookshelves against the northeast wall.

Above centre: Interior of Margaret Stonborough's private salon, postwar. Note the mirror door to the closet in the background.

Above: 'Private' corridor leading from the stairwell to Margaret Stonborough's private rooms, present situation.

117

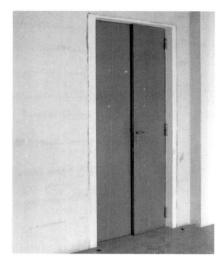

Right: The left mirror door giving access to the boudoir by way of a closet. To the left the steel door to the private corridor. Situation in 1975.
Far right: Library, folding doors to the *Saal* which have now disappeared. Situation in 1975.

Precision metal work of the drip edge on the front door.

Door and window furniture

Wittgenstein's training as a mechanical engineer and unerring feeling for the logic of mechanical construction enabled him to design the moving parts of the house with the same precision that served him in his philosophical pursuits. The design of the fastenings, latches and locks clearly imply a mechanical interpretation of Occam's Razor, 'simplicity is the hallmark of truth': if the need for additional parts could be reduced by a logically more elegant design of the essential parts, then this should be preferred. For the window and door frames Wittgenstein employed existing shaped iron parts of standard size as far as possible; door and lock handles were made of brass. The same criterion of simplicity and availability held for his selection of switches, wall and lamp sockets, taps, piping, parts of the heating system, etc.

On the ground floor the opaque doors are made of metal sheets screwed on to metal frames; the bolts are concealed beneath layers of red-lead and paint. There are no rims, mouldings, covering plates or rings: the doorhandle disappears without any visible intermediary parts in a hole of exactly its own diameter, the keyhole is cut directly out of the metal sheet. One half of the handle is just a polished brass bar bent at right angles; the complementary half is bent in a contrary manner, a bolt with ring through a transversely placed cylinder fastens it to its counterpart. The heavy doors are hinged in narrow metal doorposts and hang by three hinges each; the middle hinge lies in the point of application of force when the doorhandle is being pushed or pulled and supports the door, the lower and upper ones guide it. The leaves of the hinges fit so exactly into the doorposts as to be invisible beneath the layers of red-lead and paint.

The design of the glass doors and windows is a masterpiece of mechanical construction because of the extreme rigidity necessary to prevent the narrow tall glass panes from breaking (the largest of these measure 10 7/8 inches by 9 feet 10 inches, a ratio of about 1:10!). Therefore, the door frame

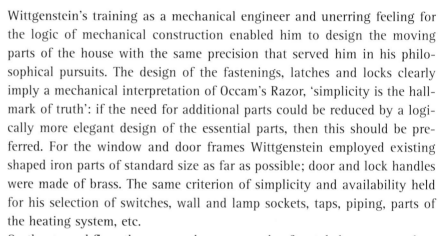

118

is constructed of screwed steel angle sections; the glass panes are set into narrow sections that also serve as cross-pieces and were specially shaped for this purpose – the glass sheets are secured in position by screwed wooden or metal strips. The lock and door-handle mechanism is enclosed in its own casing mounted on the glass door frame. According to Heinrich Postl with the help of a screwdriver all the doors and windows could easily be taken apart for maintenance.

As is common in Austria, all glass doors and windows in the façades are double-glazed to insulate the interior against winter temperatures. Both the outer and the inner doors and windows open inwards; by means of a clamp mounted on the outer doors and windows, the outer and corresponding inner wings can be fastened against each other in any position. The outer wings are locked with a simple hook, the inner ones by an espagnolette mechanism that is of a common Austrian type, but was completely redesigned by Wittgenstein. The metalwork was painted greyish-green, the door and window handles were of polished brass. The windows have roller blinds, the strips of which were originally of metal, running in two vertical grooves, invisible when not in use, with the roller mechanism hidden in the exterior wall. They were operated by narrow woven tapes.

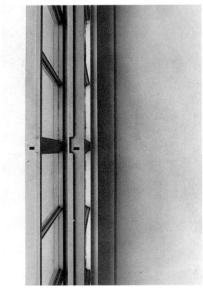

The glass doors in the outer walls of the beletage can be curtained off by metal sheets pulled up by means of a hook from the floor between the inner pair of doors and the hot air outlets in front of them. They fit exactly into the doorways and work easily by means of a counterweight mechanism and a pair of wheels guided by narrow grooves in the walls on both sides of the doorways. In sunken position they hang in niches in the basement walls; these are covered by metal sheets coated with a soundproofing material. A metal covering plate along the upper edge of the curtain, exactly level with the air outlets and flooring-slabs, hides the wheel-mechanism from view. Such curtains were also planned for the glass wall in the hallway but they do not appear in the finished house, probably due to insurmountable technical difficulties caused by the large area to be covered. The curtains were pulled up at night or when the family left the house.

Top: Glass doors between hallway and south terrace, just after completion of the Kundmanngasse.
Above centre and above: Precision metal work on the glass doors between hallway and south terrace.

119

Page 120: Hallway, the dining room doors with milk glass, present situation.

Page 121, from left to right:

Top: Doorhandles of the *Saal*-door, from left to right, hallway-side, construction and *Saal*-side second row: Fingerlock of the *Saal*-door, key of the *Saal*-door and folding doorhandle of the door to Margaret Stonborough's salon.

Third row: Doorhandles and lock mechanisms of the interior glass doors, and espagnolette mechanism of inner folding doors.

Bottom: Doorhandles and lock mechanisms of the interior glass doors, and the hook locks into the slightly raised threshold between the pair of folding doors.

Right: Glass doors in exterior wall, clamp mechanism.

Right: Glass doors in exterior wall, hook locking the outer folding doors

Far right: Window lock of boudoir and pantry windows.

122

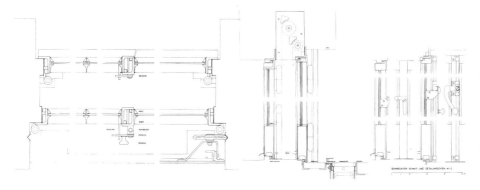

Far left: Glass doors in exterior wall, cross-section including metal curtain roller mechanism.

Left: Glass doors in exterior wall, longitudinal section inlcuding metal curtain construction and lock construction of glass doors in exterior wall, longitudinal and cross-sections.

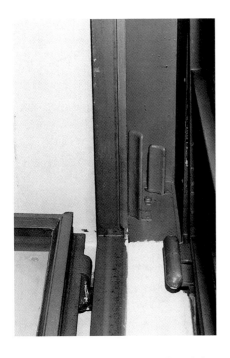

Heating and electrical installation

The ground floor is heated by three different means. Underfloor heating is used in those rooms that have artificial stone flooring; this consists of a piping system laid in the concrete floor which supports the stone slabs. Underfloor heating is indeed the only answer to the problem of keeping houses with stone flooring north of the Alps comfortable in the cold season. In the Kundmanngasse it is supplemented by hot-air outlets in front of the windows and the glass doors which open out on to the terraces. These outlets were probably inlets as well, for beneath them are reservoirs provided with a drain cock in the bottom to drain off surplus water after cleaning the floors – the hot air enters these reservoirs from an opening in one side. (Another plausible explanation might be that these reservoirs were part of a humidifier system.) Other rooms and those rooms on the upper floors are heated by hot water radiators. Most of these were placed in corners (like the usual Austrian tiled stoves) and were therefore constructed in two halves connected at an angle of 90 degrees. On stone flooring they

Above from left to right: Roller mechanism for the taffeta roller blinds between the double doors, opened niche in basement with metal curtain counterweight mechanism and detail of covering plate along the upper edge of a metal curtain, exactly level with the air outlet in front of the inner glass door.

123

rested on plain wooden blocks, possibly for acoustic or thermal insulation, elsewhere they were mounted on thin iron legs; they were unpainted, showing the anthracite colour of cast iron. The stairwell is heated by a radiator constructed of thick pipes on the terrace beneath the glass lean-to roof.

The main lighting consisted of naked 200 watt bulbs screwed into bare sockets placed into the axis of the ceiling within the symmetrical layout of the room. At first Wittgenstein experimented with coverings of translucent silk mounted on a fragile cone-shaped frame suspended from the ceiling, but these did not satisfy him. His aim seems to have been a completely even, artificial lighting in harmony with the reserved and symmetrical quality of the rooms. Floor and table lamps were used as direct light sources where needed. The switches he chose for the ground floor were black with a white knob (these were made of porcelain, as was usual at the time); all the sockets and switches on the upper floors were white. Each of the outside light fixtures above the entrance doors and on the terraces consisted again of a naked bulb and socket, mounted at a right angle at the far end of a short bar that projected straight out of the wall.

According to Heinrich Postl the internal telephone system and electric bell system for summoning servants was also ingeniously designed by Wittgenstein, but the details of these have been lost.

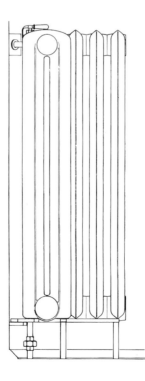

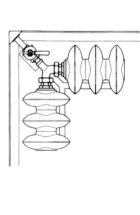

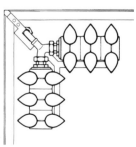

124

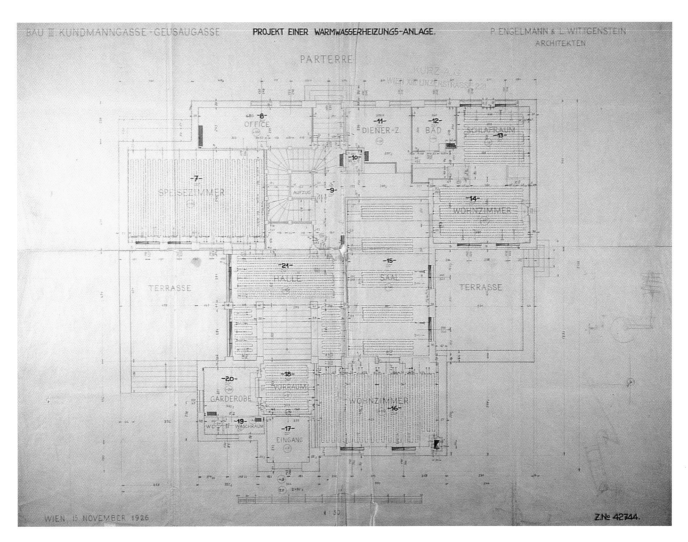

Above: Plan of the heating system on the ground floor, November 1926.
Aufzug = lift.

Opposite site, from top to bottom:
Ceiling lamp on the landing of the first floor, original porcelain switches on the ground floor and lamp above the main entrance

Opposite site: Reconstruction drawing and cross-section of corner radiator on upper floor.

Far left: Radiator in the water closet on the first floor, showing the original cast iron colour and supporting wooden blocks.

Left: Corner radiator in breakfast room.

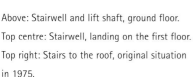

Above: Stairwell and lift shaft, ground floor.

Top centre: Stairwell, landing on the first floor.

Top right: Stairs to the roof, original situation in 1975.

Right: Corner pilaster and pilaster on stairs.

Opposit site:

Top left: Roof of lift cage as seen from the stairs.

Left centre: Lift hoisting machine.

Right: Construction drawings of lift,
March 1927 signed by Baumeister Friedl and
Ludwig Wittgenstein.

Stairwell and lift

The stairwell is supported by 12 slender pillars that form a modular grid of squares between the reinforced concrete supports in the west corner of the main block. The lift shaft is defined by the four inner pillars. The staircase ascends on three sides around it, supported on the outside by the remaining eight pillars which are visible as pilasters. On the fourth side are the landings of each floor on to which the lift doors open. The steps and skirting boards are made of fine grained grey granito; the five steps in each corner square fan out symmetrically from the inner pillar. The walls and pillars were covered with cream coloured *stucco lustro*. The stairwell receives daylight through the glass lean-to roof of the fourth block and, on the upper floors, through tall windows in the north-west elevation. The cool north-west light generates soft contrasts in the planes and curves of the

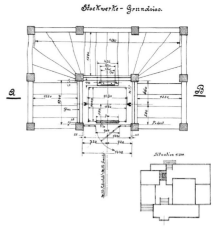

Stockwerke-Grundriss.

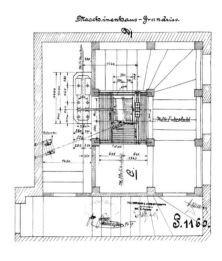

Maschinenhaus-Grundriss.

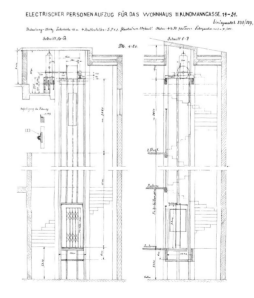

ELECTRISCHER PERSONEN AUFZUG FÜR DAS WOHNHAUS III KUNDMANNGASSE 19-21.

stairwell suggesting the experience of rising into mathematical space.

The lift shaft is separated from the staircase by glass panes between the four inner pillars. The transparency of the shaft and the movement of the lift, together with the fact that the pillars and pilasters are not covered by the granito baseboards in between them, again accentuate verticality. The lift cage also has large glass windows. Thus the functioning of the lift mechanism, constructed by the firm of Stigler in close collaboration with Wittgenstein, is not hidden from view, but is naturally incorporated in the architecture of the house; this effect includes the definite sounds of opening and closing metal doors, of bolting and unbolting relays and of the humming hoisting engine which is visible from the uppermost stairs.

Page 128: Stairwell and lift, ground floor, present situation.
Page 129, top: Landing on the first floor, present situation.
Bottom left: Sewing room with the glass lean-to roof, original situation in 1975.
Bottom right: The glass lean-to roof, original situation in 1975.

Right: Stairs to the second floor, curvature of the ceiling (far right), present situation.

Right: Stairs to the second floor and stairs to the roof (far right), present situation.

The upper floors

It has been noted in the preceding chapter that the final design contains all the rooms that had been planned in the fourth phase of Engelmann's sketchbook. Apart from the grid underlying the construction of the stairwell, one cannot conceive of any principle of symmetry, with the sole exception of the front rooms on the first floor, nor of any proportional system determining the layout of the upper floors. Their plans seem to have been chiefly determined by practical considerations and lack the harmonious character of the ground floor plan. The arrangement of rooms on the first floor even seems contrived: to fill the spacious floor area large storage rooms were planned on both sides of the dark corridors, and the second version eliminated even the intended continuation of the sham pillars of the hallway beneath on the south-west side of the main corridor. The load-bearing pillars on the north-east side of the corridor were hidden in cupboards which lined the wall, which, like the built-in cupboards in the private corridor of the beletage, may have been constructed at the instigation of Jacques Groag. The first and second versions of the first floor plan contain the private rooms of Jerome Stonborough and his servant and, presumably, a guest-room, further rooms for servants and Margaret Stonborough's secretary, and for her dressmaker and her garderobe. Alterations indicated on the blueprint dated 10 January 1927, and confirmed by the survey of 1976, mainly concern the relocation or omission of doors and partition walls.

The second floor contains rooms for the children, the governess, guests and servants in addition to two bathrooms. Originally it also had a breakfast room for the children and their governess, but the blueprint of 10 January 1927 shows the layout as it was finally executed: the room has been converted into a large landing and partition walls and doors have been relocated, changing the dimensions of most of the rooms. As on the first floor, the space between the load-bearing pillars along the corridor has been filled with wooden cupboards, while the flue in the room in the east corner was also concealed by built-in cupboards flush with it. A second alteration concerned the parapet of the terrace along the children's rooms; its sloping edge was made narrower to enlarge the terrace and provided with a railing. The smooth wooden doors on the upper floors are painted grey and hinged in wooden doorposts. The lock mechanism casing is screwed on to the door panel on the corridor side. The polished brass doorhandles, again simple bars but on both sides of identical form, are a little shorter than those of the ground floor doors, and assembled in the traditional way.

The first floor corridor consists of the same artificial stone as was used on the ground floor but without the grid. The rooms all have parquet floors laid crosswise in a rectangular grid. This type of parquet is more difficult to lay than the usual herringbone pattern, but is, of course, much more in sympathy with the architecture of the house. The bathrooms were furnished according to the standards of luxury of the day, though again the most

Top: South corner room on the first floor.
Crayon drawing by Hermine Wittgenstein.
Above: East corner room on the first floor.
Pencil drawing by Hermine Wittgenstein.

Interior of east corner room on the first floor, postwar.

functional furniture design was chosen and there was no decoration. Here, as in the toilets, the floor was covered with small hexagonal yellowish-brown tiles; the wall tiles were square and white.

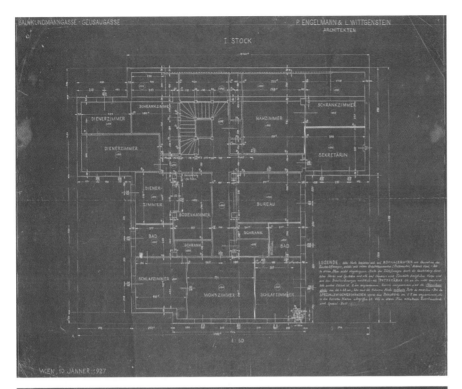

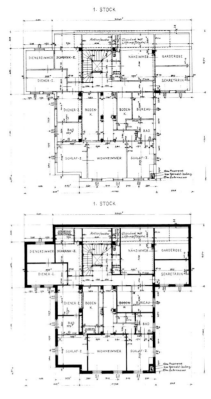

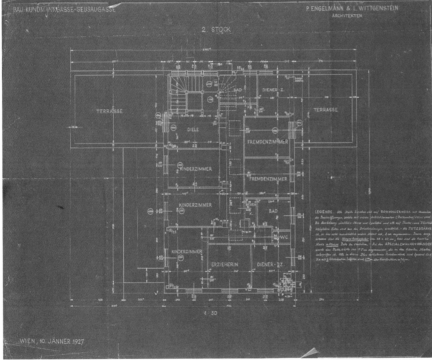

Top left: Plan of the first floor, definitive version.
Bad = bathroom; *Schlafzimmer* = sleeping room;
Wohnzimmer = living room; *Diener-Z.* = servant's
room; *Büreau* = study; *Bodenkammer* = storage
room; *Schrank* = closet; *Schrankzimmer* = closet
room; *Nähzimmer* = dressmaker's room;
Sekretärin = secretary.

Top right: Plan of the first floor, first version
and second version (centre), November 1926.

Above: First version , November 1926.

Left: Plan of the second floor, definitive version.
Terrasse = terrace; *Diele* = landing; *Kinderzimmer*
= children's room; *Erzieherin* = governess; *Diener-
Z.* = servant's room; *Besen-K.* = broom closet;
Bad = bathroom; *Fremdenzimmer* = guestroom.

133

134

Page 134:

Top left: Westernmost children's room, original situation in 1975.

Top right: The kitchen, original situation in 1975.

Bottom left: Southernmost children's room. Pencil drawing by Hermine Wittgenstein.

Right: Hand-turned key of a door on the upper floors.

Bottom right: Dumbwaiter doors in the pantry.

Page 135:

Top, from left to right: First floor, door to the front room, present situation, wooden closets lining the corridor, detail of interior and doors.

Centre, from left to right: Second floor, closet with key (left) and doors to the northeast rooms, present situation, second floor, built-in closets along the corridor, present situation.

Bottom, from left to right: Window latch in the garderobe, dumbwaiter and window latch/handle and opening the kitchen window.

Top right: First floor, view of the front room, present situation.

Right: First floor, servant's room above the dining room, present situation.

Door to the pantry and stairs to the basement.

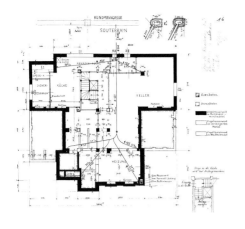

Plan of the basement, first version (top), November 1926, and second version (above). *Diener-Essraum* = servant's dining room; *Küche* = kitchen; *Abwasch-Küche* = scullery; *Keller* = cellar; *Aufzug* = lift; *Aufzugsmaschine* = lift hoisting machine; *Heizung* = central heating; *K.(urtinen)* = (iron) curtains; *Waschküche* = laundry; *Bad* = bathroom.

The basement

As for the plan of the basement it is interesting to note the presence of the niches for the metal curtains that could be drawn up in front of the ground floor windows, without doubt one of Wittgenstein's inventions, and therefore strong evidence that he was responsible for these plans. Furthermore, the lift hoisting engine, deleted from the second plan, was eventually placed in the superstructure on the roof of the main block. The servants' dining rooms were the rooms in which Milli Vogl, the cook, and butler/chauffeur Heinrich Postl lived. What is not shown on the plans is the entrance, in the boiler room below the north-east window, to the underground passage which leads to the garage and fuel storage rooms in the basements of the converted buildings at the corner of the lot.

The large and well-furnished kitchen was situated in the basement, beneath the pantry and dining room. The relatively high position of the basement windows and their design made it necessary to modify the locks and handles. These show the same precise construction as the window furniture on the ground and upper floors.

The boilers were installed in a room beneath the library, and had to be at a deeper level because of the dimensions of the system. Curved tiles linking floor and wall tiles prevent dirt accumulating. The bare concrete staircase leading to this engine room of the Kundmanngasse, the concrete pillars supporting the upper floors, and all the mechanical parts of the heating machinery were proportioned and finished with the same care as other architectural details of the house.

'Architecture is a *gesture*'   5

So far we have discussed Ludwig Wittgenstein's alterations and additions to Engelmann's design for the Kundmanngasse and described the exterior and interior as it was when Margaret Stonborough and her family lived in it before the Second World War. To be able to understand the house as an architectural achievement we must also determine to what extent its distinguishing features make it different from the origins and formal characterization of Engelmann's initial design. Furthermore, as Wittgenstein was striving for an 'authentically modern' design, we should examine what his idea of modernity, as expressed by the Kundmanngasse, amounted to and how it relates to the modern architecture of his time.

Wittgenstein did not change the overall conception of the ground floor plan and cubic arrangement of the building, and so adopted as its main roots the mixture of the traditional Viennese *Palais*-architecture and the *villa suburbana* that was basic to Engelmann's design, together with a general asymmetric layout which seems partly descended from Loos's modernist programme, partly influenced, although not explicitly acknowledged, by other, contemporary, modernist examples. The fact that the hallway of the Kundmanngasse is reminiscent of the grand staircase and *Galerie* of the Alleegasse may suggest a comparison with the nineteenth century Ringstraße *Palais*, which may help us to understand Wittgenstein's architecture. However, we also know that Wittgenstein had a great admiration for Viennese baroque, in particular for the work of Johann Bernhard Fischer von Erlach (1656–1723). Fischer is the architect of such well-known classicist baroque buildings as the Karl Borromäus Church, the *Hofbibliothek* (Court Library) and the Schönbrunn Palace, but he also designed a number of aristocratic city palaces and has been called the father of Viennese *Palais*-architecture. Among the palaces is numbered the *Palais* Batthyány-Schönborn in the Renngasse (1698–1705), the *Prunk-Etage* (main floor or beletage) of which was rented by Margaret Stonborough before she moved into the Kundmanngasse. From what follows it will become clear that some of the aspects of the architecture of the Kundmanngasse can be better understood by comparing them to Fischer's aristocratic city mansions and the nineteenth century *Palais*.

Besides the plans for Loos's *Palais* Bronner, which cannot yet be regarded as an outstanding example of his conception of New Objectivity, an example of architecture of the 1920s must also be studied; it is the Villa Moller in Vienna XVIIIth, designed by Adolf Loos and built under the supervision of the same architect who was responsible for the structural specifications and calculations for the Kundmanngasse, Paul Engelmann's friend Jacques Groag. Moreover, it was built during the same period as the Kundmanngasse was 1927–28. Admittedly its total floor area and the number of rooms amount to a little less than half the floor area and number of rooms of the Kundmanngasse, but this difference reflects Loos's concept of modern architecture – that it should be attuned to the more modest means and needs of the well-to-do businessman in the new, post-feudal, industrial society. This concept, together with the care with which the Villa Moller was executed and with which finishing materials were chosen and used, make it a perfect contemporaneous modernist counterpart of the Kundmanngasse.

The architecture of the exterior

With regard to the exterior of the Kundmanngasse, it is obvious that Wittgenstein purified Engelmann's classicizing design. Engelmann himself had never envisaged a main entablature or window pediments, and possibly he had considered but rejected employing the colossal order for the façade. Later he abandoned the window mouldings, but he kept the base, an upper storey that may be interpreted as a diminished attic storey (the wall area between the attic windows and the windows of the floor below leaves ample space for a main entablature, while the wall area between windows and balustrade does not), and a balustrade. Wittgenstein, however, removed the attic storey (which does not seem to have been a real fourth floor), thereby lowering the roof-edge of the main façade, and cleared away the last remnants of Engelmann's ornamentation. Note that the classicizing baroque architect Fischer von Erlach, in contrast to other baroque city palace designers such as Johann Lucas von Hildebrandt and Domenico Martinelli, also left out the attic storey from his *Palais* (and other buildings).

The fact that Wittgenstein accepted the twofold lineage of Engelmann's design is evidenced by his alterations to the main entrance of the house and the south terrace, both situated along the driveway. He replaced the southeast part of the low parapet of the south terrace, which formed a second entrance with direct access to the hallway, with broad, inviting steps, as was customary in the Palladian style of the country villa. On the other hand, the reason for changing the position of the main entrance, which was level with the front of the main block in Engelmann's design, to a slightly projecting low block in Wittgenstein's, may be only understood by reference to the protruding or projecting portal typical of the Viennese baroque *Palais* (not of the nineteenth century *Palais* where it is level with the façade and usually crowned by a balcony). The baroque portal has three things in common with Wittgenstein's design. First, the entrance at 'street' level, which in the *Palais* allows a coach to pass through and to stop at the foot of the stairs up to the beletage; in the Kundmanngasse it allows the motorcar to be driven as close as possible to the enclosed porch (in the elevations and perspective drawing it is provided with a pergola-like thoroughfare). Secondly, the height has been limited – in the *Palais* it corresponds to the two-storey rusticated base which is the same height as the thoroughfare, and in Wittgenstein's design, where the mezzanine between basement and beletage has been left out, it corresponds to the well chosen proportions of the entrance. Finally, Wittgenstein seems to have deducted the depth of the entrance block from the example of the baroque portal which was limited to that of a column backed by a pilaster.

The bare wall-planes with the oblong window openings, defined by their light-and-dark contrasts only, which were the result of Wittgenstein's 'purification', had to be reproportioned to restore the harmony which had previously been provided by ornamental devices. It is interesting to see that Wittgenstein found it necessary to elaborate on the asymmetrical relationships originally introduced by Engelmann to achieve the necessary tension between clearly demarcated cubic masses within a balanced compositional whole. In Engelmann's design the entrance is asymmetrically placed in the left bay of the main building, not in the centre bay, but still on its axis of symmetry. Wittgenstein, however, exploits the asymmetry by moving the entrance to the left within a low projecting block, outside the axis of symmetry of the left bay. The effect is to give greater emphasis to the entrance, humble though it is, while at the same time emphasizing the main façade as an independent wall rising behind it.

Wittgenstein made the horizontal distance between the windows of the main façade consistently smaller than the distance between the outer windows and the corners. In classicist architecture this can be found (though not with Fischer von Erlach) when the corners of the building volumes are rusticated, or emphasized by using two columns or pilasters of the colossal order between window and corner instead of one as is the case in between windows, for example, in Palladio's *Palazzo* Chiericati in Vicenza. Consequently, Wittgenstein emphasized the horizontal independence of the main façade of the Kundmanngasse from the façades of the wings in a classicizing manner, whereas Engelmann's main façade, like the frontages of baroque *Palais,* suggests organic *andante* continuation to the left and the right, taken over by the wings (and in fact taken to extremes in the Schönbrunn Palace). Vertical movement is enforced by making the height of the first and second floor windows proportionately smaller; they were of the same height in Engelmann's front. The large piece of wall-plane created by the 'abstracted', filled-in balustrade between the upper windows and upper edge of the façade, which is uninterrupted by attic windows, gives a solid and firm appearance to the whole front of the main block.

The front façade of the block which oversteps the south terrace is also outside Engelmann's horizontal window scheme: Wittgenstein made it lower than the wings while at the same time raising the breakfast room and its windows to mezzanine level and adding a smaller basement window; he also eliminated the window on the first floor. The massive appearance of the main front and the entrance block is strengthened by this façade, because the windows are placed in the axis of symmetry. Consequently, along the dominating vertical of the south edge of the main façade its mon-

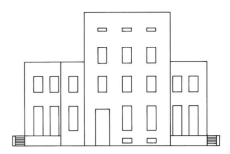

'Purified' version of Engelmann's front elevation.

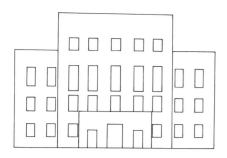

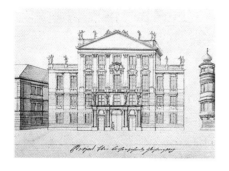

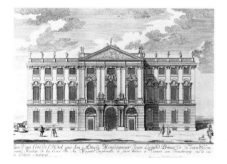

'Purified' versions of the *Palais* Schwarzenberg (top) and the *Palais* Trauthson (above), Vienna, by Fischer von Erlach.

umental height is, as it were, built up step by step by these three individual, subordinated façades – for which, by the way, the little cube of the chimney on the upper east corner forms a humorous counterpoint.

As in Engelmann's design, the wings seem to form a continuous volume, but here the regular rhythm of the bays has also been broken up. The doors on the south terrace are closer to each other than those on the east terrace and the first floor windows of the north-west wing are lower than those of the north-east wing. This creates the illusion of a greater depth between main façade and north-west wing than between main façade and north-east wing, an impression which is enforced by the broad steps of the south terrace, the receding front of the block overstepping it and the projecting entrance block. The effect is to give an openness and illusory depth to the south terrace which invites the visitor to enter whereas the east terrace, which appears to be nearer but is walled off by a parapet, forms an extension of the private part of the house.

The south-west and north-east façades, which in Engelmann's design were stabilized by groupings of windows around super- and subordinated vertical symmetry axes, now give the impression of forward movement: the equal intervals between the windows are larger than the distance between front corner and foremost window, but smaller than the distance between the rear corner and the glass door to the terraces on top of the wings. The shorter intervals between the windows of the south-west façade of the lower block overstepping the south terrace reflect its subordinate character, the eye travels along it more quickly; furthermore, because of the very narrow stretch of wall between its first window and the north-west wing façade, it seems to sprout forward from the wing. We can now be sure about Wittgenstein's rule: each plane has its own progression of vertical axes and whenever a plane stands parallel to another their vertical axes never coincide, thus creating interplanar tension; conversely, whenever the vertical axes of window bays shift, there is also the occurrence of parallel wall planes.

The north-west façade posed a difficult problem because of the addition of the block with lean-to roof and its function as a rear façade. It had to appear stable because all the forward movement originates from it. Indeed, there are only a few windows, their dimensions are small compared to the total wall area, and they form autonomous groups. About the three tall stairwell windows Hermine says:

Finally, after a construction period of I don't know how long, he had to declare himself satisfied and hand the house over as completed. Only a staircase window at the rear of the house still wasn't right to him and he later admitted to me that once he took part in a lottery because of this window; had he won a prize, the money was destined for this alteration.

If Wittgenstein did not mean moving the window triplet towards the left, possibly also reducing it to a duple and lowering its height, in order to increase the area between windows and wall edges, we can only guess what alteration he had in mind. The façade of the added block again, as in the front elevation, has a window arrangement which gives the impression of arrested movement. Its total width just includes the width of the overstepping block on the other side of the north-west wing which strengthens its buttress-like appearance.

Wittgenstein's concept of architecture consists almost completely in balancing proportions, albeit that he used a purely intuitive approach, for none of the façades convincingly reveals any underlying proportional system, unless one is satisfied with the 1:1:1 ... etc. movement of the bays. This is corroborated by an anecdote which relates that for hours on end one of the workmen had to hold the window safety railings at different heights until Wittgenstein, giving directions from the garden, was sure that the right division had been achieved with respect to each other and to the outline of the window opening. We also have a pupil's notes taken at Wittgenstein's lectures on aesthetics (1938) which connect beauty with proportional harmony as illustrated by the problem of finding the 'right' dimensions for windows and doors. The reductionist nature of Wittgenstein's architecture, which involved the complete elimination of ornamentation, an emphasis on solidity and severity achieved by utilising precisely defined clear white planes firmly established on the ground, and the resulting volumetric clarity, further demonstrate the characteristic restraint of classicist architecture. Note that the concave moulding along the base of the front and side façades has its precursors in classicist examples as well, for example in the seventeenth century Royal Palace in Amsterdam. On the other hand, the elaboration and deliberate exploitation of asymmetrical relationships between symmetrically ordered wall-planes to create a plastic effect show strong kinship with contemporary Constructivist architecture inspired by the beauty of mechanical movement. Yet, this tendency towards movement given to the 'inner' façades which

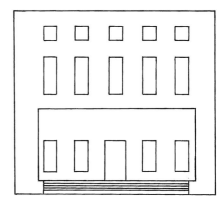

'Purified' elevation of the frontispiece of the Palazzo Chiericati by Palladio.

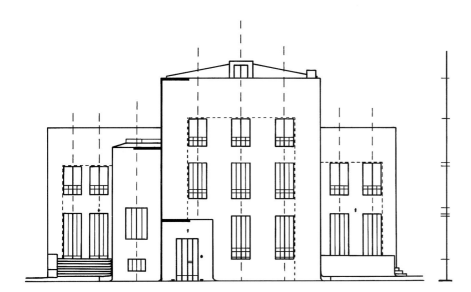

Stabilizing devices in the front façades of Wittgenstein's design.

border the terraces, is brought under control by the stability and calm of the front and rear façades. In this way Wittgenstein seems to incorporate the idea of well-controlled movement in his contemporary classicizing architectural statement.

Wittgenstein's classicism, then, is of a completely different order to Loos's, as exemplified in the Palais Bronner. For Loos it has a much more traditional architectural sense, involving the reintroduction of the simplest of classical orders – Tuscan, Doric or Ionic – and of classical ornaments and motifs, and the breaking up and re-assembling into new proportional relationships of the classical syntax. It also involved Schinkel-like clarity in a strictly symmetrical composition of well-defined cubic volumes and Biedermeier-like simplicity in the application of adornment. Asymmetry in the arrangement of the façades only results from and is justified by the building's internal structure; it is embedded in the governing symmetrical pattern of mouldings and bays to avoid any appearance of tension.

With the Villa Moller, Loos abandoned classicism and reached his final conception of modernity. What he borrowed from it was extreme simplicity in façade design and volumetric emphasis suggested by a large, well-defined wall area and relatively small window openings. These now expressed the modern need for privacy and reservation, achieved by an interior created by a fully developed *Raumplanung*. Basically, the arrangement of windows in the façades should follow logically from the position of the rooms within the *Raumplanung* and could therefore be completely asymmetrical. This is, for example the case in the Rufer House (1922), the first elaborate *Raumplanung* realized by Loos, which, by the way, still bears simplified classical ornament. The street façade of the Villa Moller, still a cube, is, however, a carefully designed abstract composition around a central axis of symmetry which can hardly be called the logical result of the *Raumplanung* of the interior. In fact, after 1923, under the influence of modernist architecture in France and elsewhere, Loos became fascinated by the abstract play of window openings of different sizes within shifting bare wall planes. The front of the Villa Moller is a perfect example of 'ornamenting with unornamented planes', by which words Paul Engelmann would later condemn this kind of abstract play, convinced that he spoke according to the ideas of his teacher. At any rate, with the exception of its bareness there could be no greater contrast to the exterior of the Kundmanngasse.

The windows of the side and rear façades of the Villa Moller do bear a more or less direct relationship to the interior, though their dimensions have also

Below: Shifting bay rhythms in the parallel planes of the north-east façade.

Centre: Shifting bay rhythms in the parallel planes of the south-west façade.

Right: Stabilizing devices and shifting bay rhythms in the parallel planes of the north-west façade.

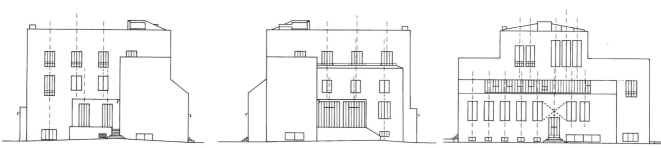

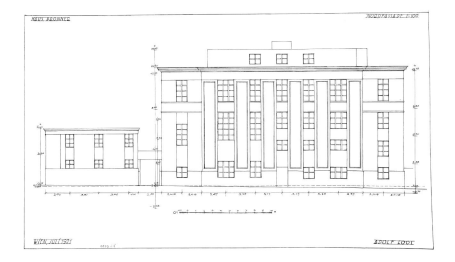

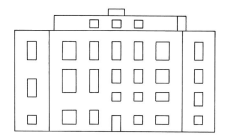

been determined with regard to the composition of the exterior wall. The garden façade, which was as important as the street façade in Loos's conception but with a contrasting, open character, shows the simplicity and clarity of design which is characteristic of the beauty of Groag's later architecture and places him somewhere in between Wittgenstein and Loos. But it also shows a strong kinship with the Kundmanngasse: the dimensions of the windows and glass doors, their slender, uninterrupted vertical framework, and the balanced play of symmetry and asymmetry in their arrangement within the wall-plane show the same classicizing restraint, albeit in a less severe manner. The hypothesis that Jacques Groag was largely responsible for the design of the garden façade seems to be supported by the degree of his involvement in the design reflected in the portion of the architect's fee he received: 35 per cent. Although Loos, who was living in Paris at that time, visited Vienna regularly during the construction period, Groag was the supervisor, and he made the decisions when they had to be taken. Some other details should be mentioned. As is typical of Loos the main entrance is executed in luxury materials: a base of natural stone flags, polished granite door jambs, and the front door itself is covered by copper plates which Wittgenstein would have deemed an unthinkable affectation. Groag's rear façade, for that matter, does not use these ostentatious materials. Furthermore, naked light bulbs as exterior lighting for the terraces are used in both the Kundmanngasse and the Villa Moller. It is also interesting that the original zinc finishing of the roof was reduced to the same absolute minimum in the Kundmanngasse as in the Villa Moller, as photographs taken immediately after the completion of each house show. Groag's purist modernism is illustrated by the fact that he once, in the design of his own parents' house, on principle refused classical ornament such as the portico with columns proposed on that occasion by Engelmann; in the case of the design of his brother's house, the fact that he was not allowed to execute a roof edge at right angles but had to provide for a projecting lip to carry away the water was a cause of endless dispute. In any event, neither in the Kundmanngasse nor in the Villa Moller did he have to make concessions on his idea of modernism.

Adolf Loos, Villa Moller, 1927-1928. Street elevation.

Adolf Loos, Villa Moller, 1927-1928.
Garden elevation, presumably mainly
Jacques Groag's design.

Spatial structure of the beletage

In the same way that he re-proportioned the exterior Wittgenstein also changed the proportions of the ground floor plan, leaving its asymmetrical layout intact. Even more so than in Engelmann's plan this arrangement again suggests movement around the hallway which finds its balance in returning to its point of origin. The search for a proportional system determining the plan of the beletage leads to a finding that approximates proportional ratios, allowing for a tolerance of 2 to 5 per cent. In Engelmann's plan the dimensions of hallway, *Saal,* dining room, and breakfast room approximate to the progression of 1:1, 1:2, 3:4, 5:6, respectively. In Wittgenstein's plan the progression is 1:1, 1:2, 2:3, 5:6, whereas the vestibule, the library and Margaret Stonborough's private salon are in the ratio's 1:1, 2:3 and 3:4, respectively. The elements of both progressions belong to the Pythagorean harmonic system, based on musical intervals – 1:1, 1:2, 2:3, 3:4, 4:5, 5:6, etc. If the Pythagorean progression was indeed employed by Wittgenstein (and Engelmann), then it is difficult to see why these slight deviations were introduced – deliberately, one must assume, and not because of a failure to achieve sufficient accuracy, for the plans have been carefully executed with a precision only allowing for deviations of less than a centimetre. If one accepts the system, that is as a guiding principle employed in the first stages of the design after which small intuitive adaptations were made, the progressions reflect the diminishing formal importance of the rooms: vestibule and hallway correspond to 1:1, the *Saal* to 1:2, the dining room and library to 2:3, Margaret Stonborough's salon to 3:4, the breakfast room to 5:6 (the ratio 4:5 is missing).

The most convincing suggestion of a proportional system, however, has been brought forward by E. Flach, and concerns *geometrical* proportioning underlying the definitive plan. Flach identifies the intersection of the

The suggestion of proportionality underlying
the plan of the beletage of the Kundmanngasse.

146

south-west/north-east axis cutting through the connecting doors of the south terrace, hallway, *Saal* and east terrace and the south-east/north-west axis cutting through the connecting doors of the library, hallway and corridor to the stairwell as the centre of a circle exactly enclosing a rectangle defining the outline of the plan (with maximum tolerance of 0.5 per cent). The intersection of these axes literally constitutes the centre point of the plan dividing the total width of the house into two equal lengths **r** (12.32 metres, again with a tolerance of 0.5 per cent) while the division of each of these lengths determines the dividing walls between the terraces and the hallway and *Saal*, respectively. This intersection, of course, also divides the total depth of the house into two equal lengths. This system is absent in Engelmann's plan while in the final, definitive plan it even accounts for the depth of the shallow rear block and therefore also for the expansion of the hallway, vestibule, corridor and stairwell.

Only the entrance block sticks out of the enclosed rectangle, but in a proportionally justified manner. From the threshold of the entrance to the hallway one traverses exactly three times length **s**, which is the distance between the centres of the two freestanding hallway pillars (3.24 metres - 3.25 metres in the final plans): the enclosed porch, the vestibule and the stairs each have this same length **s**. Moreover, vestibule and stairs are perfect squares with length = width = **s**, as is the part of the hallway defined by pillars and pilasters framing the blind wall facing the stairs. Furthermore, the length of the corridor leading from the hallway to the stairs of the service entrance is exactly 2 **s**. Interestingly, the grid of squares formed by the pillars and pilasters of the stairwell is determined by the measurement **t**=1.40 metres which is practically half the distance between two freestanding hall pillars, (that is half of 2.82 metres in the final plans). The measure **t** is important in more respects, for in the final plan of the beletage all doors have a width of **t** – the small differences between final plan and survey (**t** = 1.38 to 1.395 metres) may be accounted for by the thickness of the stucco. The main entrance and service entrance show their formal importance by deviating from it, their plan widths are 1.62 metres and 1.49 metres respectively (also in the survey of 1976).

The emphasis on proportionality in classicist architecture expresses the need for some pre-established mathematical or geometrical 'rule', such as the Pythagorean progression of musical intervals or the enclosing circle, representing an eternally valid 'artistic law' of 'absolute beauty' supposed still to have been in the possession of the ancients. Wittgenstein's method, however, to arrive at the 'right' proportions by intuition instead of by deducing them from some rule, does not in any way weaken the argument for a classicist motivation because, as will become clear in the last chapter, this is in full agreement with Wittgenstein's conviction that 'absolute beauty' is beyond rational justification and that some pre-established 'rule' can only intuitively be *shown*. The fact that a mathematical expression or geometrical section 'coincidentally' reflects some 'eternally beautiful' proportional relationship cannot add any meaning to it. If the Pythagorean pro-

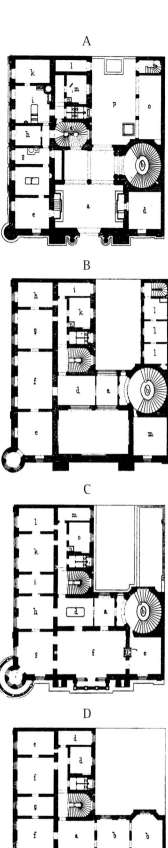

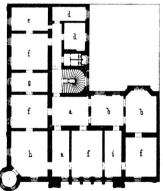

Page 147:

Example of a 19th century *Palais*,

Johannesgasse 26, Vienna.

Ground floor (A): *a* = vestibule and

b = main stairwell.

Mezzanine (B): *a* = anteroom; *d* = billiard room;

e = smoking room; *f* = dining room; *g* = study;

h = sleeping room; *i* = servant's room; *k* = valet's

room and *l* = coachman's room.

First floor (C): *a* = anteroom; *d* = dining room;

e = tea salon; *f* = large drawing room or

ball room; *g* = music room; *h* = small drawing

room; *i* = boudoir; *k* = sleeping room of the

countess and *l* = sleeping room of the young

countess.

Second floor (D): *a* = anteroom; *b* = guest-room;

d = servant's room; *e* = garderobe; *f* = sleeping

room; *g* = governess; *h* = drawing room and

i = bathroom.

Adolf Loos, *Palais* Bronner. *Raumplanung* of the

main floor. *Kanzlei* = office; *Vorraum* = landing;

Salon = drawing room; *Office* = pantry;

Speisezimmer = dining room; *Halle* = hall;

Gedeckte Terrasse = portico; *Vestibule-Luftz* =

vestibule; *Bad* = bathroom; *Gastzimmer* = guest-

room.

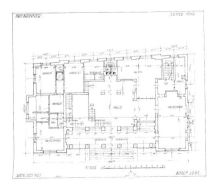

gression did indeed play a role in the proportioning of the rooms at some stage in the design process, then the slight and irregular deviations in the final plan can only be explained by the overriding importance intuition had for Wittgenstein in considerations of proportion. How exacting he could be in this respect is related by Hermine Wittgenstein in her *Family Recollections*:

The strongest proof of Ludwig's relentlessness when it came to getting proportions exactly right is perhaps the fact that he had the ceiling of a large room [the *Saal*] raised by three centimetres, just when it was almost time to start cleaning the completed house. His feeling was absolutely right and this feeling had to be followed.

It has already become obvious that the ground floor plan and the spatial structure of the Kundmanngasse has little in common with the *Raumplanung* typical of the earlier *Palais* Bronner and the contemporary Villa Moller (nor, incidentally, with the plans of contemporary bourgeois villas in historical neo-styles which were mainly influenced by the more practical layout of the English country house). Its asymmetrical layout may be seen as a remnant of Loosian design: the main floor plan of the *Palais* Bronner shows a more or less similar arrangement of rooms crosswise to the adjacent rooms around the central living hall. The contrasts between the plans and spatial structures of the respective buildings will be revealed by following the analysis of the concept of *Raumplanung* by Johan van de Beek.

Although the *Palais* Bronner still occupies a large area which allows for an ample use of space on all floors, the *Raumplanung* developed into obtaining spatial *compactness* so that ideally the interior could be enclosed within a tight cube. Loos had already expounded this ideal in the educational programme of his *Bauschule,* but it was not until the designs of the Rufer House and the Villa Moller that it was approached closely. From the standpoint of the semi-aristocratic 'garden-*Palais*' Stonborough in the Kundmanngasse the striving for compactness is indeed *bourgeois*. The wings, the terraces, the verticality of the main building all negate it, even if the stability expressed by its plain and 'reserved' façades seems to suggest a striving for compactness. Furthermore, the dimensions of the rooms on the beletage have been determined by monumentality, not by practicality or efficiency, leaving, for example, a great deal of superfluous space on the second floor which follows the ample circumference of the main floor. The height of the beletage of the Kundmanngasse measures about 12 feet 6 inches as against 10 feet 6 inches for the music room of the Villa Moller, the highest on its main floor.

By restoring the rooms of the mistress of the house on the beletage (as they had been in Engelmann's earliest plans), Wittgenstein even returned to a layout of rooms which can often be found in plans of nineteenth century *Palais*. In these plans the *Saal*, the large main drawing room, gave access to, on the one hand, a gentleman's or billiard room, on the other to a, smaller, lady's drawing room, from which her boudoir and bedroom could be reached. Exactly this aristocratic order of rooms is to be found in the Kundmanngasse, where the functions of library, gentleman's room and informal living room have been integrated in the front room. As in the Kundmanngasse it was also customary to have the study and master bedroom on a different floor. The presence of a 'formal' versus an 'informal' plan of the beletage resulting from Wittgenstein's alterations also conforms to the layout of the traditional nineteenth century and baroque *Palais*, though in the latter the reception rooms of the formal plan were always situated at the front of the house facing the street, while the informal plan covered the rooms situated around the courtyard. Just as in the Kundmanngasse, the formal plan included the grand staircase leading to the hallway or gallery of the beletage from which the *Saal* was to be entered, but excluded the back staircase connecting the basement, beletage and upper floors, which appeared less conspicuously as part of the informal plan. This is also true for the plan of a baroque country villa to which the alternative way of entering the Kundmanngasse corresponds: entrance (south) terrace - hall - *Saal* - garden (east) terrace. Regarded from the standpoint of a country villa the front façade of the Kundmanngasse is one of the garden façades and all the main rooms behind these façades open towards the surrounding garden according to their orientation. Finally, Wittgenstein logically combined the servants' entrance and stairs with the back staircase to the basement and upper floors.

The *Raumplanung*, however, makes no such distinction between a 'formal' and an 'informal' plan (though the *Palais* Bronner still kept the traditional back staircase connecting all floors), but strictly separates the floor with rooms used during the day — the main floor — from the floor with the bedrooms above it. The difference between the 'reserved' street façade and the open garden façade, present in both the *Palais* Bronner and the Villa Moller, reflects the orientation of the rooms on the main floor towards the garden, creating a private living space to include the garden and facing away from the street. The 'electrical kitchen' and the 'introverted' space of the library of the Villa Moller border the street façade, while the living hall, the music room and the dining room open towards the terrace and garden. Living hall and music room, dining room, kitchen and pantry, and the library and oriel window with seats are all on different levels connected by short flights of stairs. The stairs continue the passage through the main floor, determining the formal order of the rooms: vestibule — living hall; living hall — music room and dining room; living hall — library; dining room — upper floor. The kitchen is situated on the main floor, not, as in the plan of the traditional *Palais* (and consequently in the Kundmanngasse) in the basement. In accordance with the *bourgeois* way of life, there are no separate 'private apartments' for master and mistress of the house.

It is obvious then that in contrast to the *Raumplanung* of the Villa Moller, no such practical considerations lay at the base of the changes made in the plan of the beletage of the Kundmanngasse; they merely restored tradition.

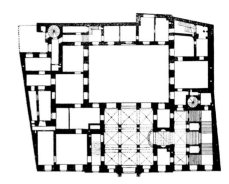

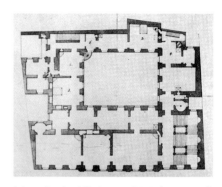

Johann Bernhard Fischer von Erlach (1656-1723), ground floor plan (top) and the beletage (above) of the *Palais* Batthyány-Schönborn.

Page 150: Section of the Raumplanung, plan of the ground floor, plan of the main floorand plan of the second floor.

Translations: *Atelier* = atelier; *Schlafzimmer* = sleeping room; *Sitzerker* = oriel window; *Küche, Speisezimmer* = kitchen, dining room; *Halle, Musikzimmer* = hall, music room; *Kleider-ablage* = vestibule; *Hausmeister-Zimmer* = butler's room; *Vestibule, Waschküche* = entrance, scullery; *Keller* = basement; *Garage* = garage; *Mädchen* = housemaid; *Küche d. Hausmeister* = butler's kitchen; *Schr.* = closet; *Speisekammer* = food storage room; *Eintritt* = entrance; *Kleiderablage* = vestibule; *Terrasse* = terrace; *Balkon* = balcony; *Blumenbalkon* = 'flower' balcony; *Esszimmer* = dining room; *Anrichte* = pantry; *Elektr. Küche* = 'electrical' kitchen; *Bibliothek* = library; *Zimmer* = (bed) room; *Office* = pantry; *Bad* = bathroom; *Dusche* = shower.

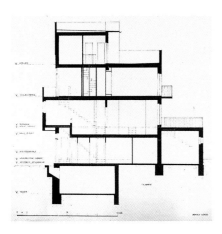

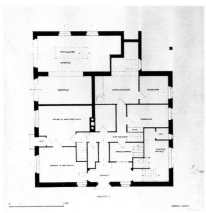

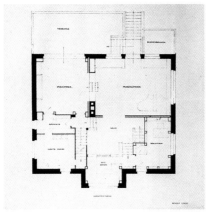

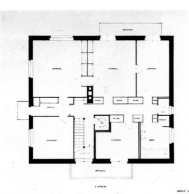

Moreover, Wittgenstein did not hesitate to achieve this spatial structure and the effects of its subsequent purification by artifice. Obvious examples are the partition walls in the library, in Margaret Stonborough's private salon and in the servant's room. As these inner partition walls are not load-bearing they were made of prefabricated sections, their function being only the division of space. Wittgenstein, however, doubled them when necessary from a purely formal point of view to realize the effect of symmetry, thereby creating lost space. The same is true of the space above the ceiling of the vestibule, or for the thickness of the plaster applied to walls which was varied according to the required total wall thickness.

Less obvious to the eye, but even more telling is the treatment of the concrete supports which are essential to the framework of the house. Some coincide with pillars and pilasters in the hallway, but others are hidden within the walls – for example between private salon and east terrace and between dressing room and bathroom – or disguised, for example as one of the pillars between the windows of the dining room. Their cross-sections are fully determined by the appearance they should have (or not have) within the interior of the rooms they are in, not by their structural function. Moreover, a number of pillars, having structurally the same load-bearing function as the outer walls, are made of brick, but their outward appearance is identical to the concrete supports. The same discrepancies between actual structure and appearance are to be found on the upper floors. Indeed, the interior architecture of the Kundmanngasse mostly hides the real structural framework of the house – even suggesting, like a convincing stage set, a beautifully consistent supporting structure that is a far cry from the actual construction characterized as it is by *ad hoc* solutions (these may have been a real cause for tensions between Wittgenstein and Groag, for the latter set great store by construction and constructional clarity, as his later work time and again shows). The Kundmanngasse again shares this stage-like, illusory approach to architecture with its nineteenth century and baroque predecessors, exemplified by the structural irregularities hidden behind regularity suggesting formal plans, of the *Palais* Batthyány-Schönborn and other city palaces by Fischer von Erlach. Though Loos, in the salon of his *Palais* Bronner, can also be caught placing a main inner wall at right angles to an adjacent wall even though its corresponding outer wall is oblique, the Villa Moller is the near perfect marriage of form and structure (as is the Rufer House).

The architecture of the interior

Entering the house and finding the way to the main floor in the Kundmanngasse is, then, a completely different experience from the same journey in the *Palais* Bronner and the Villa Moller. Though both the *Palais* Bronner and the Kundmanngasse have a driveway leading to the main entrance, the Villa Moller is on the street and one has to cross the pavement between the car and front door. In the Kundmanngasse the straight passage through the enclosed porch and vestibule towards the stairs leading to the monumental hallway of the beletage follows the layout of the aristocratic *Palais*. The hallway at once clarifies the axial structure of the beletage revealing the passage into the main reception rooms. Just as in the Alleegasse and in the baroque city palaces by Fischer von Erlach, while climbing the stairs one ascends from the dark into the light. The *Galerie* of the Alleegasse was covered by a glass roof. Fischer let light flood in through the tall windows of the beletage, as also happens in the Kundmanngasse, though the light in the latter is softened by the shade of the canopy formed by the block overstepping the south terrace.

The living hall in Loos's spatially planned houses, however, is reached by walking round right-angled corners. There is no enclosed porch in the *Palais* Bronner, only a covered walkway leading directly to a flight of stairs to the front door and the vestibule, high and light, behind it. In the vestibule the staircase is to the left, not in the centre; it turns through 90 degrees again, against a side wall, and leads into the living hall on the main floor. In the Villa Moller the dimly lit, corridor-like, enclosed porch runs parallel to the front façade, obliging the visitor to turn right as soon as he enters the front door. Steps lead to the vestibule which is at right angles to the enclosed porch and has a moderately sized window high up in the wall. To reach the living hall you must climb the stairs again and turn three times: left, right and left. By following this labyrinthine path one is, as it were, 'wrapped up into' the private space of the house.

Wittgentein's attempt to arrive at 'modern design' by an ultimate purification and clarification (partly inspired by classicizing baroque) of the traditional aristocratic architecture desired by his sister, becomes clearer when its interior finishing and furnishing is contrasted with the Villa Moller. Supports in the latter, always structurally necessary, for example in the living hall and music room, follow the typical pillar design of Loos. They are square without pedestal or capital, and support crossbeams of the same width. They are covered, as are the walls and floors, with wood veneer (okumé, oak in the library) or natural stone (travertine) which show their precious quality in the texture, colour and lustre. In the Kundmanngasse pillars are only visible in the vestibule and hallway and are finished with a simple layer of plaster. They play an architectural role which goes further than purely structural because, as in traditional *Palais* design, they are part of the formal ceremony of entering the beletage. In the vestibule there are four pilasters without capitals. They appear not to support anything but pass through the ceiling and continue up to the height of the ceiling of the beletage hallway. Their utter simplicity heralds the articulated hallway pillars and pilasters in the same way as, following the classical rules, the simple Tuscan order of the parterre heralds the more complex Ionian order of the beletage in the *Palais* Batthyány-Schönborn.

The slightly receding cushions, their height exactly half the width of the shaft, may be interpreted as an inversion of capitals, as a negation of func-

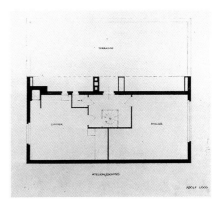

Adolf Loos, Villa Moller. Above: Plan of the second floor.

Hallway-stairs

151

tionality; they may also be understood as abaci resulting from a 'purifying' reduction of Engelmann's Egyptian columns, or as abaci reminiscent of those steel 'abaci' which are used on top of bridge piers. In any case this narrowing of the cushions, continued by the even narrower beams resting on them, suggests a certain lightness of the ceiling, which, combined with the suggestion of direction given by having only lengthwise beams (Loos invariably employed a grid of lengthwise and crosswise beams), avoids the effect of a heavy ceiling 'weighing upon' the visitor climbing the stairs. The cushions are also missing from the pillars and pilasters of the stairwell; as in the vestibule their absence gives the visitor an impression of upward movement. This impression of lightness may be seen as an aspect of the general tendency towards dematerialization which characterizes the Kundmanngasse, and is intended to counterbalance the massiveness of its architecture. It stands in strong contrast to Loos's use of finishing materials by tastefully showing its natural decorative structure and its preciousness. The white or off-white planes of the walls and ceilings and the dark floor surface of the Kundmangasse are completely smooth and evenly coloured; there are no mouldings, skirtings or thresholds. The flooring therefore does not demarcate a room but seems to stretch out endlessly under the dividing walls that just touch the ground at the place where they stand, their position only confirmed by the grid of joints of the flooring slabs. With the exception of the vestibule, hallway and stairwell where pilasters define the corners, walls and ceilings seem to be the intersections of limitless planes, flat when they define the rooms, or 'mathematically' curved when forming the rising ceiling of the stairwell. The silky gloss of the plain white stucco lustro wall covering and the polished dark floor suggest translucency, which is emphasized by the lack of an identity of the walls and floor, which have no natural decorative articulation. In this manner architecture has been reduced, or refined, to the absolute minimum – to light, and intersecting planes.

Doors and windows and, at night, the iron window curtains partition off the spaces; they are consequently more noticeably there as tall greyish-green framework or planes. The opaque doors opening to the *Saal* emphasize the importance of the rooms they guard; the glass doors and windows form slender tall latticework. The dual aspect of some of the double doors – transparency alternating with translucency, or with opacity – makes their role as intermediaries even more striking. The extremely simplified door and window furniture attract just sufficient attention because of their cool brass colour that never becomes glossy by long use. The two-winged double doors of the beletage are typical of aristocratic mansions, while the doors in the Villa Moller are all single one-winged. Single one-winged doors of wood in the Kundmanngasse, relatively light and easy to move, belong to the upper floors; but, like the doors of the wooden cupboards along the corridors, they are painted smooth grey to conceal their texture instead of veneered with precious wood. The parquet of the upper floor rooms (which made a minimal skirting necessary) is in fact the only material that shows it natural texture. It gives the rooms a warmer, sheltered feeling, which complements their informal function.

The materials used for the finishing not only contribute to the architectural abstraction because of their neutral appearance, but also because of their lack of intrinsic structure which would otherwise have had to be taken into account – they can be shaped into any desired form. This is true for the plaster and *stucco lustro*, for the artificial stone flooring, but also for the steel framework and plates of windows and doors and for the brass door and window handles (and is also suggested by the grey painted wooden doors of the upper floors). It is interesting to note that plaster, *stucco lustro* and artificial stone flooring were among the materials used in Viennese *Palais*-construction during and after the baroque period and their use had again flourished during the construction of the Ringstraße; skilled workers in these trades could still pride themselves on a long tradition of craftsmanship, and an appreciation of craftsmanship was something that Wittgenstein and Loos had in common. The skills necessary to work with metal were of course the very skills Wittgenstein himself had practised since childhood and studied as a student of engineering.

If Loos had a special talent for combining the decorative quality of precious natural woods and stones and for combining them with built-in furniture, Wittgenstein's gift for mechanical construction found full expression in the design of doors and windows and their furniture and in other mechanical elements of the Kundmanngasse. The execution of the steel windows and doors reveals a degree of precision, at that time unsurpassed, which allows for the utmost simplicity and nobility of form. It is clear that their design was prompted on the one hand by purely formal considerations of a proportional nature, for example, the positioning of espagnolette handles exactly at the intersection of the diagonals of the doorway, or making the fastener of a window latch exactly as wide as the window jamb on which it is mounted and the heads of its bolts level with the surface of the fas-

Page 152: Stairs towards the beletage in the *Palais* Batthyány-Schönborn, the grand staircase of the Alleegasse with on top of the stairs The *Squatting Woman* by Max Klinger, and the Galerie of the Alleegasse.

Above: Adolf Loos, Villa Moller. Vestibule with stairs leading to the living hall.

Bottom, from left to right: Tuscan column from the exterior and pillar from the interior of Loos' *Haus am Michaelerplatz*, Egyptian chalice column (Horustemple, Edfu) used in Engelmann's hallway design without plinth, Wittgenstein's pillar from the Kundmanngasse, pillar from the Villa Moller.

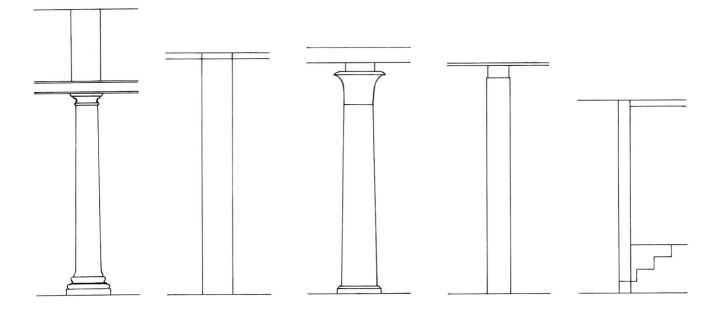

tener; on the other hand by the requirements for ease of maintenance, durability, and well-controlled movement of the functioning parts. The lift exhibits its straightforward mechanical structure while the confident sounds of its working are clearly audible.

Because of the straightforward design of the fastenings, locks and handles, and ingenuous details like the clamps fastening the outer leaf of window or door against the inner leaf, and the inescapable confrontation with them, one is at first easily tempted to ascribe a functionalist tendency to Wittgenstein's design in the context of the emerging functionalism in contemporary modern architecture. However, a strictly functionalist interpretation could not explain the dimensions and enormous weight of the doors which, despite their smooth movement, require quite some effort to set them in motion. Their weight could indeed justify the high position of the door and window handles on the beletage – approximately at shoulder height so that pushing or pulling the doors becomes easier. This cannot, however, account for the differences in height of the handles for the glass doors at 5 feet 3 inches, which is at the intersection of their diagonals, at 4 feet 8 1/2 inches for the *Saal* door, and at 4 feet 1 inch for the main entrance doors. The differences in size between the door handles of the ground floor and those of the upper floors are also unaccountable, and the same is true for the presence of crosspieces on the entrance and servant's entrance doors and their absence on other doors.

It is interesting to recall the correspondence between Wittgenstein and Eccles, cited in an earlier chapter. In his letter Eccles mentions the design principles advanced by Wittgenstein, as seems obvious, on which both agreed: 1. Utility, 2. (giving preference to the easiest method of) Construction, 3. Absolute simplicity. Utility, or functionality, is, although mentioned first, only one of three principles. As will be explained in the last chapter, the second and third principles concern guidelines which were for Wittgenstein rather of a moral and aesthetic importance, over and above considerations of a merely factually concrete, structural nature. These principles were to be *shown* in a kind of transcendental technical insight; they echo the idea of 'elegant mathematical proof' (Wittgenstein then believed that logic and mathematics improved one's aesthetic judgment) and were represented for him by the well-designed and well-functioning machine. As a mechanical engineer he could, of course, in the design of the mechanical parts, go further in blending symbolic formal features with the structural ones than he could as the dilettante architect without professional knowledge of building construction. In any event, the symbolic value mechanical design had for him may explain Wittgenstein's strong objections to a bed on rollers, though they may very well have served as functional extras for the person who had to clean Eccles' bedroom. This may also throw light on something Wittgenstein wrote in 1942: 'Architecture is a gesture. Not every functional movement of the human body is a *gesture*. No more is every functional building architecture.'

As in the baroque aristocratic mansion, the rooms of the Kundmanngasse

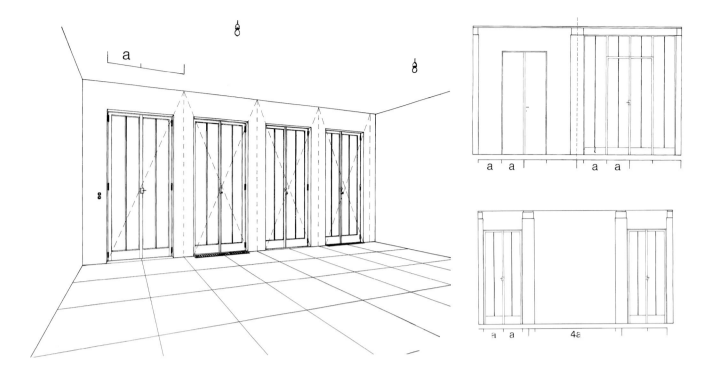

are comparatively independent of their furnishing (this disconnection of room and furniture has its origin in medieval practice – when aristocrats progressed from one castle to another they took their furniture with them). They are autonomous spaces defined only by their proportions and symmetries which include the positioning of the chandeliers (reduced by Wittgenstein to naked light bulbs), and by the finishing of their walls and floors. The transitory spaces – vestibule, hallway, corridor, and stairwell – have pillars and pilasters; like the bars in a score they measure the distance covered. The absence of pilasters and the symmetry of the rooms around the vertical axial planes puts them completely at rest and suggests a feeling of repose. The architecture of the rooms, therefore, functions only as a background framework, or grid, for furniture of whatever type and style.

The vestibule and hallway had no furniture; as in the *Palais* Batthyány-Schönborn and the Alleegasse the hall had a bare wall facing its main axis,

Proportioning of the dining room wall facing the south terrace (above left) and proportioning of the hallway wall (top and above).

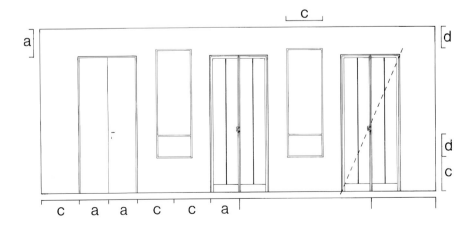

The mirror arrangement in the *Saal* of the Kundmanngasse

separated by pilasters from doors on both sides. It is a space for display – a painting (over a mantelpiece), and a Gobelin and sculpture, repectively in the *Palais* Batthyány-Schönborn and the Alleegasse, and a sculpture only in the Kundmanngasse. As in the baroque *Saal* between the glass doors of the *Saal* in the Kundmanngasse there were gilt framed mirrors, there were folding screens, and groups of tables and chairs were arranged in different corners. *Objets d'art* displayed on pedestals or in glass cases can be traced back to the nineteenth century fondness for creating museum-like surroundings to live in. The arrangement of the dining room again reflects the aristocratic tradition: a large table in the centre and small side tables against the wall with chairs on both sides ready to be drawn up if required. In the same tradition the library bookshelves are part of the interior design of the room, as is the bed in Margaret Stonborough's rooms, though she placed it, eccentric as she was, *between* dressing room and salon. In the salon the marble of the mantelpiece is, of course, replaced by artificial stone. The breakfast room has at least symbolic value in that, as Jan Turnovský's analysis shows, the solution to creating symmetry, chosen by Wittgenstein in the plans, tries to combine the solutions of the architects he respected: Johann Bernhard Fischer von Erlach and Adolf Loos.

The modern bourgeois way of living is rooted in the idea of settling in one place, which is the city where one makes a living. The house one lives in is one's permanent residence and therefore Loos integrates furniture and architecture and has built-in alcoves with sofas, built-in shelves, sideboards and cupboards; he uses materials for their finishing which are similar to those used for the finishing of floors, walls and ceilings. Because of the limited floor area of the Villa Moller there is no room for idle play with proportions and symmetries; spaciousness is suggested by leaving out dividing walls between rooms on different levels. For practical reasons, functions originally assigned to separate rooms are extended to neighbouring rooms, for example, by the use of sliding doors and a folding flight of steps between music room and dining room. The rooms acquire identity by different relationships with the *Raumplanung* and a different emphasis on the choice of materials used. Thus the music room is characterized by the rich use of wood, not only for decoration, but also for obtaining excellent acoustics. (We know that Loos was preoccupied with the problem of acoustics, possibly because he was rather deaf.) It is only within the informal plan of the ground floor and on the private upper floors of the Kundmanngasse that we find a practical feature also shared by the Villa Moller: the wooden cupboards lining the corridors. It would be interesting to know whether Jacques Groag suggested these; all his interior designs show elegant solutions for creating practical storage space.

Wittgenstein's architectural gesture

We cannot expect a mature architectural style to arise from the design of a single building which, while meeting the specific demands of the client, is bound to specific surroundings and historical circumstances. It is also true that there is no sign that Wittgenstein had such pretensions. The restrictions arose from the owner's lifestyle which was more suited to pre-twentieth century aristocratic mansions than to twentieth century houses and, also, from a preliminary design which had proved unsatisfactory in this respect. Wittgenstein could accept the commission because he himself grew up in the same nineteenth century upper class surroundings of semi-aristocratic scale as the client, his sister. As we shall see, however, his own conception of architecture was also rather pre-twentieth century than twentieth-century. What he could, and would, undertake was an attempt to formulate an authentic, and genuine answer to this particular challenge to him as the serious dilettante architect.

If he succeeded, then the design would necessarily be 'modern' though it might be fundamentally different from the 'New Architecture' of his time. As we shall see in the next chapter, Wittgenstein believed that if there was a unifying, centripetal force inherent in the culture of a given historical period, authenticity implied its expression through the creative individual – this was what, in his eyes, made Fischer von Erlach's architecture so great during the flowering age of baroque. If not, and he was convinced his own times lacked such a centripetal force, the best he could achieve in seeking for authenticity was a statement of purification as an answer to weak and inauthentic contemporary architecture. Wittgenstein had had serious discussions with one of the founders of modern twentieth century architecture, Adolf Loos, who himself took an idiosyncratic position within the modern movement. These exchanges may have confirmed Wittgenstein in his own conception of authenticity or modernity in architecture, though it resulted in a design that stands in many respects in remarkable contrast to the work of Loos. Wittgenstein's Kundmanngasse should therefore be understood as a single purifying gesture *vis-à-vis* the modern architecture of his time being made by a serious dilettante and thus unique; as such it may serve as a paradigm for those who find inspiration in it. An attempt to analyse what this paradigm amounted to has been made above and can be summarized as follows.

Above: Furniture arrangement of the *Saal* of the Kundmangasse. Charcoal drawing by Hermine Wittgenstein.

Opposite page: Top: Mirror arrangement in the *Saal* of the *Palais* Batthyány-Schönborn Centre: Baroque furniture arrangement of a drawing room in the *Palais* Batthyány-Schönborn.

Bottom: Fin de siècle furniture arrangement of the Red Room of the Alleegasse.

Adolf Loos, Villa Moller. View from the living hall into the oriel window (above), and view from the dining room into the music room (right).

The preliminary design of Paul Engelmann, from which Wittgenstein started, should be typified as classicist, with its origin in the classicism taught at the *Adolf Loos Bauschule,* and characterized by its rigidly defined masses, its volumetric clarity, and the simplified and rearranged application of classical ornament. The influence of twentieth century architecture can be felt in the asymmetrical arrangement of cubic volumes and the asymmetrical layout of the plan of the beletage which underlies it. It should be added that the blending of the spatial structure of the classical *villa suburbana* and the traditional Viennese city *Palais* into the plan of the Kundmanngasse lent itself pre-eminently to Wittgenstein's classicizing re-interpretation.

Dissatisfied with Engelmann's modern classicism Ludwig Wittgenstein developed his own 'authentically modern' classicizing approach, apart from making alterations in the plan which restored a traditional *Palais*-layout which for Engelmann had been problematic. He could do this because the conception of aesthetics he held during the period of the design and construction of the Kundmanngasse can be described as 'classicist' and could even serve as an 'eternal artistic rule', albeit of an intuitive nature, which should govern the design in order to preserve its classical purity. As will be explained in the last chapter this rule is reflected in the special significance he attached to the adage *simplex sigillum veri* – simplicity is the hallmark of truth.

As regards the characteristic classicist tendency to lay emphasis on volumetric definition and clarity, Wittgenstein went to the limit. He eliminated classical ornament altogether and thus reduced architecture to undisturbed straight lines running parallel or perpendicular to each other, to the intersection of planes formed by them, to symmetry and proportion, to the pure perception of depth and shallowness, and to the pure effect of light and shadow. As in romantic neoclassical architecture (and in opposition to the geometrical garden layout of Engelmann's design), the contrast between the building itself and the relatively unstructured natural surroundings of the garden only heightened the resulting effect of superb restraint and austere monumentality. A personal note of Wittgenstein comes to mind: 'My ideal is a certain coolness. A temple providing a setting for the passions without interfering in them.'

Thanks to the possibilities of modern building techniques he could go further than any pre-twentieth century classicism. These modern techniques concerned the use of concrete supports and beams allowing for an open internal structural framework and flat roofs, a roof covering with minimal edges, prefabricated wall panels enabling thin partition walls to be used where appropriate, and the use of steel for door and window frames, all creating the maximum adaptability and flexibility necessary to comply with his wishes. With the exception of the steel doors and windows these modern structural features are also the most obvious connection to Adolf Loos's architecture for the preliminary design by Loos's pupil, Paul Engelmann, had the same structural organization, and its execution was in the hands of Loos's pupil Jacques Groag.

Extreme flexibility as a consequence of modern techniques was also at the core of Wittgenstein's classicizing application of proportionality for it enabled him to realize his conception of proportionality governed by 'absolute' intuition without let or hindrance. Even if one is not convinced by the supposed presence – slightly 'corrected' by intuition – in the interior of dimensional ratios based on the Pythagorean harmonic progression, nor by the presence of the circumscribing circle with its significant centre and the role of the distance **s** between the centres of the hallway pillars – proportional devices meant to represent cosmic order in earlier classicisms – Wittgenstein's pure intuitional proportionality still acknowledges classicist architectural tradition, because, as we shall see, in his opinion aesthetic intuition originated from cosmic, transcendental order.

Architectural tradition, in particular the classicizing Viennese baroque *Palais* architecture of Johann Bernhard Fischer von Erlach, provided Wittgenstein with the starting point for the remaining formal purification. He reduced the portal of the baroque mansions to the shallow projecting entrance block. He stressed the traditional symmetrical organization of the rooms by removing all ornament and all disrupting elements – skirting, thresholds, etc. – which modern techniques could make superfluous and, subsequently, by introducing the symmetrical grid of the flooring slabs and leaving out meaningless horizontals in the design of doors and windows – now executed in neutrally painted steel and brass, the twentieth century construction materials for mechanisms. Pillars and pilasters were employed to reflect *andante* tempo in the transitory rooms; their absence in the other rooms indicates repose in spaciousness. The grids of the joints of the flooring slabs suggest unlimited horizontality; the dominance of verticals in pillars and pilasters and in the design of windows and doors emphasizes verticality. At the same time Wittgenstein relieved the resulting severity by using finishing materials that were anthracite grey for the flooring or some shade of white for walls and ceilings polished and without texture or articulation of their own, aiming at breaking up the masses they cover into the play of light and the suggestion of translucency. The nature of these finishing materials was again borrowed from or akin to earlier baroque finishing materials – *stucco lustro* for the walls, synthetic marble for the floors. Lastly he replaced the chandelier by its twentieth century equivalent: the naked 200 watt light bulb.

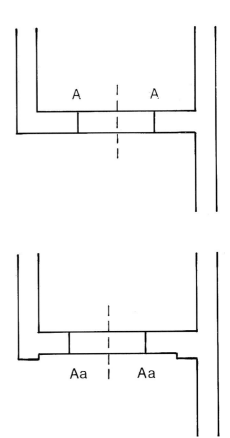

Two solutions of symmetrically proportioning the wall of a receding adjoining room by Adolf Loos (top) and Johann Bernhard Fischer von Erlach (above). Ludwig Wittgenstein tried to combine both in the first plan of the breakfast room of the Kundmanngasse (not executed). (After Turnovský, 1987)

As suggested above he expressed the idea of well-controlled, mechanical, movement in his design by preserving the asymmetry of Engelmann's plan of the beletage and by incorporating it in the shifting of bay rhythms laying in different parallel façade-planes. The tension thus created by the suggestion of movement arrested or finding equilibrium should be understood as a second modernist aspect. It seems narrowly related to the third one, the formal incorporation into the architecture of the Kundmanngasse of actual mechanical elements – the construction of the metal doors and windows and their locks and handles, of the lift (at that time still unusual in private houses), of the various parts of the heating system, etc. Considering the degree of integration of mechanical engineering and architecture in Roman construction and the often ingeniously clear and simple design of the mechanical elements employed, this incorporation is, most literally, consistent with the architecture of classical antiquity.

The essence of the Kundmanngasse as an architectural gesture *vis-à-vis* contemporary modern architecture – and therefore its place in in the history of architecture – can now be fairly accurately established by comparing its features to the basic characteristic of the process of functionalizing architecture and the subsequent change in the conception of space that took place between 1850 and 1930. As expounded by Manfred Bock (1977), the concept of space in traditional architecture, which invariably meant aristocratic or religious architecture, entails the creation of space within a well-defined, closed plan and mass that was articulated according to a preconceived or a priori form-scheme such as a classicist form syntax. It was shaped mass that symbolically – as a *meaningful* gesture – represented the act of architectural creation; as a classicizing gesture it represented the act of architectural creation as it had existed since the master builders of classical antiquity and therefore could claim 'eternal Beauty'. In that sense traditional architecture was monumental architecture expressing itself first and foremost in the volumetric plasticity of the building. Characteristic of the traditional, monumental conception of space is that there is no explicitly causal connection between the volumes of the building and the specific function they should fulfill; furthermore, that there is a similar lack of an explicit causal relationship between the building itself and the surrounding architectural environment, such as the city in which it stands.
It is clear that the Kundmanngasse perfectly complies with this conception of architecture, even if it incorporated asymmetry and mechanical functioning into its a priori form-scheme. Its strong dematerializing aspect appears to be a feature of its finishing, as one would expect with contemporary modern architecture, adding to its monumentality and balancing it rather than destroying it. Its modern construction techniques have been completely subordinated to the traditional aims and only serve to perfect its classicizing design. The Kundmanngasse was probably the last commission for a dwelling in the Viennese aristocratic tradition.
The New Architecture, developing in accordance with the way of life of the

industrial bourgeoisie and reaching maturity in the second half of the 1920s, combined space and function in a way exemplified in many respects by the Villa Moller. Space came to be conceived as a limitless outstretching a priori, from which, starting from some point defining a centre, architecture sliced off volumes, sized and organized around it according to function, while keeping its basic relationship towards limitless space by an open plan. This conception of articulating space instead of articulating mass is a 'literal hollowing-out' of the monumental aspect. It was equivalent to the structural consequences of modern building techniques, because the open plan was achieved by an open framework of steel or reinforced concrete beams and supports – in Loos's Villa Moller and Rufer House quite literally fanning out from the centre. Thus the function of dividing walls was taken over by partitions breaking up space; their construction could be light and therefore prohibited heavy ornamentation in favour of the decorative texture of the material of the wall itself. It also readily brought forth the sliding wall, as in the Villa Moller, enabling the occupants to adapt the space to temporarily changing functions. The use of large glass areas in outer walls – in Loos's designs limited to the garden façade only – emphasized the fundamental openness of the New Architecture towards limitless space outside. In addition, structurally, floors and roofs no longer needed to end at the façades; they could extend further, to form balconies and canopies, as with the terraces of the Villa Moller, and the oriel window above its entrance. Finally, since the city was now understood as a surrounding articulation of the same limitless space, separate dwellings were seen as part of a structural coherence forming the plan of the city, and their individual articulations of space had, therefore, to be attuned to each other. The Villa Moller, with its deliberately reserved front facing towards the city contrasting with the openness of the façade facing the private garden, establishes this emphatic spatial relationship with the surrounding city. (The *Palais* Bronner should then be seen as a transitional phase in which, like the Kundmanngasse, a monumental mass adorned with a neo-classicist style has been realized with the help of modern construction techniques, while, unlike the Kundmanngasse, the contrasting aspect of the front and garden façade was introduced around a *Raumplanung.*) It was in architecture like this, proudly exhibited in the *Wiener Werkbundsiedlung* of 1932, that Loos and Jacques Groag (and Richard Neutra) participated – the 'indecent' openness of which would later provoke Wittgenstein to remark: 'Look at all these houses. They are grinning at you, as if to say, "Look at me, how pretty I am."'

Ludwig Wittgenstein, Margaret Stonborough and
Arvid Sjögren taking a walk in the *Wiener
Werkbundsiedlung*. Photograph sent to Gilbert
Pattison: 'Dear old blood, I'm sure you'll be interested to see me as I walk with a sister and a
friend of mine in an exhibition of bloody modern
houses. Don't I look enterprising?! You can gath-
er from this picture that we had very hot weath-
er but not that there was a terrific thunderstorm
half an hour after this was taken. I am, old god,
yours in bloodyness, Ludwig'

Simplex sigillum veri   6

To establish a meaningful connection between Ludwig Wittgenstein's classicizing 'architectural gesture' and his philosophical thinking, based on the imperative of an intuitively clear 'rule' of absolute beauty, we should begin with the assessment of his ideas on philosophical aesthetics during the period of the design and construction of the Kundmanngasse. Wittgenstein finished his first main philosophical work, the *Tractatus logico-philosophicus* in 1919 and at that time regarded his philosophical pursuits to be accomplished. He then decided to live by the ethical conclusion of the work and live humbly as a schoolteacher to the poor in order to be a decent and good human being. He resumed his philosophical activity in a limited way when the English mathematician Frank Ramsey visited him, in 1923, to discuss problems concerning the English translation of the treatise. However, these discussions did not lead to overt changes in his thinking. The first documents which reveal his renewed interest in philosophical thinking date from the months immediately following the completion of the Kundmanngasse, when, motivated by contacts with the *Vienna Circle*, he returned to Cambridge to start a second career as a philosopher. One of these documents is a more or less popularizing lecture on ethics delivered to the intellectual society called *The Heretics* in November 1929, which contains thoughts on aesthetics. A comparison, therefore, of these thoughts with his conception of aesthetics as expressed by the *Tractatus* should presumably result in a reliable reflection of his aesthetic ideas relevant to the design of the Kundmanngasse.

The mechanism of *showing*

The *Tractatus logico-philosophicus* mentions the subject of aesthetics only once, almost at the end and between brackets. Proposition 6.421 says:

It is clear that ethics cannot be expressed.

Ethics is transcendental.

(Ethics and aesthetics are one.)

The coincidence of ethics and aesthetics, of the Good and the Beautiful, thus asserted would incline us to study the paragraphs on ethics, but these comprise only a few propositions. The rest of the eighty pages in which Wittgenstein expounds his philosophical system, deals with the logical relationship between language and the world. Yet the *Tractatus* has an ethical purport; however, according to the premises of the treatise, ethics cannot meaningfully be put into words. We cannot formulate an ethical 'rule' dealing with how to live as a good human being nor, consequently, an aesthetic 'rule' stating how to create beauty in objects of art. What we can do is to isolate ethics, and consequently aesthetics, from whatever can be meaningfully expressed – which is what remains after the establishment of what can be meaningfully said – in that way they can be *shown*. To elucidate the idea of *showing* in relation to aesthetic matters, including Wittgenstein's 'architectural gesture', it is necessary to understand to some degree the special content of the idea of *showing* in relation to logic and ethics.

The *Tractatus* is a system of assertions, or propositions, founded on seven basic propositions meant as self-evident truths, very much like the Euclidean system of geometry, or the ethical system *more geometrico* of Spinoza. The propositions are given decimal numbers according to their relative role within the whole; thus the sixth basic proposition has number 6, which is elaborated by propositions numbered 6.1, 6.2, 6.3, 6.4, etc., and the last number in its turn is further elaborated by 6.41, 6.42, etc., and 6.42 by 6.421 and so on. As Wittgenstein was an engineer, we could regard the *Tractatus* as a complex mechanism receiving its energy from seven main gear wheels, which in their turn drive the wheels subordinated to them. Once set in motion, the logic of its mechanism as a whole will become self-evident.

The *Tractatus* 'calculates' what can meaningfully be said in language, in order to show what is beyond language. This is the realm of the non-factual or transcendental, the realm of values usually referred to as ethics and aesthetics. The factual is expressed for instance by the sentence 'The door is open', because it can be empirically established whether this is true or false. The value judgment 'The door is beautiful' cannot be empirically verified and is therefore, in Wittgenstein's opinion, a meaningless sentence, a piece of 'non-sense'. Whether it is beautiful or not lies beyond facts and language and can only be transcendentally acknowledged or *shown*. The method of 'calculating' the factual in order to show the valuable proceeds in a manner comparable to drawing a figure, and then acknowledging it as such so as to perceive the space outside it as the space that *excludes* the figure.

This calculation can be made according to Wittgenstein's conception of logic: logic concerns the relationship between the facts that constitute the world. Facts – objects, situations – are combined in certain ways from supposed basic or smallest facts (atomic facts); logic determines the possible combinations of facts and therefore the structure of the world. Language can say something about the facts of the world because of its capability to form logical relationships between its elements identical to the corresponding facts; thus language mirrors the world. Combinations of language elements in an assertion are identical to at least possible combinations of facts, which therefore form the meaning of that assertion. The sentence 'The door is open' has the same logical configuration as the door being open. 'The door is closed' has a different logical configuration to the actual state of affairs, but it is a logically possible configuration and, though false, it is

164

still a meaningful sentence. The logical configuration can now be represented in logical signs, or symbols, similar to the method of algebraic symbolism, which enable one to make calculations with the elements of language, just as algebra makes it possible to calculate with variables. This calculation, then, is performed by the *Tractatus*, and its result is a formula representing all possible combinations of language elements that can express meaning, thus corresponding to all possible combinations of facts. It determines everything that may ever constitute the world and be expressed by language. This done, everything that does not belong to the world, which therefore cannot be expressed by language is being *shown* in the manner explained above.

The realm of the non-factual, the transcendental or mystical as the *Tractatus* describes it, is also the realm of logic itself, for if logic is the mirror between world and language, it follows that a logical configuration itself cannot be mirrored in language or in reality: one can never see the reflective quality of the mirror itself. One only sees the image and this *shows* that the mirror is there – logic *shows* itself in the mirroring of facts. Logic, like ethics–aesthetics, is transcendental, but unlike ethics–aesthetics, which are complementary to the world, it is inextricably bound to the world, or, as Wittgenstein formulates it, logic fills the world and its limits are the limits of the world. The complementary relationship between the world of facts and its transcendental logical framework on the one hand, and transcendental ethics–aesthetics on the other can be illustrated by the example of the magnifying glass. A magnifying glass does not change the relative positions and dimensions of the letters on the page, which is determined by the framework of the type area, but magnifies the typeface as a whole in an absolute sense and thus facilitates reading. In the same way, the absolute viewpoint of the ethically Good and the aesthetically Beautiful makes the world and life happier (and, conversely, the absolute viewpoint of the Evil and the Ugly makes it unhappier) without changing the relatively determined facts of the world.

Showing, then, whether it concerns logic or its complement ethics–aesthetics, coincides with the same transcendental, absolute viewpoint. Because of its transcendental nature it is an a priori viewpoint that precedes experience: it cannot itself be seen, just as the seeing eye, as the origin of seeing, cannot see itself as its object of seeing. What is *shown*, then, is immediately given with the transcendentally originating act of thinking and of experiencing the world; it is 'at once clear' although it cannot meaningfully be put into words, or therefore argued or rationally justified. It is the flash of insight, the *Einfall*, which was so important to Wittgenstein, as Paul Engelmann tells us:

For W[ittgenstein]. the flash of insight was everything. ... [H]e would never commit himself to anything that did not occur to him as a flash of insight. I believe that this was the criterion by which he decided between true or false: did it occur to him as a flash or not? And it is that which distinguishes him from an ordinary philosopher who constantly searches through a mist, without real flashes of inspiration, for something which can only follow from an original flash of inspiration and which leads to a (tenable) result. It is, of course, also conceivable that where there is as yet no flash of insight, one first starts searching for it. But then the flash must happen. If not everything *else* is hopeless. The flash of inspiration is, so to speak, the a priori.

Thus far this has been referred to here as intuition, but a better term would be 'transcendental' or 'absolute intuition', or (a moment of) 'contemplation'. It is important to stress that the a priori viewpoint from which fact and value originate, entails *activity*. The logic expounded in the *Tractatus* goes further, therefore, than a mere body of rules, the one to be rationally deduced from the other like the axiomatic system of Euclidean geometry, by incorporating the idea of a priori activity into it. It must be conceived of as the *functioning of a mechanism*. Wittgenstein borrowed the idea of a priori activity as the basic state of experiencing the world and *showing* logic and ethics–aesthetics through it from his experience with mechanical functioning. Engelmann corroborates this: 'At that time the [...] machine [was] for him before all else the paradigm of a logically organized and con-sistently interlocking, and because of that *de facto* functioning, whole, and [valid] as a real, irrevocable proof for the rightness of such thought.' (As for the *Tractatus* itself, the book *shows* its point by thinking it; it should there-fore be compared to a calculating *machine*, not to a calculation.)

Philosophical problems arise when the careless use of language hides whether an assertion is properly factual and verifiable or whether it also attempts to express matters of value. If that happens the application of logic should reveal what is factual and what belongs to the realm of val-ues. The factual then ceases to be problematic, for it can be verified. The elements trying to express value can be removed from the assertion for they are inexpressible; consequently the problem has disappeared. This approach to solving philosophical problems has been called the 'method' of logical clarification.

But then one may ask what is the criterion of logical clarity, how is it that we know whether logical clarity has been achieved? The application of logic again shows to which elements no facts can correspond and which therefore have no use. The criterion thus realized is Occam's Razor, *simplex sigillum veri*, or simplicity is the hallmark of truth, which is not, according to Wittgenstein, an arbitrary or practically successful rule but the very prin-ciple of logic, the contents of which can only be *shown*. In proposition 5.4541 he writes in architecturally, or at least geometrically, evocative lan-guage:

The solution of logical problems must be neat for they set the standards of neatness.

Men have always thought that there must be a sphere of questions whose answers - a priori - are symmetrical and united into a closed regular structure.

A sphere in which the proposition, simplex sigillum veri, is valid.

But Occam's Razor is not only the principle of logical *showing*, it appears to be the principle of *showing* itself, including ethical–aesthetic *showing*. It is at once the very 'law of eternal Beauty', found in transcendental intuition only, to which Wittgenstein's classicizing architectural gesture tries to return.

Aesthetics as clarification

Though the reference to aesthetics in the *Tractatus* is extremely limited, some notes in the preliminary *Notebooks 1914–16* reveal that Wittgenstein had given the subject profound thought during his stay in Olomouc (which, by the way, justifies to some extent Engelmann's authority). Wittgenstein retained these ideas with only minor variations until after the completion of the Kundmanngasse, as his lecture on ethics given in 1929 shows. For him *simplex sigillum veri* as an ethical standard meant resignation to the reality of the world and one's place in it, which was that of a humble cogwheel, and to neatly perform one's task in life *shown* in that way. This attitude towards life was the prerequisite for happiness, for the world would 'wax as a whole'. By analogy with the effect of the magnifying glass mentioned above, it coincides with the absolute viewpoint of *showing* logic and the complementary ethics–aesthetics. The aesthetic aspect seems confirmed by the (last) notes, of 20 and 21 October 1916:

The artistic miracle is that the world exists. That what exists, exists.

Is it the essence of the artistic point of view that it contemplates the world with a happy eye?

For there is something to the opinion that the beautiful is the purpose of art.

And the beautiful is just that what makes one happy.

The aesthetic experience, which Wittgenstein in his lecture on ethics calls the 'wondering at the existence of the world' and which, one may safely assume, has been characterized by others in other contexts as 'aesthetic rapture', does not bear on one's conduct, but concerns the absolute experience of the things:

The work of art is the object seen *sub specie aeternitatis*; and the good life is the world seen sub specie aeternitatis. This is the connection between art and ethics.

The ordinary point of view sees objects, as it were, from in between them, the view *sub specie aeternitatis* from outside.

This would imply that any object could become a work of art when contemplated from the absolute point of view, for which Wittgenstein employs the expression of Spinoza, the view *sub specie aeternitatis* ('under the aspect of eternity'). Indeed, he gives the example of a stove, the contemplation of which may well elicit an aesthetic experience which *shows* it against the background of the logical framework of the world as a whole, and as such is experienced in an absolute sense *with* time and space instead of in a relative sense *within* time and space, as he suspects. He started this train of thought, however, on 19 September, with the assertion that art is expression and that the good work of art entails perfect expression, which followed immediately on remarks concerning the logical order of the world and the relevance of *simplex sigillum veri* that most probably led to proposition 5.4541 in the *Tractatus*. From the *Tractatus* it can be inferred that any facts possessing a logical structure, may be called an expression if one is willing to generalize Wittgenstein's application of the term *Ausdruck* (expression) from language to everything factual — for this very reason objects can symbolize other objects. If this is so, then perfect expression amounts to the expression of the object from the absolute viewpoint thereby *showing* the logical framework of the world, which is ordered, as we have seen, according to Occam's Razor. It must be concluded that aesthetic *showing* also amounts to *simplex sigillum veri*.

The difference between the work of art and an ordinary object is that the maker of the former deliberately strives after perfect expression, whereas this is not necessarily the case for the latter. The artist must necessarily be concerned with clarification, for perfect expression can only be *shown*. If the result is successful, the work of art achieves an effect which is described by Wittgenstein in a personal note from 1930, and which connects philosophical clarification with artistic clarification — they both have 'aesthetic detachment' or the absolute point of view in common:

Engelmann told me that when he rummages around at home in a drawer full of his own manuscripts, they strike him as so splendid that he thinks it would be worth making them available to other people. (He says this is also the case when he is reading through letters from his dead relations.) But when he imagines publishing a selection of them, the whole business loses its charm and value and becomes impossible. I said that was like the following case: nothing could be more peculiar than seeing a man who thinks he is unobserved performing some quite simple everyday activity. Let us imagine a theatre; the curtain goes up and we see a man alone in his room, walking up and down, lighting a cigarette, sitting down, etc. so that suddenly we are seeing a man from outside in a way in which, ordinarily, we can never see ourselves — surely this would be uncanny and wonderful at the same time. It would be more wonderful than anything a playwright could arrange to be acted or spoken on the stage: we would be seeing life itself. — But then we do see this every day without its making the slightest impression on us! True enough, but we do not see it in *that* perspective. — Well, when E. looks at his writings and finds them wonderful (though he would rather not publish them separately), he is seeing his life as a work of art created by God and, as such, it is surely worth contemplating, as is every life and everything else. But only an artist can so represent the particular that we acknowledge it as a work of art; those manuscripts should *rightfully* lose their value when you consider them separately, and they lose it anyway when you consider them without bias, that is without being enthusiastic about them beforehand. A work of art forces us — so to speak — to see it in the right perspective, but without the artistic, the object is a piece of nature just like any other. The fact that we may exalt it in our enthusiasm gives nobody the right to confront us with it. (I keep thinking of one of those insipid nature photographs which the maker finds interesting because he was there himself and had some experience; but a third party justifiably looks at them coldly, in so far as it is justifiable at all to look coldly at something.)

But it seems to me that in addition to artistic creation there is another way to catch the world *sub specie aeterni*. It is — so I believe — the way a thought may go that, as it were, it flies above the world and leaves it as it is — contemplating it from above, looking down from its flight.

The mechanistic interpretation of *simplex sigillum veri*, which is Wittgenstein's conception of logic in combination with the accomplishment of perfect expression by absolute intuition in an object of art, leads to some interesting observations concerning the architect as an artist. Anyone who invents, designs, or creates new objects, composes new configurations of facts corresponding to certain logical forms. (Wittgenstein employs the expression 'logical form' for the specific logical framework which represents the structure of a fact or composition of facts.) We may now conceive of a continuum representing the degree of clarification the maker of such an object achieves. For example the mechanical engineer designing a machine may realize its functional aim in an inferior design by employing too many or wrongly designed parts, thus wasting energy, or by using materials of inferior quality which wear out, with the same result. He may, on the other hand, possess superior technical insight which enables him to design an efficient, reliable and durable machine. According to Wittgenstein, the first machine does not correspond well to the logical form of its functional aim; but the second does so, thanks to the *showing* of the logical form to the designer through his technical intuition, embodying *simplex sigillum veri*. The upper limit of such a continuum of creation would be the *showing* of the logical form of the object in perfect degree; the machine would then be a work of art. In this way art and technique are connected to each other. This is true for any craft with its idiosyncratic techniques and for every craftsman pursuing them. Honest craftsmanship strives after clarification and good craftsmanship is unthinkable without the drive for clarification. Moreover, if talents are regarded as gifts, exploiting them to the full is a duty. The coincidence of ethics and aesthetics within this conception of craftsmanship speaks for itself. The artist approaches perfect craftsmanship or perfect engineering and the resulting product, art, cannot but *show* this because the expression is perfect.

Wittgenstein strove for clarification in the design of the Kundmanngasse by purifying architecture in the way described in the preceding chapter. In doing so he transposed the activity of clarification from philosophy to architecture, which corresponds to his own conception of artistic pursuit; at the same time it confirmed that for him, architecture was an art form. This is borne out by the respect he showed towards the craftsmen working on the building site, and by the letter of thanks he wrote to the engineering firm of M. Weber & Co. Indeed he referred to the ethical unity of the clarifying approach for philosophy and for architecture when he wrote, in 1931:

Philosophical work — just as, often, work in architecture — is really more working on oneself, on one's own outlook, on one's way of seeing things. (And what one expects of them.)

Wittgenstein's conception of art also throws light on his 'dilettantism' as an architect. The commission to build a house for his sister challenged his ideas on design, his sense of proportion and his technical gifts as well as his understanding of his sister's lifestyle. Although he was not trained as a professional architect his own conception of ethics–aesthetics implied that complete dedication and perseverance in an effort for clarification would necessarily lead to a satisfying result in at least those aspects of architecture to which his talents were relevant (the remaining architectural responsibilities lay, of course, in the hands of Jacques Groag). As soon as Wittgenstein had agreed to take the commission, he regarded architecture not so much as a profession but as a vocation. He acquitted himself of the task with the same devotion as he had shown before in designing the jet propelled engine, in devising the *Tractatus logico-philosophicus*, and in teaching children, and would demonstrate again in philosophy after the completion of the Kundmanngasse and in designing a medical apparatus while working as a volunteer during the Second World War.

The classicizing gesture

Just as the Kundmanngasse should be regarded as an example of traditional monumental architecture, though realized by the application of modern building techniques, Ludwig Wittgenstein's conception of the architect as an artist performing an assignment dictated by the 'Higher Things' is part of the same traditional outlook. It stands, therefore, in remarkable contrast to contemporaneous architects' ideas on the relationship between architecture and art, and because he, like them, consciously strove for some 'authentically modern' architecture, Wittgenstein's attitude may again be clarified against the change the architectural profession went through during the process of the functionalizing of architecture between 1850–1930 as a consequence of the Industrial Revolution.

The relative separation of the formal and structural aspects of the Kundmanngasse, and of Wittgenstein's and Groag's respective tasks corresponds closely to the nineteenth century division between the disciplines of construction and design, which in previous periods were both the responsibility of the architect. These were divided during the latter half of the nineteenth century, into the respective tasks of the constructional engineer, the city-planner, the building inspector and of the architect now solely responsible for the formal aspects of the design. The Ringstraßeproject in Vienna, realized 1855–96, indeed played a key role in this redefinition of the architectural profession and clearly demonstrates its consequences. The architect as a purely formal designer 'lost in time and space' because traditional structural considerations were no longer his responsibility while, at the same time, structural limitations were overcome by the scientific approach of the constructional engineer who employed new and powerful techniques, was forced into what now appeared like one of the liberal arts, into artistry as a 'will to form', albeit limited to façades and interior finishing. This resulted in the unrestrained flowering of the neo-styles of the Ringstraße architecture.

In reaction to this anarchy of forms which in their opinion also entailed conformism to the dominant and somewhat petty *bourgeois* tastes – and for which reaction they would later find support in the idea of Alois Riegl of an a priori 'will to style' – architects started to search for the 'true' style of their period. That style would have to express the unifying cultural force of their age, finally resulting in the aesthetic merging of form and structural function in the New Architecture. It is significant to note that about the same time (1913) that Walter Gropius characterized the developing industrial style of the age with the words:

The coming age demands its own expression. Exactly moulded form leaving nothing to chance, clear contrasts, the ordering of elements, the joining of equal forms and the unity of form and colour will become the aesthetic armamentarium of the modern architect as artist, corresponding to the energy and economy of our public life.

Adolf Loos, following Riegl, harked back to the prototype of antique ornament which became for the next ten years his classicizing inspiration for modern architecture.

It was also around this time that Loos discussed the essence of modern architecture with Ludwig Wittgenstein. After 1922 Loos abandoned his modern classicism and his own conception of functionalist design matured into his interpretation of New Architecture. However, four years later the serious dilettante architect, Wittgenstein, without seeking an aesthetic *rapprochement* between the modern division of tasks between constructional engineer and artistically liberated architect, 'continued' in a classicist manner – leading to a result deceptively close to Gropius's characterization – and found an aesthetic foothold in his 'mechanical' reinterpretation of the adage *simpex sigillum veri*.

A second, closely related contrast between Wittgenstein's architectural aesthetics and the process of the functionalizing of architecture going on around him concerns the relationship between the machine and art. The nineteenth century separation between the artist and the engineer reflected the initial abhorrence of the machine, expressed by John Ruskin, as a thing incapable of producing well-designed, let alone artistic forms. This led to the ambivalent attitude of William Morris pleading for mastery of the machine, so that it would at least produce objects formed as well as possible within its intrinsic limitations. All this resulted from the opposition of 'divine' craftsmanship and the 'evil' machine, and the subsequent merging of the artist and the craftsman, which motivated the flowering of the decorative arts in the Arts and Crafts Movement in England and, in its wake, the *Wiener Werkstätte* in Austria. On the other hand the developments in mechanical and constructional engineering had already produced an impressive field of design, with an aesthetic vocabulary of forms entirely of its own, on a large scale in England and the United States. This was the *Maschinenstil,* or 'machine-style', of railway station roofs, bridges, exhibition halls, steam ships, etc. The standardization of parts, which was fundamental to the constructional activity of the engineer, led to simplified and rationalized ornament and eventually, when it became aesthetically incorporated into the New Architecture, to the rejection of ornament altogether as the form of expression typical of the ages of craftsmanship, which were over now.

Ludwig Wittgenstein was born in the midst of both these currents; his father was on the one hand a patron of the *Wiener Werkstätte* and financed the closely related 'ornamentist' painting of the *Wiener Secession,* on the other hand he was the engineer and industrialist who modernized Austria's steel industry and who was the country's main supplier of the standardized parts of the *Maschinenstil.* For Ludwig the engineer, growing up at the lathe while surrounded by works of the finest craftsmanship, there was no fundamental rift between the machine and the arts and crafts. As expounded above, the engineer and the craftsman were cast in the same mould and the upper limit of both craftsmanship and engineering was the lofty upper end of the creative continuum, the work of art. Although it was a reaction against nineteenth century ornamentation, Wittgenstein's elimination of ornament did not result from the opposition between engineering and art or craft and the eventual aesthetic merging of engineering and architecture. His most authentic aesthetic expression coincided with the 'method' of clarification which originated in the 'mechanical' reinterpretation of *simplex sigillum veri.* For that reason his most authentic expression of modernity as an architect was necessarily the purification of architecture, which for him entailed the continuation of the traditional, monumental idea of architecture, in which now ornament simply had no place.

Wittgenstein's architectural gesture, then, not only rejects the New Architecture in the actual formal characteristics of the Kundmanngasse, but also in the *Weltanschauung* from which its underlying aesthetics originated and which is reflected in the philosophy of the *Tractatus.* In addition, it is full of nostalgia for a world of 'aristocratic' values, in the original sense of 'noble', that had vanished, but in which his conception of the machine, that is the mechanism embodying *simplex sigillum veri,* would have meant true modernity. This was the world of Romantic neoclassicism to which he, in his personal notes, mostly referred in terms of music (with which he more than once compared architecture):

I often reflect whether my ideal of culture is a new one, that is a contemporary one, or one stemming from Schumann's time. At least it seems to me a continuation of that ideal, that is to say not the continuation that it actually had by then. That is excluding the second half of the nineteenth century. I ought to say that this has become so purely instinctively and not as the result of reflection.

As has been noted in the previous chapter Wittgenstein's purifying clarification embodied in the design of the Kundmanngasse should be associated with the classicizing trends that occur repeatedly in the history of architecture. It has in common with them a tendency towards restraint in articulation and ornamentation, guided by some 'absolute rule of Beauty' which expresses itself in the overriding importance of proportionality. This classicizing tendency stood for control of the passions and domination of the impulse, leading to *edle Einfalt und stille Grösse* (noble simplicity and calm grandeur), as Winckelmann characterized the art of Greek antiquity which was believed still to have been inspired by this eternal, even divine, rule. Wittgenstein's adoption of the adage *simplex sigillum veri* to express his absolute 'rule' of proportion may certainly be connected with this harking back to classical standards. However, with the advent of Romanticism, as Sir Ernst Gombrich wrote:

the work of art as such (...) was valued as a symptom of the artist's state of mind, as an 'expression of personality', and this, at once, raised the issue of the genuine *versus* the false expression.

By merging formal artistic expression with the moral sincerity of the artist the work of art received an ethical charge, and terms such as 'nobility', 'purity' and 'restraint' applied to the formal aspects of a work of art entailed at the same time an ethical judgment. Thus the classicizing tendency had become the expression of moral Truth.

It will be obvious now that Wittgenstein's classicizing architectural gesture finds its origin in the Romantic conception of classicism. Probably under the influence of Sigmund Freud and Otto Weininger, whose works he studied, control over the passions and emotions came to mean control over the instinctive impulses. This seems to be reflected in a personal note, written in 1940 in one of the moments of profound self-doubt to which he more than once fell prey during the decade preceding the Second World War:

In all great art there is a WILD beast: *tamed*. Not, e.g., with Mendelssohn. All great art has, as its ground bass, the primitive drives of man. They are not the *melody* (as is perhaps the case with Wagner), but they are what gives the melody its *depth* and force.

In *this* sense one may call Mendelssohn a 'reproductive' artist.

In the same sense: my house for Gretl is the product of a definitely refined hearing, of *good* manners, the expression of a deep *understanding* (of a culture, etc.). But the *primordial* life, the *wild* life that strives to be given free rein — is lacking. One could as well say, it lacks *health* (Kierkegaard). (Hothouse plant.)

The judgment on the Kundmanngasse inherent in the last two paragraphs should, by the way, not be taken too seriously. Wittgenstein often, and with pleasure, showed photographs of the house to friends. He was certainly proud of it, as can be seen, for example, in the letter to Keynes, and in the postscript to the letter to his sister, sent a number of years after he wrote the above remark.

Wittgenstein expressed his feeling of alienation in the actual modern world surrounding him (which was in the industrialized world after the First World War, in the founding of which his own father played a leading role) most clearly in the draft for a foreword to a philosophical typescript of 1930. In it he contrasts his self-imposed role as purifying *clarificator* with the constructive forces striving for 'progress' provoked by the contemporary spirit of the age, characterizing it by an architectural metaphor that may as well be applied to his architectural gesture:

This book has been written for those who sympathize with the spirit in which it was written. This spirit is, so I believe, a different one from the main current of European and American civilization. The spirit of this civilization, which is expressed in the industry, architecture, music, in the Fascism and socialism of our times, is alien and uncongenial to the author. This is not a value judgment. This is not to say that what passes for architecture today, he would believe was architecture, neither that what is called modern music he would not profoundly distrust (without understanding its language), however, the vanishing of the arts does not justify a deprecatory judgment of mankind representing such an age. For in our times of all times true and strong natures turn away from the realm of the arts towards other things, and somehow the worth of individual man finds expression. Not so, however, at a time of great cultural flourishing. (...) Our civilization is characterized by the word 'progress'. Progress is its form, it is not one of its attributes that it makes progress. It is typically constructive. It is its work to build a more and more complicated construction. And again also, clarity only serves to this end; it is not an end in itself. For me on the other hand clarity, perspicuity, is an end in itself.

I am not interested in erecting a building, but in perspicuously presenting to myself the foundations of all possible buildings.

This remark may be related to a note written much later, in 1948, in which he emphasizes indirectly the incomparability of the duty of the architect of genius in an age of decline *versus* his duty in a flourishing period. He mentions Eduard van der Nüll, one of the fathers of the Ringstraße architecture, as an example of the former – and he might have suggested Johann Bernhard Fischer von Erlach as an example of the latter. The duty of van der Nüll would have been a purifying one, instead of making the fashionable neo-styles the main feature of the Ringstraße. This idea set for Wittgenstein a criterion of sincere, true architecture: 'Architecture immortalizes and glorifies something. That's why there can be no architecture where there is nothing to glorify.' In periods of decline, that is in the absence of a unifying cultural force, and therefore of a style of the period, the sincere architect would limit himself to clarification and not try to glorify by succumbing, as he formulated it, to the temptation of empty forms.

Architecture and philosophy

In the past various parallels have been drawn between the Kundmanngasse and the *Tractatus logico-philosophicus*. If Wittgenstein had meant the Kundmanngasse to symbolize his philosophy, then, following that same philosophy, they should literally have a common logical structure. Though both share the same ethical–aesthetic principle of *simplex sigillum veri* it will be obvious that this cannot be the case. The function of the Kundmanngasse – inhabitation in accordance with a (in all senses) noble lifestyle – is something quite different from the effect the *Tractatus* aims to achieve – *showing* the realm of ethics–aesthetics.

However, reference to certain stylistic similarities between the Kundmanngasse and the *Tractatus* may be made on good grounds, though they explain little and mainly affirm a common mental attitude in their creator which is only in accord with the inner consistency of Wittgenstein's conception of aesthetics between 1916 and 1930. Both the Kundmanngasse and the *Tractatus* express *simplex sigillum veri,* albeit in different material forms – building materials in the former case, language elements in the latter. This makes it difficult to elaborate their perceived similarities on a more specific level than by such general and intuitive characterizations as 'expressing a subtle sense of proportion' (in the *Tractatus*, for example: the seven main propositions, the system of decimal numbering, the logical symbolism expounded, etc.), or as 'creating an austere atmosphere' (for example, in the concise language of the *Tractatus*, forcefully making its point with uncompromising restraint, corresponding to the complete omission of ornament in the Kundmanngasse).

It is only plausible, therefore, that *simplex sigillum veri* should be equated with the 'effort for precision' presented as a semiotic explanation for the stylistic affinity between the Kundmanngasse and neoclassicism on the one hand, and the Kundmanngasse and the *Tractatus* on the other. Not taking this as an explanation but as a starting point, the last chapter tried to give meaning to *simplex sigillum veri* as a stylistic typification closely related to classicist currents within the history of architecture. Apart from recognizing the adage as the aesthetic principle underlying both Kundmanngasse and *Tractatus* it still remains difficult to compare the connections between architectural precision, consisting in visual–spatial–tactile relationships and in a certain use of building elements, with philosophical or linguistic precision, consisting in semantic relationships and in a certain use of words and concepts.

Though not specifically with regard to *simplex sigillum veri*, Wittgenstein did, however, acknowledge the affinity that may exist between architectural and conceptual structures – as he did between architecture and music – centering around the importance for him of the a priori *act* of thinking. He once compared architecture with thought by way of the gesture: 'Recall the impression made by good architecture, that it expresses a thought. One would want to express architecture as well by making a gesture.' He did not work this idea out because he himself thought such a specification impossible; like music, the gesture, and thus architecture, may express a thought that cannot be adequately captured in language. Recalling the remark quoted above, that architecture glorifies something, one may think of a glorifying thought, which in the case of the Kundmanngasse would have been the classicizing thought that glorifies the classical tradition in Western culture. In any case, the remark stresses again the symbolic nature of great architecture in Wittgenstein's conception. It is very likely that his admiration for Fischer von Erlach originated partly in the symbolic, even allegorical quality characteristic of baroque architecture, and pre-eminently of Fischer's works, for example the Karl Borromäus Church, which in its abundance of allusions and images glorified the classical tradition in the reign of the Holy Roman Emperor Charles VI.

By *showing* what cannot be said the *Tractatus* is, in that sense, also a gesture; in fact, the problem of the unbridgeable gap between what can be expressed in language and what can only be expressed in non-verbal ways of communication lies at the foundation of the philosophy of the *Tractatus* and it was, among other problems, the problem of the meaningful gesture that led Wittgenstein to his later revised philosophy of the *Philosophical Investigations* built around the idea of language games.

In the *Philosophical Investigations* Wittgenstein introduced the language game by the example of the activity of erecting a building, in which it should be noted that the actual game seems to spell out the abridged syntax of a classical column:

A is building with stones: there are blocks, columns, slabs and beams. B has to pass the stones, and do so in the order in which A needs them. For this purpose they use a language consisting of the words 'block' (*Würfel*) [= pedestal], 'column' (*Säule*), 'slab' (*Platte*) [=abacus], 'beam' (*Balken*) [=architrave]. A calls out the words; - B brings the stone which he has learnt to bring at each particular call. - Conceive this as a complete primitive language.

Wittgenstein's rooms in Whewell's Court, on the top floor, Cambridge.

From reminiscences of Maurice O'C. Drury, who shortly after Ludwig Wittgenstein's return to Cambridge in 1929 became a close friend, we catch glimpses of buildings condemned or admired by Wittgenstein, confirming his criterion that architectural honesty embodies architectural greatness. While sitting in Trafalgar Square and talking about its architecture he denounced the historicizing classicizing forms of Canada House, just being completed: 'That's *bombast*; that's Hitler and Mussolini.' On the other hand, he admired the Georgian architecture of houses in Dublin: 'people who built these houses had the good taste to know that they had nothing very important to say; and therefore they did not attempt to express anything.' In the interior decoration and furnishing of his own rooms in Cambridge he went to considerable pains to avoid the 'empty' design of the time. The walls were bare, with the exception of a silhouette of a young woman in an elaborate gilt frame, a small bookcase and, in his bedroom a zinc bathtub which hung against the wall when not in use. The other furniture consisted of one

176

simple wooden chair and a few deck chairs (during lectures more deck chairs were brought in from the corridor) and, in front of the window, a folding card table used as a writing desk on which stood a fan which muffled the noise from neighbours. On the mantelpiece was a low-powered bulb on a retort-stand for lighting. Instead of the fireplace, Wittgenstein used an old-fashioned black stove, the pipe of which disappeared straight through the ceiling. As in the Kundmanngasse there were always flowers in a vase on the windowsill, and there was a houseplant. Wittgenstein changed the proportions of the (neo-Gothic) window by gluing black strips of paper across it. He once remarked to Drury:

See what a difference it makes to the appearance of the room when the windows have the right proportions. You think philosophy is difficult enough but I can tell you it is nothing to the difficulty of being a good architect. When I was building the house for my sister in Vienna I was so completely exhausted at the end of the day that all I could do was go to a 'flick' every night.

True glorification in architecture, in contrast to clarification, implied freely speaking 'the language of its time', to quote from Margaret Stonborough's letter to her brother, and this could very well include ornamentation. This is in accordance with Wittgenstein's admiration of the Viennese baroque in general and of the still ornamented, classicist baroque of Fischer von Erlach. Visiting Ely Cathedral with Drury, Wittgenstein was impressed by the late-Romanesque chapel forming the south wing of the west front. This has three tiers of columns and arches and two elaborate triforia piled on top of each other, and, as such, is far removed from the simple and austere earlier Romanesque of the continent. They continued on to the Lady Chapel, built in Decorated Gothic, where Wittgenstein remarked: 'Once the arch becomes pointed, I don't understand it any more.' One should here envisage the hyperbolic concave point of the Decorated Gothic arch, which is different from the simple convex point of the Gothic arch, and may be seen as an indication of its decline. With regard to Gothic architecture, as to music, Wittgenstein once observed a 'meaningful irregularity' akin to the meaningful irregularity of language (a development in his philosophical thinking of about 1929 closely related to his photographic experiments to clarify the notion of family resemblance). 'The towers of St. Basil's Cathedral also come to mind' he added. He had been in Moscow in 1936. He thought of Lenin's tomb as one of the very few well designed contemporary buildings; St. Basil's, only a few steps away, was:

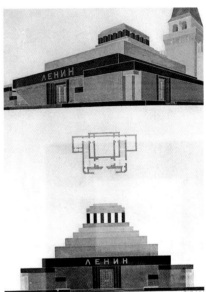

Top: Saint Basil Cathedral, Moscow.
Above: Lenin's mausoleum, Moscow.

One of the most beautiful buildings I have ever seen. There is a story — I don't know whether it is true but I hope it is — that when Ivan the Terrible saw the completed cathedral he had the architect blinded so that he would never design anything more beautiful.

177

Bibliography

- Amendolagine, F. & Cacciari, M. (1975): La casa di Wittgenstein. In: F. Amendolagine & M. Cacciari, OIKOS da Loos a Wittgenstein. Rome: Officina Edizioni.
- Barrett, C. ed. (1967): Wittgenstein. Lectures & Conversations on Aesthetics, Psychology and Religious Belief. Berkeley: University of California Press.
- Beek, van de, J. 1987. Adolf Loos — Patronen stadswoonhuizen. In: M. Risselada ed., Raumplan versus plan libre. Delft: Delft University Press.
- Bernard, M. (1986): Les mécènes de la Secession. In: Vienne. l'Apocalypse joyeuse. Exhibition catalogue. Paris: Centre Pompidou.
- Bock, M. (1977): Vom Monument zur Städteplanung: Das Neue Bauen. In: Tendenzen der Zwanziger Jahre. Exhibition catalogue. Berlin: Reimer.
- Bouveresse, J. (1973): Wittgenstein: La rime et la raison. Paris: Éditions Minuit.
- Bouveresse, J. (1986): Wittgenstein et l'architecture. In: Vienne. l'Apocalypse joyeuse. Exhibition catalogue. Paris: Centre Pompidou.
- Černoušek, T., Šlapeta, V. / Zatloukal, P. (1981): Olomoucka Árchitektura 1900-1950. Olomouc.
- Eccles, W. (1963): Some letters of Ludwig Wittgenstein. In: Hermathena, 97, pp. 57-65.
- Eggert, K. (1976): Der Wohnbau der Wiener Ringstrasse im Historismus 1855-1896, Wiesbaden: Steiner.

- Engelmann, P. (1911): [Das Haus auf dem Michaelerplatz]. In: Die Fackel, 317/318, 28. February, p. 18.
- Engelmann, P. (1913): Studie zu einer Villa. In: Der Architekt, XIX, plate 148.
- Engelmann, P. (1929): see: Ostdeutsche Bauzeitung, 27, p. 654.
- Engelmann, P. (1946): Adolf Loos. Tel Aviv: Paul Engelmann. Facsimile edition 1984, Vienna: Architektur- und Baufachverlag.
- Engelmann, P. (1948): Ludwig Wittgenstein. Tel Aviv: Paul Engelmann.
- Engelmann, P. (1967): Letters from Ludwig Wittgenstein. With a Memoir. Translated by L. Furtmüller. Oxford: Basil Blackwell.
- Engelmann, P. (1967): Dem Andenken an Karl Kraus. Edited by Elazar Benyoetz. Vienna: Kerry.
- Fann, K.T. (ed.) (1967): Ludwig Wittgenstein. The Man and His Philosophy. New York: Dell.
- Feigl, H. (1981): Inquiries and Provocations. Selected writings 1929-1974. R.S. Cohen ed. Boston/Dordrecht: Reidel.
- Feyerabend, P. (1966): Herbert Feigl: A biographical sketch. In: Mind, Matter, and Method. Essays in Philosophy and Science in Honor of Herbert Feigl. Minneapolis.
- Ficker, L. (1951): Rilke und der unbekannte Freund. In memoriam Ludwig Wittgenstein. In: Der Brenner, 18, pp. 234-248.
- Fischer von Erlach, J.B. (1721): Entwurff Einer Historischen Architectur. Vienna. Republished in 1988 in the series 'Die biblio-

philen Taschenbücher'. Dortmund: Harenberg.
- Fischer von Erlach, J.E. (Edition of 1715): Wiener Ansichtenwerks Joseph Emanuel Fischers von Erlach. Vienna.
- Flammersfeld, M.-L. (1974): Het sluitwerk van Ludwig Wittgenstein. In: De Revisor, 8, pp. 17-21.
- Frank, J. (1931): Architektur als Symbol. Vienna: Schroll.
- Frey, D. (1923): Johann Bernhard Fischer von Erlach. Vienna: Hölzel.
- Gasking, D.T.A. / Jackson, A.C. (1951): Ludwig Wittgenstein. In: The Australasian Journal of Philosophy, XXIX, pp. 234-248.
- Gebauer, G. / Grünenwald, A. / Ohme, R. / Rentschler, L. / Sperling, Th. / Uhl, O. (1982): Wien, Kundmanngasse 19. Munich: Wilhelm Fink.
- Giacomini, U. (1965): Un'opera architettonica di Wittgenstein. In: Aut, aut, May, pp. 88-92.
- Gombrich, E.H. (1978/1963/ 1952): Visual metaphors of value in art. In: Meditations on a Hobby Horse. London: Phaidon.
- Gombrich, E.H. (1984/1979): The Sense of Order. London: Phaidon.
- Graf, O.A. (1985): Otto Wagner. Das werk des Architekten. 2 Vols. Vienna: Böhlau.
- Gravagnuolo, B. (1981): Adolf Loos. Milano: Idea. Engl. (1982). Translated by C.H. Evans. Milano: Idea and Löcker.
- Greenhalgh, M. (1990): What is Classicism? London: Academy Editions.
- Grimschitz, B. (1944): Wiener Barockpaläste. Vienna: Wiener Verlag.

- Gropius, W. (1913): Die Entwicklung moderner Industriebaukunst. In: Jahrbuch des Deutschen Werkbundes. Berlin.
- Hänsel, L. (1951): Ludwig Wittgenstein (1889-1951). In: Wissenschaft & Weltbild, 4, p. 274-277.
- Hård af Segerstad, U. (1970): Huset som Wittgenstein byggde. In: Svenska Dagbladet, 6 February, p. 5.
- Hayek, F.A. (1953): Sketch of a Biography of Ludwig Wittgenstein. Written in 1953 for private circulation by F.A. Hayek, with some later corrections and insertions. Unpublished manuscript.
- Hermans, W.F. (1968): Wittgenstein en Wittgensteinboeken. In: Literair Paspoort, 23, 222, pp. 181-189.
- Hermans, W.F. (1971): Van Wittgenstein tot Weinreb. Amsterdam: De Bezige Bij.
- Hoffmann, W. (1969): Ludwig Wittgenstein, ein Philosoph als Architekt. In: Bau, 1, pp. 3-8.
- Indiana, G. (1985): Ludwig Wittgenstein, Architect. In: Art in America, January, pp. 112-133.
- Janik, A. (1985): Essays on Wittgenstein and Weininger. Amsterdam: Rodopi.
- Janik, A. / Toulmin, S. (1973): Wittgenstein's Vienna. New York: Simon and Schuster.
- Johnston, W.M. (1972): The Austrian Mind. Berkeley: University of California Press
- Kapfinger, O. (1984): Haus Wittgenstein. Eine Dokumentation. Vienna: Kulturabteilung der Botschaft der Volksrepublik Bulgarien.

- Kapfinger, O. (1989): Kein Haus der Moderne. In: M. Huter ed. *Wittgenstein. Biographie, Philosophie, Praxis.* Vienna: Wiener Secession.
- Kapfinger, O. / Leitner, B. (ed.) (1989): *Wittgenstein-Haus. Ein Pressespiegel Juni/Juli/August 1971.* Vienna: Wiener Secession.
- Kieslinger, A. (1972): *Die Steine der Wiener Ringstrasse.* Wiesbaden: Steiner.
- Kraft, V. (1951): Ludwig Wittgenstein. In: *Wiener Zeitschrift für Philosophie/Psychologie/ Pädagogik,* 3, pp. 161–163.
- Kraft, W. (1961): Ludwig Wittgenstein und Karl Kraus. In: *Neue Rundschau,* LXXII/4, pp. 812–844.
- Kulka, H. (1931): *Adolf Loos.* Vienna: Schroll. Republished in 1979/1985 by Löcker, Vienna.
- Kurrent, F. / Spalt, J. (1970): Unbekanntes von Adolf Loos. In: *Bauforum,* 3, 21, pp. 29–48.
- Lee, H.D.P. (1979): Wittgenstein 1921–1931. In: *Philosophy,* 54, pp. 211–220.
- Lee, H,D.P. (ed.) (1980): *Wittgenstein's Lectures, Cambridge 1930-1932. From the Notes of John King and Desmond Lee.* Chicago: University of Chicago Press.
- Leitner, B. (1970): Wittgenstein's Architecture. In: *Art Forum,* February, pp. 59–61.
- Leitner, B. (1973): *The Architecture of Ludwig Wittgenstein. A Documentation.* Halifax: Nova Scotia College of Design (New York, 1976: New York University Press).

- Leitner, B. (1985): Zur Architektur von Ludwig Wittgenstein. In: *Parnass,* 2, pp. 24–31.
- Leitner, B. (1989): Das Haus in Bewegung. In: M. Huter ed. *Wittgenstein. Biographie, Philosophie, Praxis.* Vienna: Wiener Secession.
- Levin, M. (1988): *White City. International Style Architecture in Israel. A Portrait of an Era.* Tel Aviv: The Tel Aviv Museum.
- Loos, A. (1908): *Ornament und Verbrechen.* Vienna.
- Loos, A. (1910): *Architektur.* Vienna.
- Loos, A. (1911): Mein Haus am Michaelerplatz. In: *Parnass* Sonderheft, 2.
- Loos, A. (1912): *Verzeichnis der Vorlesungen an der Bauschule Adolf Loos.* Vienna.
- Loos, A. (1913) Meine Bauschule. In: *Der Architekt,* XIX, pp. 69–76.
- Loos, A. (1919): *Richtlinien für ein Kunstamt.* Vienna: Lanyi.
- Loos, A. (1921): *Ins Leere Gesprochen. 1897-1900.* Paris: Georges Crès. 2. revised ed. (1932) Innsbruck: Brenner. Reprint of the 1st ed. (1981) Vienna: Prachner.
- Loos, A. (1931): *Trotzdem 1900-1930.* Innsbruck: Brenner. Reprint (1982) Vienna.
- Loos, A. 1962. *Sämtliche Schriften. Band 1.* Edited by Franz Glück. Vienna/Munich: Herold.
- Loos, A. (1983): *Die Potemkin-'sche Stadt. Verschollene Schriften 1897-1933.* Edited by Adolf Opel. Vienna: Prachner.
- Malcolm, N. (1984/1958): *Ludwig Wittgenstein. A Memoir.* With a

biographical sketch by G.H. von Wright. Second edition with Wittgenstein's letters to Malcolm. 2nd revised edition. Oxford: Oxford University Press.
- Mays, W. (1955): Note on Wittgenstein's Manchester period. In: *Mind,* IXIV, 1955, pp. 247–248.
- Mays, W. (1967): Recollections of Wittgenstein. In: K.T. Fann ed., *Ludwig Wittgenstein. The Man and His Philosophy.* New York: Dell.
- McGuinness, B.F. (1966): The mysticism of the Tractatus. In: *Philosophical Review,* 75, pp. 305–328.
- McGuinness, B.F. (1985): Ornament und Askese in der Denkweise Wittgensteins. In: A. Pfabigan ed., *Ornament und Askese im Zeitgeist des Wien der Jahrhundertwende.* Vienna: Brandstätter.
- McGuinness, B.F. (1988): *Wittgenstein. A Life.* London: Duckworth.
- Methlagl, W. (1969): Erläuterungen zur Beziehung zwischen Ludwig Wittgenstein und Ludwig von Ficker. In: G.H. von Wright ed., *Briefe an Ludwig von Ficker.* Brenner Studien I. Salzburg: Müller.
- Meyer, Chr. (ed.) (1981): *Josef Hoffmann. Architect and Designer 1870-1956.* Vienna/New York: Galerie Metropol.
- Micheletti, M. (1967): *Lo schopenhauerismo di Wittgenstein.* Bologna: Zanichelli.
- Monk, R. (1990): *Ludwig Wittgenstein. The Duty of Genius.* London: Jonathan Cape.

- Mulder, H.L. (1968): Wissenschaftliche Weltauffasung. Der Wiener Kreis. In: *Journal of the History of Philosophy,* 6, pp. 386–390.
- Münz, L. / Künstler, G. (1964): *Der Architekt Adolf Loos.* Vienna: Schroll. Engl. 1966, London: Thames & Hudson.
- Muthesius, H. (1908): *Das englische Haus.* Berlin: Wasmuth.
- Naredi-Rainer, P. von (1986): *Architektur und Harmonie.* Cologne: DuMont.
- Nedo, M. (1989a): Familienähnlichkeit, Philosophie und Praxis. In: M. Huter ed., Wittgenstein. *Biographie, Philosophie, Praxis.* Vienna: Wiener Secession.
- Nedo, M. (1989b): Eine medizinisch-technische Apparatur. In: M. Huter ed., *Wittgenstein. Biographie, Philosophie, Praxis.* Vienna: Wiener Secession.
- Nedo, M. / Ranchetti, M. (1983): *Wittgenstein. Sein Leben in Bildern und Texten.* Frankfurt/ Main: Suhrkamp.
- Nierhaus, I. / Kamenicek, E. (1989): Der Kopf. Wittgenstein als 'aufrichtiger' Dilettant. In: M. Huter ed., *Wittgenstein. Biographie, Philosophie, Praxis.* Vienna: Wiener Secession.
- Parak, F. (1978): *Wittgenstein prigioniero a Cassino.* Roma: Armando Armando.
- Pevsner, N. (1970/1960). *Pioneers of Modern Design.* Harmondsworth: Penguin.
- Plaisier, P. (1987): *De leerlingen van Adolf Loos.* Delft: Delft University Press.

• Plattus, A. (1974): On Bernhard Leitner's 'The Architecture of Ludwig Wittgenstein: A Documentation'. In: *Oppositions*, 3, pp. 107–109.

• Posch, W. (1986): Die Österreichische Werkbundbewegung 1907-1928. In: *Geistiges Leben im Österreich der Ersten Republik*. Vienna: Verlag für Geschichte und Politik.

• Rave, P.O. (ed.) (1950–1979): *Karl Friedrich Schinkel. Lebenswerk*. Berlin: Deutscher Kunstverlag.

• Rhees, R. (ed.) (1984): Recollections of Wittgenstein. Oxford: Oxford University Press.

• Riegl, A. (1923/1893). *Stilfragen*. Berlin: Siemens.

• Risselada, M. (1987): Documentatie van 16 woonhuizen. In: M. Risselada ed., *Raumplan versus plan libre*. Delft: Delft University Press.

• Rukschcio, B. (1986): Een analyse van het Huis am Michaelerplatz. In: *Archiv*, 7, pp. 17–23.

• Rukschcio, B. / Schachel, R. (1982): *Adolf Loos. Leben und Werk*. Salzburg: Residenz.

• Safran, Y. (1983): The curvature of the spine: Kraus, Loos and Wittgenstein. In: *9H*, 4, pp. 17–22.

• Scheu, R. (1909): Adolf Loos. In: *Die Fackel*, 283/284, 26 Juni, pp. 25–37.

• Schwanzer, K. ed. (1964): *Wiener Bauten 1900 bis heute*. Vienna: Österreichisches Bauzentrum.

• Sedlmayr, H. (1976): *Johann Bernhard Fischer von Erlach*. Vienna: Herold.

• Sedlmayr, H. (1984/1959): Allegorie und Architektur. In: M. Warnke ed., *Politische Architektur in Europa vom Mittelalter bis heute*. Cologne: Dumont.

• Sekler, E.F. (1971): *Zur Wertung des Hauses Wien III. Kundmanngasse 19. (Villa Stonborough-Wittgenstein)* Unpublished expert opinion commissioned by the Bundesdenkmalamt, Vienna.

• Sekler, E.F. (1982): *Josef Hoffmann. Das architektonische Werk*. Salzburg: Residenz.

• Sekler, E.F. (1986a): *Josef Hoffmann, Adolf Loos und die Vereinigten Staaten. Akten des XXI. Internationalen Kongresses für Kunstgeschichte*. Vienna 4.-10.IX 1983.

• Sekler, E.F. (1986b): Josef Hoffmann, Adolf Loos et le 'Kulturgefälle' est-ouest. In: *Vienne. l'Apocalypse joyeuse*. Catalogue to the exhibition. Paris: Centre Pompidou.

• Sjögren, C. (1989): Die Familie. In: M. Huter ed., *Wittgenstein. Biographie, Philosophie, Praxis*. Vienna: Wiener Secession.

• Šlapeta, V. (1978): Paul Engelmann und Jacques Groag, die Olmützer Schüler von Adolf Loos. In: *Bauwelt*, 40, pp. 1494–1501.

• Spadoni, C. / Harley, D. (1985): Bertrand Russell's Library. In: *The Journal of Library History*, 20, pp. 25–45.

• Stoessl, O. (1911): Das Haus auf dem Michaelerplatz. In: *Die Fackel*, 317/318, 28 Februar, pp. 13–17.

• Tranøy, K.E. (1976): Wittgenstein in Cambridge 1949-1951: Some personal recollections. In: *Acta Philosophica Fennica*, 28, pp. 11–22.

• Turnovský, J. (1987): *Die Poetik eines Mauervorsprungs*. Braunschweig/Wiesbaden: Vieweg.

• Uhl, O. (1966): *Moderne Architektur in Wien*. Vienna: Schroll.

• Vrooman, R. (1978): Hoe er werd gesold met 't huis van Wittgenstein. In: *Furore*, 10, pp. 32–35.

• Wagner, O. (1895): *Moderne Architektur*. Vienna.

• Wagner, O. (Vol. 1: 1889, 2: 1897, 3: 1906, 4: 1922): *Einige Skizzen, Projekte und ausgeführte Bauwerke*. Vienna. Reprint (1987): Otto Wagner. Tübingen: Wasmuth.

• Waismann, F. (1967): *Ludwig Wittgenstein und der Wiener Kreis*. Oxford: Basil Blackwell.

• Walden, G. (1989): Fotografie als Beschreibung. In: M. Huter ed., *Wittgenstein. Biographie, Philosophie, Praxis*. Vienna: Wiener Secession.

• Wittgenstein, H.. *Familienerinnerungen*. Unpublished manuscript.

• Wittgenstein, L. 1926/1977): *Wörterbuch für Volksschulen*. Vienna: Hölder-Pichler-Tempsky.

• Wittgenstein, L. (1922/1933): *Tractatus logico-philosophicus / Logisch-philosophische Abhandlung*. London: Routledge & Kegan Paul.

• Wittgenstein, L. (1953): *Philosophical Investigations / Philosophische Untersuchungen*. Oxford: Basil Blackwell.

• Wittgenstein, L. (1961/1983): *Notebooks 1914–1916*. Oxford: Basil Blackwell.

• Wittgenstein, L. (1964): *Philosophical Remarks / Philosophische Bemerkungen*. Oxford: Basil Blackwell.

• Wittgenstein, L. (1965): A lecture on ethics. In: *The Philosophical Review*, LXXIV, Januar, pp. 3–27.

• Wittgenstein, L. (1969): *Briefe an Ludwig von Ficker*. Brenner Studien I. Salzburg: Müller.

• Wittgenstein, L. (1974/1977): *Letters to Russell, Keynes and Moore*. Oxford: Basil Blackwell.

• Wittgenstein, L. (1980b): *Briefwechsel*. Frankfurt/Main: Suhrkamp.

• Wittgenstein, L. (1980b): *Culture and Value*. G. H. von Wright, ed.. Oxford: Basil Blackwell.

• Wright, G.H. von ed. (1982): *Wittgenstein*. Oxford: Basil Blackwell.

• Wünsche, K. (1985): *Der Volksschullehrer Ludwig Wittgenstein*. Frankfurt/Main: Suhrkamp.

• Zeibig, E. (1989): Arbeiten auf den Gebiet des Luftzeugbaues. In: M. Huter ed., *Wittgenstein. Biographie, Philosophie, Praxis*. Vienna: Wiener Secession.

• Zemach, E. (1984): Wittgenstein's philosophy of the mystical. In: *Review of Metaphysics*, 18, pp. 39–57.

• Zevi, B. (1974): Il filosofo tra i mattoni. In: *Espresso*, XX, 26. May, pp. 82–83.

• Zweig, M. (1987): *Lebenserinnerungen*. Gerlingen: Bleicher.

Index

Illustrations

*Graphische Sammlung Albertina,
Vienna:* page 30, 34, 77 (bottom),
78, 92 (bottom), 145 (top left and
bottom right), 146 (top), 148, 150,
151 (top), 153,158.

Paulus Auer, Liebenfels: page 114
(bottom right), 117 (top right and
center),132, 148, 158.

Avraham Eilat, Haifa: page 60.

Archiv Baupolizei, Vienna: page 36
(top), 94, 95, 96, 97, 98 (bottom),
102 (top), 103 (center and bottom), 104 (left), 106, 127 (right),
133 (right), 138.

*Bildarchiv Preussischer Kulturbe-
sitz, Berlin:* page 76, 103 (bottom).

Hanna Blum, Hoofddorp: page 45.

*Bandesdenkmalamt, Vienna, cour-
tesy P.H. Stonborough, Genolier:*
page 16, 52, 75, 79, 81, 82, 83, 84,
85, 86, 87, 88, 89, 102 (top).

*T.Černousek, V. Šlapeta, and S.
Zatloukal, Olomouc/Prague:*
page 57.

*Sigmand Freud-Gesellschaft,
Vienna:* page 68 (top).

*Collections of the Getty Center for
the History of Art and the
Humanities, Santa Monica,
California:* page 93.

Willi Groag, Maanit: page 36 (bottom).

*The late Dr. Willem Frederik
Hermans, Brussels:* page 98 (top
left).

Hölder-Pichler-Tempsky, Vienna:
page 35 (top).

Ing. Arch. Zdeněk Hynek, Olomouc:
page 55 (top).

*The Jewish National and University
Library, Jerusalem:* page 28 (top),
29 (bottom), 48, 54, 58, 59, 61.

Landesbildstelle, Vienna: page 71,
74.

*Prof. Bernhard Leitner/Herbert
Urban, Vienna:* page 121 (top, left
and right, center top right), 125
(bottom right).

Margherita Krischanitz: page 11,
100, 101, 102 (bottom), 109, 110
(top left), 111 (center), 112, 113,
116 (top left), 117 (bottom), 120,
122, 123 (center), 127 (center
left), 135 (top and center) 136.

*Moritz Nähr, courtesy Pierre H.
Stonborough, Genolier:* page 103
(top), 119 (top).

*Moritz Nähr, courtesy Michael
Nedo, Cambridge:* page 12, 37, 38,
39, 40 (top), 42, 98 (top center),
99, 110 (center and top right), 116
(top right and center), 126 (top
center), 151 (bottom).

Michael Nedo, Cambridge: page
14, 21, 23 (center), 24, 25, 26, 27
(bottom), 33, 35, 43, 51, 67, 70,
72, 115 (bottom), 152 (center, bottom), 156 (bottom).

*Museum für Angewandte Kunst,
Vienna:* page 64, 65, 116 (bottom).

Neue Pinakothek, Munich: page
62.

Österreichische Nationalbibliothek:
page 32, 66, 69, 91, 104 (top), 125
(top), 133 (left), 142 (center, top
and bottom), 152 (top), 156 (top,
center).

Gilbert Pattison, Maldon, Essex:
page 162.

Pepin Press, Amsterdam: 107 (right,
from top to bottom), 108, 121
(center top left, center bottom),
122, 126 (center), 129 (top), 130,
134 (bottom right), 135 (bottom).

Thomas Römer, Vienna: page 121
(top, center).

Cecilia Sjögren, Vienna: page 22,
63.

Pierre H. Stonborough, Genolier: 27
(top), 40 (bottom), 41, 44, 114 (top
left and bottom), 115 (top), 116
(center left), 117 (left), 131, 134
(left), 157.

*Prof. O. Uhl, T. Sperling, and collab-
orators, Munich:* page 123.

RIA NOVOSTI, Moscow: page 178.

*Universiteitsbibliotheek
Amsterdam:* page 29 (top), 46.

*Universiteitsbibliotheek Technische
Universiteit Delft:* page 92 (top),
179.

Rudy Vrooman, Amsterdam: page
28 (bottom), 111 (left), 118, 124,
125 (top), 126 (top right), 129
(bottom), 134 (top right, center
right), 135.

Galerie Weltz, Salzburg: page 23
(top)

Wiener Secession, Vienna: page 23
(left).

*Wiener Stadt- and Landesarchiv,
Vienna:* page 68 (bottom).

Paul Wijdeveld, Amsterdam: page
47, 55 (bottom), 56, 85 (bottom),
98 (top right), 102 (center), 105,
110 (center left and right), 111
(right), 118 (left), 119 (center and
bottom), 126 (top), 134 (left top,
right bottom), 137, 141, 142 (top
and center bottom) 144, 145 (top
right), 177.

Eredi Yehuda Kurt Unger, Haifa:
page 49, 53.